STARDUST LOST

STARDUST LOST

THE TRIUMPH, TRAGEDY, AND *MISHUGAS*
OF THE YIDDISH THEATER IN AMERICA

STEFAN KANFER

ALFRED A. KNOPF · NEW YORK 2006

This Is a Borzoi Book Published by Alfred A. Knopf

Copyright © 2006 by Stefan Kanfer

All rights reserved under International and Pan-American Copyright Conventions. Published in the United States by Alfred A. Knopf, a division of Random House, Inc., New York, and simultaneously in Canada by Random House of Canada Limited, Toronto. Distributed by Random House, Inc., New York.
www.aaknopf.com

Knopf, Borzoi Books, and the colophon are registered trademarks of Random House, Inc.

Due to limitations of space, permissions to reprint previously published material can be found on page 325.

Library of Congress Cataloging-in-Publication Data

Kanfer, Stefan.
Stardust lost : the triumph, tragedy, and mishugas of the Yiddish theater in America / by Stefan Kanfer. —1st ed.
p. cm.
ISBN 1-4000-4288-7
1. Theater, Yiddish—United States—History. I. Title.
PN3035.K36 2006
792.089′924073—dc22   2006041034

Manufactured in the United States of America

First Edition

פֿאַדלאָדענעד שטעדנשטויב
אלי וויזעלן און מײַן מוזע

If statistics are right, the Jews constitute but one percent of the human race. It suggests a nebulous dim puff of stardust lost in the blaze of the Milky Way.

Properly, the Jew ought hardly to be heard of, but he is heard of, has always been heard of. He is as prominent on the planet as any other people, and his commercial importance is extravagantly out of proportion to the smallness of his bulk. His contributions to the world's list of great names in literature, science, art, music, finance, medicine and abstruse learning are also way out of proportion to the weakness of his numbers.

He has made a marvelous fight in this world, in all the ages; and has done it with his hands tied behind him.

— MARK TWAIN, *"Concerning the Jews"*

CONTENTS

ACKNOWLEDGMENTS

✦

E XPLORING THE HISTORY of the vanished Yiddish Theater amounts to an archaeological dig. A good deal of the spadework took place in the great trove of material at YIVO, and at the 42nd Street Library and the Lincoln Center Library, all in New York City. In addition there were forays into the backwaters of the Sterling Library at Yale University, and, sometime back, in the shelves of Brandeis University.

The primary and most vital researcher on *Stardust Lost* was Villette Harris, a scrupulous and knowledgeable ally who has worked on some of my previous books, and who can find almost anything, including photographs and song sheets thought to be lost or beyond retrieval. Many of the translations from the Yiddish were done by Jocelyn Cohen, whose work was particularly valuable on unpublished memoirs recalling the work of David Kessler. Throughout, Jeremy Dauber, the Columbia University Yiddishist, proved to be a knowledgeable and patient counselor.

Nahma Sandrow, whose pioneering volume *Vagabond Stars* traced the Yiddish Theater from its infancy, was a generous provider of information and eyewitnesses. Others were helpful in guiding me backward to the heyday of Second Avenue, principal among them my parents, Allen and Violet Kanfer. I am grateful for accounts by Mina Bern, Shifra Lehrer, Lillian Lux, Viola Harris, Sholem Rubenstein of WEVD, and Victoria and Gene Secunda. In addition there were sage contributions from Elie Wiesel, Joseph and Harry Stein, Steve Zeitlin of City Lore, Zalmen Mlotek of the Folksbiene Yiddish Theater, Sidney Lumet, Caraid O'Brian, and the late Arthur Rosenblatt.

When this book was little more than an idea, and I was working at *Time* magazine, the subject of the Yiddish Theater came up in conversations with the late Herschel Bernardi, Chaim Ehrenreich, Walter Matthau, Harry and Teddy Thomas (né Thomashefsky), Seymour Rexite, Zero Mostel, Zvi Scooler, and Jack Gilford.

I continue to be grateful for the astute counsel and encouragement given by Myron Magnet of *City Journal,* Myron Kolatch of the *New Leader,* Professor Renata Adler of Boston University, Jess Korman, Hugh Nissenson, the intrepid Kathy Robbins, the ultrademanding, and uncommonly correct, Peter Gethers, and the late and very much missed Henry Anatole Grunwald.

I must also thank my fellow pongers who kept me going during this demanding period, among them Will Shortz, Rob Bernstein, Paul Indenbaum, Trevor Mack, Fred Gordon, Fred Ellman, Peter Wolf, Robert Mankoff, Alex Porush, Leo Trubman, Amy Hsu, and Rishi Gupta. In addition I am grateful for the companionship of my fellow bloggers on the old duckseason.org Web site: Lance Morrow, Priscilla Turner, Thomas Dworetzsky, James Morrow, John McWhorter, Jess Korman, Lisa Reitman-Dobi, Michael Walsh, and James Meigs; and to the Aestas Aeterna group, Alan Fine, Steve Becker, Robert Rittner, Jack Damann, Kevin, Andrew, and Timothy Ettinger, Robert Tucker, and Howard Weishaus.

My serious, encouraging, and amusing family is mentioned last but leads the gratitude parade: enduring and undying thanks and love to May, to Lili and Andy, to Ethan and Daniela, and to those bright and beautiful students, hope of the twenty-first century: Lea and Aly.

INTRODUCTION

✦

TWO EXTREMES

i

IN HIS 1902 BESTSELLER, *The Spirit of the Ghetto,* journalist Hutchins Hapgood urged readers to visit the Jewish quarter on the Lower East Side. The exotic territory was bounded by 14th Street on the north, the East River on the east, Broadway on the west, and Catherine Street on the south—hardly the place for Manhattan's uptown crowd. But Hapgood insisted that visitors would not only be safe, they would be nourished in every sense of the word. For at the heart of the district were Yiddish theaters offering New York City's most exciting dramas, comedies, and operettas. And while the tourists were in the area, he added, they could visit cafés "where excellent tea and coffee are sold, where everything is clean and good, and where the conversation is often the best."

A century after Hapgood published his guidebook, hardly a trace of the old times can be found. A few blocks to the south, Chinatown is still a vibrant community of Asian immigrants. To the west, Little Italy remains the scene of the Scuola Italiana, and the dialects of Naples and Sicily can be heard in the neighborhood shops. Artists seek places in Greenwich Village, as they always have. But on the Lower East Side, not one of those theaters is extant. No spirited Yiddish colloquies take place because none of the cafés and tearooms survive. Yiddish itself, the Velcro language that picked up idioms and words from every European nation, has vanished from the streets. With it has gone the audiences who once crammed dineries and emporia, and who filled the balcony and orchestra seats, night after night. Hardly any synagogues are left, and those that remain are attended by the elderly and the curious.

Hippies who moved in during the era of low rents in the 1960s; young couples who want proximity to their workplaces on Wall Street; adolescents in search of navel piercing and tattoo establishments—all have turned the area into the opposite of what it was, the focal point of American Jewry. Once upon a city, the Lower East Side was the place of sights and sounds and smells that remained in the minds of its denizens long after they had graduated to high-rises and suburbs.

Eddie Cantor, the child of Russian immigrants, was raised in that ghetto. He called himself the "world's supreme delicatessen eater, absorbing more salami, pastrami, bologna, and frankfurters in that short span than most families do in a lifetime." Along with many such youths, he could recall the powerful aromas of Kosher food and drink well into old age. Others, like children's book writer Sydney Taylor, re-created the bygone scene in detail: "Heaped high with merchandise," the pushcarts in the ghetto "stretched into endless lines up and down the main streets. They were edged up close to the curb and wedged together so tightly that one could not cross anywhere except at the corners. The pushcart peddlers, usually bearded men in long overcoats or old women in heavy sweaters and shawls, outdid each other in their loud cries to the passers-by."

Not that the Lower East Side was a continual pageant of bounty and delight. For every greenhorn success story there were scores of early deaths and abject failures. A great deal of human misery was hidden from public view. Sweatshops used the immigrants mercilessly; sixty-hour weeks were not uncommon, and the overcrowded tenements were a breeding ground for mental illness, tuberculosis, felonies, and murder. In *Looking Back*, the novelist Belva Plain imagined a Hester Street apartment house at the turn of the century: "The stench surged from the street door . . . cooking grease, onions, an overflowing toilet . . . the sickening steam of pressing irons; a noxious drenching of tobacco from the front apartment where the cigar makers lived." Another novelist, Meredith Tax, made her heroine, Hannah, wander through a place where "colors glowed more garishly, dirt was greasier, people grew bigger, and all the latent exaggerations in their characters flowered. Hannah heard her own voice come out louder than before."

But these truths could not obscure the significance of the New York ghetto. In her study *Lower East Side Memories,* historian Hasia R. Diner notes that the pawnshops and eateries, the factories and workplaces, the tumultuous thoroughfares and teeming flats, the meeting halls and theaters, provide the iconography of the American Jewish experience. The turf below 14th, she observes, "has entered the realm of the sacred."

Nothing about that realm is more hallowed than the Yiddish Theater. Most of the immigrants had never seen a drama or operetta before, and they regarded them with a child's credulity. When the ticket-holders witnessed scenes from the Bible, from czarist Russia, from American tenements and workplaces, they believed every speech and every incident. They were swept up in the narratives of avaricious bosses and passionate union organizers, autocratic parents and defiant children, whores and innocents, intellectuals and big shots. And as they watched, they came to understand the roles they themselves were playing in the New World.

Thus the history of that theater is more than merely a show business account; it is the saga of a people in the New World, illuminated by spotlights and scenery, backed by mood music, enacted by some of the most luminous talents of the twentieth century. As we will see, before the story was done it had not only changed the ghetto dwellers, it had altered the history of Broadway and Hollywood, and thus, to a certain extent, America.

THE CREATION of most art forms is lost in history. The Yiddish Theater is unique; it was born on a precise night in a precise year, and its lineage can be traced to an actual father. Its last, lingering illness can also be traced to a specific decade, although the causes of the malady are varied and subtle.

Late in the 1960s the celebrated Jewish actress Ida Kaminska came to New York with her troupe. The USSR had been currying favor with Arab nations of the Middle East, and yet another wave of anti-Semitism had been encouraged by the Soviet government. Kaminska and her actor husband, Meir Melman, no longer felt at home in their native country, Czechoslovakia. In the 1965 feature *The Shop on Main*

Street, she had played an elderly Jewish shopkeeper at the beginning of the Holocaust. Nominated for an Academy Award, Kaminska was endlessly praised and interviewed, a new face at the age of sixty. Everyone in the film and stage business knew her name. Roles were tendered. America seemed a likely place for the Melmans to relocate.

But en route to the United States, the actress had an unsettling premonition: though her touring troupe played to astonishingly full houses in Germany and to unsurprisingly enthusiastic audiences in Tel Aviv, Kaminska kept thinking of an old Yiddish folktale. A *schlimazel*— "luckless soul" in Yiddish—appeals to his rabbi for help. The ragpicker is advised to relocate; the move will change his luck. Packing up, he sees the Ghost of Poverty leaping with joy in a dark corner. "What are you jumping for?" demands the poor man. "Why shouldn't I?" chortles the apparition. "I'm coming, too!"

Despite her reservations and Old World superstitions, Kaminska settled the troupers in New York and booked Carnegie Hall for a night. Advance sales were outstanding. Then, on the eve of the performance New York was hit by the worst blizzard in more than twenty years. "Many people who had tickets couldn't come," states Kaminska's memoir. "The results for the impresario were disastrous, and for us they were not too good either. In a word, *schlimazel.*" Nevertheless, she stayed in the city, hoping for another chance at a New York audience.

She was to get her wish. In 1970, the poet Louis Zukofsky published his lyrical *Autobiography.* "My first exposure to letters at the age of four," he wrote, "was thru the Yiddish theaters, most memorably the Thalia on the Bowery. By the age of nine I had seen a good deal of Shakespeare, Ibsen, Strindberg and Tolstoy performed—all in Yiddish." A handful of investors had similar memories; they agreed to back a project that mixed nostalgia with modernism. They founded the Ida Kaminska Yiddish Theater, rented an appropriate downtown location—the Roosevelt Auditorium on Union Square—and made ready for the renaissance.

But they had failed to consider a few details. Dressing rooms needed to be constructed, press agents hired, acoustical equipment rented. Because a language barrier stood between the actors and a large part of the audience, headphones were wired to every seat. Those who could not follow the Yiddish could listen to a simultaneous translation. Just when all seemed in place, more troubles piled on. The Roosevelt was owned by the Amalgamated Workers Union, and its directors had a new stipulation. When they needed the auditorium for a meeting, performances had to be canceled. The investors wearily agreed. By now the project was an *idée fixe* and judged to be worth any price.

Reviews were uniformly favorable; standing ovations greeted the players. Yet attendance fell off after the first several nights. Foul weather kept some people away; others attended and registered complaints. Kaminska recalled, "Once, when I left the theater after a performance, two young men in their mid-twenties were waiting for me. They seemed to be fine, intelligent young men. They apologized for stopping me and expressed their warm thanks for the performance, which stimulated much feeling and thought in them. At the same time, my husband emerged from another door. An old lady met him and said, 'Are you a member of this company? Then I must tell you that you've shown us a terrible play and we didn't understand a thing.' Two extremes." The season ended on January 4, 1970, severely in debt.

No more was said about a new Yiddish Theater, run by Ida Kaminska or anyone else.

SOME SIX DECADES EARLIER there had been two dozen Yiddish theaters in New York. Now only a handful of productions made it to off-Broadway venues. None had a permanent home; all were short of cash. The audience had dwindled to a few hundred loyal fans, most of them in their seventies. Their colleagues had died, or retired to Florida, or gone to the suburbs. Those who remained in the city preferred to see plays spoken in English, the language they now regarded as their native tongue, even when they spoke it with an accent.

The Yiddish Theater was so far gone that even its melodies, some of them popular enough to have made the Hit Parade in the 1930s, were forgotten. To introduce the tunes to a new generation, the *New York Times* published *Great Songs of the Yiddish Theater,* a compilation of melodies from better times. A number of lyrics had been written by the Yiddish superstar Molly Picon; in 1975 she was signed to write the book's introduction and notes. Her chipper prose refused to acknowledge reality. "Recently I went to the Yiddish Theater to see *Hard to Be a Jew,*" she said, "and frankly was surprised to see a line stretching around the corner, buying tickets at the box office. As I approached the entrance, I overheard one woman say to another, 'I've been waiting here for half an hour and the line doesn't seem to move. No wonder the

Yiddish Theater is dying—you just can't get tickets!' " A pretty tale, but fiction nonetheless. After the second week of any such fare, tickets went begging.

That year another book about the Jewish experience was published, and this one made no attempt to avoid the truth. Irving Howe's massive history, *World of Our Fathers,* was subtitled *The Journey of the East European Jews to America and the Life They Found and Made.* The author sought to detail the entire immigrant experience in and around New York City, from the 1880s onward. Nothing seemed to escape his notice, from the tribulations of entering at Ellis Island, to the harsh overcrowded neighborhoods and sweatshops, to the labor agitations and the rise of Yiddish journalism and politics, to the intellectual ferment and the escape to the Catskills and the suburbs. Only thirty-six pages were devoted to the Yiddish Theater, though, shortchanging an art form for which Howe proceeded to sit *shivoh*—the Jewish mourning period for the dead.

Howe allowed that the dramas and operettas "reached everyone in the immigrant world, collapsing distinctions between serious and popular." But that inclusiveness was to be both its glory and its curse. In order for the Yiddish Theater to have survived "some sort of leap was necessary . . . from folk to cosmopolitan." Unfortunately this could happen "only if there had been more time, only if there had been several generations that used Yiddish as their native tongue yet were also at home in Western culture." The rush to assimilate destroyed that possibility. In the end, "it was a theater blazing with the eloquence of its moment, and in the memories of a few the glow would remain."

Howe's cheerless assessment was amplified in 1977, with the appearance of Nahma Sandrow's *Vagabond Stars.* The daughter of a rabbi, Sandrow was well versed in the literature and lore of the Yiddish Theater. Her volume covered early productions and performers in Europe, Latin America, and the Middle East, bringing the account up-to-date by reporting an incident that took place in New York City. Facing a faculty committee at Bronx Community College, Sandrow was asked to list her accomplishments. "I said I was writing a book about Yiddish Theater. The committee members sat doodling or taking notes, the atmosphere was formal but friendly. One professor said he had a question: 'What's a nice girl like you doing writing about Yiddish Theater?' The laughter lasted for minutes. The questioner and half the committee were Jewish."

. . .

NOW THAT ITS STARS HAD FADED, the Yiddish Theater and its once boisterous audience were ripe for satire. Broadway composer Robert Merrill (*Funny Girl, Take Me Along*) wrote the book, tunes, and lyrics for *The Prince of Grand Street*. The musical followed the later life of the fictional Nathan Rashumsky, a turn-of-the-century Jewish idol, no longer young and constantly in hot water with women, playwrights, and drama critics. Mark Twain made an appearance; the actor wanted permission to stage *Huckleberry Finn,* and the author almost acceded until he learned that Rashumsky wanted to play the title role. The show seemed very promising at a run-through. But during its out-of-town tryout, laughs came infrequently, and no one went out whistling the songs. That spring *The Prince* was booked to open at the Alvin Theater in New York. It never got out of Philadelphia.

Two other pastiches followed. The Broadway musical *Rags* (book by Joseph Stein, who had written the book for *Fiddler on the Roof*) told the story of Jewish immigrants at the turn of the century. In a key scene, three of the principals, Rebecca, David, and Saul, pay a visit to a Yiddish theater where the impresario/actor Boris Kaminsky is giving his version of Hamlet.

BORIS: To be or not to be. A terrible question. In other words to live or to die. Both bad! Living we know about—suffering without end.

AUDIENCE (*Mixed reaction*): That's true. Listen to him. Ssh, let him talk.

BORIS: But dying is better? That's also no life. Because after you're dead, what have you got?

AUDIENCE: Nothing.

BORIS: Nothing! I'm going crazy thinking about it. I once said to my friend Laertes, the more we think, the more mixed up we get. I'm the saddest person in the world.

AUDIENCE (*Mixed cries*)

MAN IN AUDIENCE: You think you got it bad? You should know my boss.

(*Enter* OPHELIA)

OPHELIA: Hamlet, you shouldn't say such mean things about your mother. Your mother is your best friend. I don't know what's happening to you lately, always talking to yourself.

AUDIENCE: Maybe he's sick. He should see a doctor. Go out in the sun more.

DAVID: Why is he so angry, Saul?

SAUL: Well, his father died and his mother married his uncle.

REBECCA: Terrible . . . a second marriage. It's always the children who suffer.

Rags lasted for four performances.

Jewish pride in Broadway's preeminent composers continued through the 1970s. The musicals of Richard Rodgers, Jerry Herman, and the emerging Stephen Sondheim drew loyal followings of Hadassah ladies at Saturday matinees; Leonard Bernstein's ballet *The Dybbuk,* based on a Yiddish play, was well attended; the comedies of Neil Simon, obviously written about Jewish characters but deliberately cast with gentiles, drew similar crowds. But as for the roots of all this—the Yiddish Theater—hardly anyone cared to attend its modest, live presentations.

One last attempt was made to send up the past imperfect. *The Great Ostrovsky* had songs by Cy Coleman (*Sweet Charity; Little Me*) and book and lyrics by Avery Corman (*Kramer vs. Kramer*). Like *The Prince of Grand Street,* it told the story of a Second Avenue actor in the old days. The score mixed sentimental ballads with light-handed klezmer orchestrations, and the jokes were genial and essentially nonsectarian. And, like *The Prince,* the show never made it to Broadway. Philadelphia was its final stop.

. . .

CERTAIN THAT THEIR CULTURE was in decline, Yiddish-speaking New Yorkers grew despondent. Then came the morning of October 5, 1978, when a dramatic reprieve sounded from Stockholm. The Swedish Academy of Letters sent word that Isaac Bashevis Singer had won the Nobel Prize for Literature. The press release cited his "impassioned narrative art which, with roots in a Polish-Jewish cultural tradition, brings the universal human condition to life." Lars Gyllensten, permanent secretary of the academy, added praise for Yiddish, the language in which the laureate wrote. It was, he said, the tongue "of the simple people and of the women, the language of the mothers who preserved fairytales and anecdotes, legends and memories for hundreds of years past, through a history which seems to have left nothing untried in the way of agony, passions, aberrations, cruelty and bestiality, but also of heroism, love and self-sacrifice."

In the wake of the announcement Singer gave hundreds of interviews. A charming, formally dressed figure, he captivated reporters, who quoted him on his favorite subjects, from vegetarianism, "I don't eat meat because I'm worried about my arteries. I don't eat meat because I'm worried about the arteries of the *chicken,*" to philosophy, "We have to believe in free will. We have no choice," to the future of Yiddish, "The language is ailing, yes. But in Jewish history, the distance between sickness and death can be a long, long time." He iterated the last observation during his Nobel speech, begun in Yiddish:

"Der groyser kovad vos di Shwedishe Acadamie hot mir ongeton is oich an anerkenung fun Yiddish—a loshon fun golus, ohn a land, ohn grenitzen, nisht gshtitzt fun keim shum meluchoh. . . . The great honor that the Swedish Academy has afforded me is also a recognition for Yiddish, a language of exile, without a country, without frontiers, that is not supported by any government."

At a banquet given by the king of Sweden, Singer continued to praise Yiddish in a manner that ranged from wistful to tongue-in-cheek and back again. "His Majesty, ladies and gentlemen: People are asking me often, why do you write in a dying language? And I want to explain it in a few words. First, I like to write ghost stories, and nothing fits a ghost better than a dying language. The deader the language, the more alive is the ghost. Ghosts love Yiddish; they all speak it. Secondly, I believe in resurrection. I'm sure the Messiah will soon come, and millions of Yiddish-speaking corpses will rise from their graves one day, and their first question will be, 'Is there any new Yiddish book to read?' Thirdly, for two thousand years, Hebrew was considered a dead language. Suddenly it became strangely alive. What happened to Hebrew may also happen to Yiddish one day." When this gentle old man spoke, his lively blue eyes sparkled and his voice grew strong and persuasive. He was young again. So were his listeners and so was his language. That evening, anything seemed possible. Even rebirth. The illusion lasted until sunrise.

SEEN FROM THE INSIDE, the Yiddish Theater was an institution in need of celebration. From the outside, it was perceived as an antique, an instance of naive art whose time had come and gone. Serious appraisals began. At the Museum of the City of New York, "A Celebration of Yiddish Theater in New York" was mounted; more than three hundred items of memorabilia went on display, including production snapshots, drawings, and posters. And in Washington, D.C., the Klutznick Museum mounted a show called "Hurray for Yiddish Theater in America!" It guided the visitor chronologically through the Yiddish Theater's peaks and valleys. Both exhibits treated the subject with esteem and dignity; both embalmed it.

Bridge of Light, J. Hoberman's study of Yiddish cinema, added another valedictory. The medium in which so many Yiddish Theater stars found roles was long gone. Analyzing the film *Brussels-Transit,* the story of a family's flight from Poland to Belgium in the years of the Holocaust, Hoberman praised the Yiddish narration by the director's mother. "Postscripting the tumultuous history of Yiddish mass culture," he concluded, "Samy Szlingergaum's austere film has the modesty of the pebble one places atop a Jewish grave. (This book, I put beside it.)"

Musicologist Jack Gottlieb weighed in with *Funny, It Doesn't Sound Jewish,* subtitled *How Yiddish Songs and Synagogue Melodies Influenced Tin Pan Alley, Broadway, and Hollywood.* He noted that Jewish composers of the last century (Irving Berlin, George Gershwin, Richard Rodgers, Harold Arlen, Leonard Bernstein, Arthur Schwartz et al.) borrowed from what they knew—Yiddish operettas and musicals. But Gottlieb also showed that gentile composers ransacked the products of Second Avenue. Cole Porter's "You'd Be So Nice to Come Home To," for example, bears a strong resemblance to the Yiddish Theater song "Oyfn Pripetshik" ("In the Fireplace").

Indeed, in that melody "Porter conjures up a Russian-Jewish world to such an extent that Gregory Ratoff, the Russian-born movie producer-director, on first hearing it, thought it came from the Caucasus." Porter confessed that he paid close attention to Yiddish musicals and once boasted to Richard Rodgers that he had discovered the secret of writing hits. Said Rodgers, "As I breathlessly awaited the magic formula, he leaned over and confided, 'I'll write Jewish tunes.'"

That he did. And in the process, Porter and his colleagues slowly brought the Yiddish Theater to Broadway, off-Broadway, and Hollywood. It took decades to make the crossover, and that once vital art form got lost in the transfer. Later, the lamentations were long, loud, and futile. For no matter how great the debt of the American stage to its sources, no "foreign" theater has ever endured for very long in New York. When the French Comédie Français does Molière, or an Italian company *commedia dell'arte,* or a Greek troupe Aristophanes, it is widely regarded as a novelty, lauded by critics but ignored by the general public. Only when classics put on English garb do they find popular favor. Such was the case of *Sly Fox,* based on Italian, Elizabethan, and German sources and reworked by Larry Gelbart, *Tartuffe* in the translation by Richard Wilbur, and the Seamus Heaney version of Sophocles' *Philoctetes.* For the enthusiasts of Yiddish Theater to expect any other fate was to indulge in fantasy.

Yet had they dug a little deeper, they would have found many reasons to rejoice. For if the Yiddish Theater barely had a pulse, its impact on American show business was profound and enduring. When Marlon Brando began filming *The Godfather,* the awed cast members could barely converse with him. Al Pacino, James Caan, and Robert Duvall in particular were especially reverential. Producer Al Ruddy understood their attitude: "In a sense Marlon had created these guys."

And Brando himself had been created by his teacher, Stella Adler, the daughter of a Yiddish Theater superstar. "If there wasn't the Yiddish Theater," he once reflected, "there wouldn't have been Stella. And if there hadn't been Stella, there wouldn't have been all those actors who studied with her and changed the face of theater—and not only acting, but directing and writing."

Among the Yiddish Theater's graduates and associates were actors Paul Muni, John Garfield, Zero Mostel, Walter Matthau, the acting teachers Lee Strasberg and Sanford Meisner, the playwrights Clifford Odets and Ben Hecht, the directors Harold Clurman and Sidney Lumet, and the stage designer Boris Aronson. The Yiddish Theater was their university, and when they left the ghetto and went out into the world, they altered whatever they touched. Neither Broadway nor Hollywood has been the same since then.

IN *HASIDIC TALES: THE LATER MASTERS,* Martin Buber relates one of the classic stories: "Whenever the Jews were threatened with disaster, the Baal Shem Tov would go to a certain place in the forest, light a fire and say a special prayer. Always a miracle would occur, and the disaster be averted.

"In later times when disaster threatened, the Maggid of Mezritch, his disciple, would go to the same place in the forest and say, 'Master of the Universe, I do not know how to light the fire, but I say the prayer.' And again the disaster would be averted.

"Still later, his disciple, Moshe Leib of Sasov, would go to the same place in the forest and say, Ribono Sehl Olam, I do not know how to light the fire or say the prayer, but I know the place and that must suffice.' And it always did.

"When Israel of Riszhyn needed intervention from heaven, he would say to God, 'I no longer know the place, nor how to light the fire, nor how to say the prayer, but I can tell the story and that must suffice.' And it did."

DISTANT FROM ITS RELIGIOUS underpinnings, bereft of its fire, without a permanent place, the story of the Yiddish Theater must suffice. We have no choice.

STARDUST LOST

CHAPTER ONE

✦

THE FOUR INGREDIENTS

F OR ALMOST FIVE THOUSAND YEARS the Jews needed no
theater to relate their story. They saw themselves as participants
in an epic teeming with conquests and enslavements, revela-
tions and miracles. A burning bush that speaks, the parting of the Red
Sea, a rod turned into a snake, a woman turned into a pillar of salt—
where was the playwright that could match God's imagination? Even
the setbacks were of a grand scale: expulsions from Eden and Egypt,
lost wars, subjugation. What stage could reproduce these incidents?

The scholar Max I. Dimont was so impressed by the theatrical quality of Jewish history that he divided it into three acts. "When the curtain rises on the first 2,000 years," he wrote in *The Indestructible Jews,*

"we will note that it proceeds like a Greek predestination drama, with God seemingly the author and divine director." But there was a difference. In the classic Greek plays, the characters remain unaware of their destinies. In the Jewish predestination drama, Jehovah gives them their parts and tells them of His expectations—expectations that will require martyrdom and perseverance.

The Old Testament's pivotal scene is the essence of dramatic tension. Abraham, the man Kierkegaard dubbed the Father of Faith, makes ready to offer up his son Isaac—until Jehovah reprieves him. A covenant is struck between man and Jehovah: if this true believer remains obedient to the divine will, he and his descendants will be the Chosen People: "I will make of thee a great nation," promises the Voice, "and I will bless thee and make thy name great." From then on, human sacrifice is no longer necessary in this tribe; worship and a moral life are sufficient unto the day.

Unlike the multitude of pagan gods who surrender to temptations and war amongst themselves, Dimont observes, "the God of Abraham acts with a moral purpose and a preconceived plan. He is not a capricious god who acts on a day-to-day basis. The Jews know what God expects of them and can therefore make long range plans."

By the time Abraham's descendants settle in Egypt, they are suffused with the idea of monotheism. It will not be relinquished in the presence of their enemies. There will be many such adversaries over the course of history. Often these enemies come from without, like the Philistines; but sometimes they come from within, irresistible temptations that change the individual and threaten his people.

Those enticements become an integral part of the melodrama. The gods of the Hittites, the Assyrians, the Egyptians, the Greeks and Romans are subject to follies, passions, and mistakes. Jehovah never exhibits such weaknesses. He leaves the scandals to his all-too-human followers, who never experience a shortage of family violence. Cain murders Abel. Jacob betrays his brother Esau. Absalom rebels against his father, dies in the field, and King David's cry resounds through the eons: "Would God I had died for thee, O, Absalom, my son, my son!" Joseph is cast out by his jealous brothers, who rend his coat of many colors and falsely report his death.

And should the reader's attention flag, sexual adventures are there to pique it. Sodom is destroyed because of the uncontrolled lives of its citizens. David is so besotted by Bathsheba that he sends her husband off to war so that he can disport with her. The mighty Samson, seduced and weakened by Delilah, is destroyed for lust. The elders leering at Susannah, the ruinous fleshpots of Gomorrah, and, on a higher plane, the explicit love songs of Solomon ("My beloved put in his hand by the hole of the door, and I was moved by him") all speak of the pleasures and snares of carnal desire.

And this is only the beginning. After the Holy Writ comes the second part of the Jewish saga, when Jehovah can no longer be seen in a burning bush or heard on Mount Sinai. Twice the great Temple in Jerusalem is destroyed, first by the Babylonians in 587 B.C. After it has been rebuilt and the city regained by the Hebrews, Roman troops raze the Temple and slay thousands of Jewish men, women, and children. This catastrophe in A.D. 70 marks the end of the Jewish state and the beginning of the Diaspora.

"Without Zion," remarks historian Nathan Ausubel, the Jews are "like children deprived of their mother." Wherever they disperse, they remember Jerusalem, setting up scrolls of the Torah—the first five books of the Bible—in their makeshift temples, nourishing the hope of a Messiah who will deliver them from their exile, endlessly poring over the scriptures in search of meaning, speaking in prayer—and sometimes in one-sided conversation with a silent Jehovah. This monological style, popularized by the "Tevye" short stories of Sholem Aleichem, and musicalized in *Fiddler on the Roof,* can be heard to this day: "Dear God, why did you have to make my poor old horse lose his shoe just before the Sabbath? That wasn't nice. It's enough you pick on me, bless me with five daughters, a life of poverty. What have you got against my horse? Sometimes I think that when things are too quiet up there, You say to Yourself, 'Let's see, what kind of mischief can I play.' "

The going out from the Middle East is only the first of many such sorrows. In the early Christian era, the Jews are singled out for refusing to accept Jesus as the Messiah. Preachers find a ready target: Gregory of Nyssa sees Hebrews as "Murderers of the Lord, assassins of the prophets, rebels and detesters of God." Saint John Chrysostom thunders, "Brothel and theater, the synagogue is also a cave of pirates and the lair of wild beasts." The legend of the Wandering Jew, whom Jesus condemned to roam the earth endlessly, though mentioned nowhere in the New Testament, is related by Christian speakers and takes root from the thirteenth century on.

By the Middle Ages this antipathy hardens into doctrine. Pockets of tolerance exist throughout Europe—the Jews enjoy an unprecedented economic and religious freedom in the Arab-Christian culture of Spain. Yet a sword dangles over them at all times. Some nations force them into ghettos; others make them wear special clothing and caps to identify them as outsiders. In Germany they are forced to swear an oath of fealty on the carcass of a pig. The Passion Play at Oberammergau features Jews in horned hats to suggest their connection to Satan, and Jewish religious figures are portrayed as evil and sadistic. The sights and sounds affront rabbis; they condemn theater as "the seat of frivolity."

Jews are considered the devil's allies whenever a plague surfaces. Martin Luther excoriates them when they fail to embrace his doctrines. "Therefore be on your guard against the Jews," he warns, "knowing that wherever they have their synagogues, nothing is found but a den of devils." Spain turns from oasis to killing ground during the Inquisition. Jews are burned, murdered, tortured, and finally expelled from the country in 1492, just as Columbus sets sail for America.

For centuries they're forbidden to live in England. The absence of Hebrews makes no difference; anti-Semitism without Jews is all the rage during the Elizabethan era. In *The Jew of Malta,* Christopher Marlowe makes his villain a scheming, outspoken Jewish merchant named Barabas: "Now I will show myself to have more of the serpent than the dove." Shakespeare, in his turn, seizes on the incident of Dr. Rodrigo Lopez, a visiting Spanish convert who has been supplying information about his native country to the queen. Lopez runs afoul of the Earl of Essex. The aristocrat dislikes foreigners who have greater royal access than he has, and attempts to frame the doctor for espionage. At first Elizabeth will have none of it; but Essex persists and eventually gets his way.

En route to the block, the crowd shouting with excitement, the executioner's sword glinting in the sun, Lopez protests that he loves Elizabeth even more than he adores Jesus Christ. It does no good; the converted Jew is publicly hanged, castrated, his carcass pulled into pieces by four horses, to the amusement of the crowd. Shakespeare follows the incident with his own contribution. The Bard, states Anthony Burgess in his biography, "was not above exploiting the general bitterness towards Jews by writing a play in which a Jew is the villain—not a treacherous one, however, but a usurious one. Barabas is a Machiavellian monster; Shylock merely, and literally, wants his pound of flesh."

Shakespeare, of course, is incapable of creating a two-dimensional character, and the man is immortalized by his famous plea: "Hath not a Jew eyes? Hath not a Jew hands, organs, dimensions, senses, affections, passions?" All very well for the modern playgoer, but in the Bard's time and long after, audiences would see only a beaky moneylender rubbing his hands, alternately purring at his Christian enemies and planning their destruction.

On rare occasions the Jews find a welcome. The city of Vilna is created by Gedymin, ruler of the grand duchy, when he ventures out on a hunt for game. He sleeps where one of his arrows falls, and dreams of a big wolf wearing an iron shield and howling as loudly as a pack of a hundred wolves. Awakening in fright, he asks his priest for an interpretation. The wolf, says the holy man, represents an important place that will rise where he stands, and the roar indicates its future reputation. Accordingly, Gedymin builds a city on the site and names it for the river Vilia flowing through it. Anxious for a population to fill his new streets, he invites *all* newcomers regardless of their religion, and Jews crowd into this newly safe place. But as always in Europe, East and West, they remain subject to someone else's dream.

They prosper for long periods in the Netherlands, where the heretical Baruch Spinoza finds a home for his ethical philosophy. And in post-revolutionary France there are Jewish statesmen, bankers, musicians, and philosophers. In Berlin a free education becomes available to indigent Jews willing to study German, French, and European history. Still, menace is never far away. The nearest approximation to Hitler's genocidal procedures comes in the seventeenth-century Ukraine, where Cossacks, urged on by a maniacal leader who blames the Jews for all evils, go on a lethal rampage. Historian and Holocaust survivor Alexander Kimel describes the results: The Ukrainian Jews "were destined to utter annihilation, and the slightest pity shown to them was looked upon as treason. Scrolls of the law were taken out of the synagogues by the Cossacks, who danced on them while drinking whisky. After this the Jews were laid down upon them and butchered without mercy. Thousands of Jewish infants were thrown into wells or burned alive."

Russia handles its Jews with slow-motion malice. Beginning in the eighteenth century its hundreds of thousands of Hebrews are forbidden to travel beyond the rural towns—*shtetls*—in which they already live. An invisible moat rings the Jewish communities of Poland, the Ukraine, and Russia. The Romanov czars, fearful of revolution in the wake of foreign wars and increased taxes, use them as convenient scapegoats. Pogroms are encouraged during the frequent periods of social unrest.

The mortality rate among Jews is twice as high as for Christians in the territories. That rate is accelerated by the military draft, which sweeps up Jewish boys and puts them into training schools far away from their homes. The Russian author Alexander Herzen witnesses one forced march in 1835. The officer in charge confides that less than half of the children will reach their destination. "They just die off like flies. A Jew boy, you know, is such a frail, weakly creature, like a skinned cat; he is not used to tramping in the mud for ten hours a day and eating biscuit—then again, being among strangers, no father, no mother, nor petting; well, they cough and cough until they cough themselves into their graves. And I ask you, what use is it to the government? What can they do with little boys?"

This method is judged insufficient to deal with the Jewish Problem. Some fifty years later Czar Alexander III resolves to find a way to deal with the obdurate, stiff-necked people once and for all. Konstantin Pobiedonostev, procurator of the Holy Synod, offers a three-pronged scheme: "one-third conversion, one-third emigration, and one-third starvation."

And yet, wherever Jews congregate, a saving remnant always manages to survive. What is the formula for their endurance against millennia of savagery, persecutions, murders, evictions? There are four ingredients.

THE FIRST IS LITERACY. These, after all, are people of the Book. Sometime around A.D. 200, an epochal resolution is made. Some of the greatest wise men and teachers have perished at the hands of the Romans and they have left nothing behind. From here on, Judaism's traditions must be set down on paper, lest they be forgotten and lost forever.

The product of this decision is the Mishna. It deals with Jewish laws of diet, behavior, worship, justice, marriage. During the centuries following the writing of the Mishna, rabbis write down their discussions and commentaries in a series of books known as the Talmud. Together, the Torah, Mishna, and Talmud provide Jewish children with their moral education even in the worst of circumstances. Such study stays with them for a lifetime.

Well over a millennium later, the power of this textual base was still evident. An old book, preserved from the millions burned by the Third Reich and now housed in a New York City library, bears the stamp of the Society of Woodchoppers for the Study of Mishna in Berditchev. These axmen required no literacy to do their jobs, but that was beside the point. They were Jews, and therefore they met regularly to discuss Talmudic matters. The outside world, with its threats and exclusions, is forgotten during those hours. If they argue about religious matters, they agree about the special nature of their lives: gentiles drink away their leisure time; Jews analyze the Law.

The Yiddish novelist Mendele Sforim describes the education of a typical *shtetl* boy during this long period. From the Middle Ages to the eighteenth century there is hardly any variance: "Little Shlomo had accumulated before his bar mitzvah as much experience as if he were a Methuselah. Where hadn't he been and what hadn't he seen! Mesopotamia, the Tigris and Euphrates rivers, Persia, Egypt and the Nile, the deserts and the mountains. It was an experience which the children of no other people knew. He could not tell you a thing about Russia, about Poland, about Lithuania, and their peoples, laws, kings, politicians. But you just ask him about Og, King of Bashan. He knew the people who lived in tents and spoke Hebrew or Aramaic; the people who rode on mules or camels and drank water out of pitchers. . . . He knew nothing concerning the fields about him, about rye, wheat, potatoes, and where his bread came from; didn't know of the existence of such things as oak, pine and fir trees; but he knew about vineyards, date palms, pomegranates, locust trees. He knew about the dragon and the leopard, about the turtledove and the hart that panteth after the living waters; he lived in another world."

Shlomo is allowed to live in that place until the Enlightenment (*Haskalah* in Hebrew) transfigures Europe in the 1800s. The prime minister of England, Benjamin Disraeli, a Christianized Jew, proudly identifies himself as the missing page between the Old Testament and the New, and pushes for greater tolerance. The Rothschild family of bankers rises from "Jew Street" in Frankfurt to enjoy an unmatched global reach. Within the city ghettos as well as the contained world of the *shtetl,* ambition is no longer something to be held in check. The sounds of laughter and desire serve as a powerful counterpoint to the sighs of resignation.

The gates of opportunity swing open again, and power of learning acquired at *cheder,* Hebrew school, is turned toward the other world—the real one—where for the first time Shlomo can be more than an obscure scholar in an unknown village.

THE SECOND INGREDIENT is adaptability, as reflected in two old Jewish stories. In the first, a new flood covers the earth. After thirty-eight days and nights of rain, scientists forecast the end of the human race. A Catholic priest addresses his congregation: "My children, it is time to make our confessions and offer up our souls to God." A Protestant sermonizer says: "Let us bow our heads together and recite the Lord's Prayer over and over again until the final annihilation." A rabbi speaks to his people: "My children, we have forty-eight hours to learn how to breathe underwater."

In the other, a rabbi visits Poland. Returning to Lithuania, he informs the congregation, "The Jews of that place are especially remarkable people. I saw a Jew who all day long was scheming how to get rich. I saw a Jew who's all the time waving a red flag and calling for revolution. I saw a Jew who was running after every woman. And I saw a Jew who was an ascetic and preached religion all the time." A listener responds: "Why's so surprising? There are many Jews in Lithuania, all types." "You don't understand," says the rabbi. "It was the same Jew."

For Hebrews of any age, social and governmental restrictions are a way of life. The trick is not to get around them but to use them. Are we forbidden to enter any other guild but the diamond cutters? Very well then, we'll learn the trade and dominate it. Are we kept from owning land? Then we'll move into the cities, seek livelihoods there and invigorate the culture. Are Christians not allowed to lend money? Then we will become the world's bankers. When *Haskalah* provides new opportunities we take whatever comes our way—law, medicine, finance, education, politics, it doesn't matter.

This pliability exacts a high price. For their efforts, Jews are called disloyal, usurers, cosmopolites, plotters. Since they have no way to win this age-old battle for unconditional acceptance, a vast collective neurosis settles in. Sigmund Freud detects it in himself and others; he thinks it may be embedded in the genes. "Though we may admit for the memory-traces in our archaic inheritance we have so far no stronger proof than those memories evoked by analytical work," he writes in *Moses and Monotheism,* "yet this proof seems convincing enough to postulate such a state of affairs." It is an odd endorsement of Carl Jung's theories, which Freud so often opposes. Jung's monograph on analytical psychology posits a "collective unconscious" that constitutes "the residue of the life of the ancestors." Whether the doctors are correct or not remains debatable to this day. But there is no arguing the psychology of apprehension among the world's Jewry, perhaps inherited, perhaps acquired in early childhood. If it is a source of unhappiness, it is also responsible for their social cohesion and their urge to make a place for themselves, however prohibitive the cost.

THE THIRD INGREDIENT is humor. Just as the word "laughter" is buried in the word "slaughter," so the tragedies of Jewish history hide a subversive wit. We know that even in Auschwitz jokes made the rounds; common sense tells us that a people, no matter how oppressed, will find moments of humor in the long day's journey. Many times the Bible instructs the Hebrews to take harps, trumpets, cymbals, and lyres, and make "a joyful noise unto the Lord in all the earth." Surely that noise must have been accompanied by merriment. In the post-biblical era, there are many descriptions of Jewish celebrations accompanied by hilarity. And in the Middle Ages, a new Jewish occupation is born: the *badkhn,* Hebrew for jester. A sixteenth-century poem speaks of a merchant who "danced so merrily/with the beautiful maidens/that he became thirsty/he forgot all his cares/to the jesters he nodded/that they stop not too soon." Regulations regarding the Jews of Hesse in 1690 prohibit "the custom in vogue to date of riding to meet the bridegroom—except for waiters and jesters." The method of compensation has not varied from that time to this: a Jewish wedding song of the eighteenth century pleads, "Give also gifts today to the clowns and to the musicians."

The roots of modern comedy lie in the Jewish past. "The merrymaker did not occupy a prominent social position," notes historian Ezekiel Lifschutz. "He was feared on account of the rhymes which he freely utilized to his own purposes and frequently caused embarrassment. People exploited his friendship for their personal advantage, they were amused by his apt parables, paraphrases and merry songs and then proceeded to censure him as a sinner."

Comic stories, spread orally through the centuries, eventually catch Freud's attention. In a letter to his colleague William Fleiss in 1897, he writes, "Let me confess that I have recently made a collection of deeply significant Jewish jokes," psychical productions that he finds analogous to dreams. Some of the most meaningful stories, he goes on, are those concerned with Jews hiding under layers of pretension: "The doctor, asked to look after the Baroness at her confinement, pronounces that the moment has not come, and suggests to the Baron that in the meantime they should have a game of cards in the next room. After a while a cry of pain from the Baroness strikes the ears of the two men: '*Ah, mon dieu, que je suffre!*' Her husband springs up, but the doctor signs for him to sit down: 'It's nothing. Let's get on with the game!' A little later there are again sounds from the pregnant woman: '*Mein Gott, mein Gott was fur Schmerzen!*' 'Aren't you going in, Professor?' asks the Baron. 'No, no, it's not time yet.' At last there comes from next door an unmistakable cry of '*Oy vay!*' The doctor throws down his cards and exclaims, 'Now it's time.' "

Such tales are usually told by Jews in mixed company, and they tend to make gentiles uncomfortable. But that is their point—to discomfit the outsider. Somerset Maugham describes a relevant incident in "The Alien Corn." A wealthy Jew, Fred Robenstein, mimics the accent and ghetto mannerisms of a pushcart peddler until his listeners are weak with laughter. But the listener cannot join in the amusement: "I was not quite sure of a sense of humor that made such cruel fun of his own race."

Freud's disciple Theodor Reik explains that kind of uneasy comedy in a paper entitled *Jewish Wit.* In desperate times, "the Jew sharpens, so to speak, the dagger which he takes out of his enemy's hand, stabs himself, then returns it gallantly to the anti-Semite with the silent reproach: 'Now see whether you can do as well.' " In less threatening situations, the humor acts "to bring relaxation in the ardor of battle with the seen and with the invisible enemy; to attract as well as repel him; and to conceal one's self. Jewish wit hides as much as it discloses. Like the seraph in the Temple of the Lord, it covers its face with two of its wings."

· · ·

THE FOURTH INGREDIENT is Judaism's other language, Yiddish. The primary tongue of the Jews is Hebrew, the language of the Bible and of prayer, and therefore sanctified. Yiddish is the common speech of the ever mobile people. It begins as a kind of slang, stirring Old High German with backchat from the Western European ghettos. As the Jews are forced to the Middle Countries, then north and east, they pick up phrases from the Romance languages and Slavic tongues. Although Yiddish is written in phonetic Hebrew, it is pronounced with greater expression and a more musical cadence. In time the irony, spirit, and rhythms of this polyglot vernacular begin to shape Jewish culture.

Condensed folktales spring up. Not quite jokes, not quite anecdotes, they find a home in the wry, ironic attitude and rapid pulse of Yiddish:

· Two Jews decide to assassinate the czar. They bring sharp instruments and conceal themselves behind trees in a park where the Russian leader takes his daily stroll. Hours pass and the czar fails to appear. At sundown one of them worries: "I don't know what's wrong. I hope nothing happened to him."

· One Jew sighs to another, "It would be best never to have been born." His friend agrees: "True, but how many are that lucky? Maybe one in a hundred thousand."

· Two Jews are sentenced to be executed by a firing squad. The captain offers Sol and Mendel blindfolds. Sol accepts. Mendel spits in the officer's face: "Keep your lousy blindfold!" Sol demurs: "Mendel, don't make trouble!"

· As a magnificent funeral procession passes by the *shtetl* gates an old man weeps. "You're a relative?" asks an astonished friend. "No." "Then how come you're crying?" "That's why."

In time a literature rises from the chatter-poems, romantic stories, moral fables. By the middle of the nineteenth century Yiddish has developed from a kind of enriched patois, claimed one poet, into "the language which will ever bear witness to the violence and murder inflicted on us, bears the marks of our expulsion from land to land, the language which absorbed the wails of the fathers, the laments of the generations, the poison and bitterness of history, the language whose precious jewels are undried, uncongealed Jewish tears."

Not everyone agrees with this assessment—including some very prominent Jews. In his lavish *omnium gatherum, The Joys of Yiddish,* Leo Rosten notes that from the start purists derided Yiddish for its "bastard" origins, its "vulgar" idioms, its "hybrid" vocabulary. "Germans called it a 'barbarous argot'; worse still, Hebraicists called it uncivilized cant."

An intense battle gets under way. On one side are the pedants who want Hebrew to be the one and only Jewish language—and their unwitting allies, the assimilationists who want Jews to discard Yiddish in favor of demotic German, French, and the Slavic tongues.

Against them are the common people who have no intention of abandoning what they called their *mamaloshen*—mother tongue. A *badkhn* known as Sanye of Bialystok foretells the outcome of this language war by voting with his feet. A nineteenth-century account describes the jester as one who "possessed great gifts of mimicry and comedy. He carried with him a suitcase with false beards, various costumes, even women's costumes, and portrayed every role with mimicry and comic gesture like a true artist." By the end of the century, however, as the Jews drained out of the Pale, Poland, and Lithuania, seeking the freedom of Western Europe and the New World, life became insupportable for professional comedians. "Once, early in the morning on a summer day I met Sanye coming from a wedding. He complained to me: 'Brother, things are bad. There is no longer any room for me here.' Six months later he left for America."

Sanye is not alone.

CHAPTER TWO

✦

THE FATHER

i

LOOKING BACK IN OLD AGE, Abraham Goldfaden came to recognize New York as Zion, the fulfillment of Jewish dreams. But it would not have seemed so back in Zhitomir. He was twenty-five when the United States finished its notorious Civil War. He had read about that conflict for nearly five years. Early on, the papers made much of the order from a General Ulysses S. Grant, who disliked Jewish peddlers catering to the Union soldiers: "The Jews, as a class violating every regulation of trade established by the Treasury Department are hereby expelled from the department." This dictum was rescinded by Abe Lincoln, but look what happened: scarcely three years later the president was shot by a maniac, an actor. Who could tell what was in store for the Jews of America?

Goldfaden was content to stay put. On the one hand, Russia was not such a wonderful country for its Jewish residents. On the other hand, things were beginning to loosen up. The Enlightenment had brought big changes. There were now a few progressive Jewish academies, places where you could read not only the Torah and the Talmud, but also Western novels and plays. Abraham's parents sent him to one, and were delighted with the results. Their son had turned out to be intelligent, original, and funny—Abie the Jester, they called him. When he graduated, the young man shocked the neighborhood: he took a leading role in an amateur production. This was not a normal thing for a Jewish boy, and even his liberal parents cautioned against it. He went ahead anyway.

From the first rehearsal Abraham was aisle-struck. Performing exerted very little appeal—almost every member of the cast had more stage presence. But writing; that was different. He could see himself as the first Yiddish playwright. Maybe the first Yiddish composer. Early signs were encouraging: Abraham couldn't read a note, but he managed to pick out one-fingered tunes on a piano. Verse was written to accompany the melodies, and a student hired to write down the notes. (Another thirty years and a musically illiterate Jewish youth would do the same thing. Irving Berlin had genius, Goldfaden was to concede, but he was not the first of his kind.)

Abraham's songs caught on; they were published and played in Jewish neighborhoods. Royalties, however, amounted to pennies. Clearly, he needed some other way to make a living. Well dressed, clean-shaven, except for a carefully trimmed military mustache, the young man went out to meet his destiny.

First he fancied himself a *maggid,* a teacher, but the salary was too small. Next, he went to Odessa, where he tried his hand at retailing. Not enough ladies came to his millinery store and he closed it. What about medical school, then? Czar Alexander II had liberalized some of Russia's conditions, but he was not ready to allow Jews to be doctors. Off went Abraham to Vienna, where he entered an academy. The study proved to be tedious, and his mind wandered. Journalism, he decided; this was a career for the Coming Man.

Returning to Russia, he founded several Yiddish periodicals, did some serious reporting as well as humorous pieces, tirelessly edited and publicized his work. No one could accuse Goldfaden of an energy shortage—only of an inability to find his vocation. Each paper, in turn, failed to find an audience and stopped publishing. By 1876 he seemed to have no future at all. Was it time to emigrate? He thought so; but not to the United States, a strange and uncivilized country. Talk about the whims of the czars; what about America, where a Civil War hero, a General George Armstrong Custer, had just been slain by wild Indians? How safe could a Jew be in a nation like this?

And so, at the age of thirty-six, a married man still in search of recognition, Abraham went off to Jassy, Romania, hometown of many progressive Jews. The name of Goldfaden was not unknown here; people had heard of his newspapers and they were familiar with some of his songs. Perhaps this was the place where he could establish a new Yiddish journal. One evening, elegantly attired in frock coat complete with carnation in the buttonhole, white gloves, and pince-nez glasses, radiating a new hauteur, the visitor went for a promenade. He stopped in at the Green Tree café, where Israel Gradner, a popular Jewish singer, was appearing.

After the first show, Goldfaden introduced himself. The two men hit it off, and following the consumption of much wine, the singer made a proposal to the writer. Suppose Israel and Abraham were to team up? He would do the songs, Abraham would recite his lyrics and poems. The men shook hands and outlined a show. The next day, when both were sober, it still seemed like a good idea. They scheduled a dual performance and advertised it all over town. On the appointed day a large crowd gathered, anxious to witness the results of this ballyhooed collaboration.

In his memoirs, Goldfaden is unusually candid. "The place was packed, but whether with people or wild animals I can't say. Instead of the usual comedian with tattered shoes and stockings to his knees, the audience beheld an elegant gentleman, a man with a serious air that commanded respect. In a deep silence, I begin my well-known poem, *Dus Pintale Yid* [The Essential Jew]. I recite slowly, ecstatically. They hold their breath. I end. I bow. Silence. The silence would have been all right, but when I go off I hear whistles—hisses!" Gradner's performance was greeted with generous applause, making Goldfaden's humiliation all the more painful.

That night he lay in bed trying to figure out what had gone wrong.

And then it came to him. Hardworking Jews had come to the Green Tree to be amused, to forget their tribulations for a few hours. And what had he given them? Moral instructions, history lessons. No wonder they replied with catcalls. Diversion they wanted? Diversion they would get. Sitting down at a makeshift desk he spent a sleepless night and day knocking out two acts of a slam-bang farce in the style of *commedia dell'arte:* a love triangle complete with songs. All he needed now was a person to write down the music, plus a few actors. Some sixty years later, a playwright named Moss Hart was to write, "In the theater, the difference between failure and success can be a matter of three or four hours." He thought himself original; Goldfaden had preceded him.

The exhausted playwright summoned Gradner, read him the dialogue, and croaked the numbers. The performer liked what he heard. Abraham was to recall that "Out of this came a piece—a nonsense, a hodge-podge! I don't even remember the name of it!" Nevertheless, on the evenings of October 5 and 8, 1876, that anonymous comedy was greeted with unbridled enthusiasm. Not a soul whistled or hissed. No one was aware that the Yiddish Theater had just been born.

ii

GOLDFADEN COMPARED those first enthusiastic spectators to toddlers. He wrote down to them, he claimed later, because to do any more would be to court public embarrassment. That first night at the Green Tree had taught him well. "I could not have dressed the children up in a frock, in trousers with suspenders. I had to put them in a pair of breeches with the seam buttoned up at the back."

The youngsters took their first significant steps in the Romanian city of Bathsan, another favorite of forward-thinking Jewry. Goldfaden, Gradner, and a small company of actors had journeyed there, seeking a larger venue. The timing could not have been less propitious. Hostilities between Turkey and Russia suddenly erupted into a shooting war, and the czar's army charged through towns looking for cannon fodder. In the late 1880s conscription meant state-sanctioned arrests of young men, on the street and in their houses. No appeal was possible. Once captured, the youths were presented with a choice: don a military uniform and follow orders, or face death by firing squad. It was persecution as before: long forced marches, the possibility of death en route, and the guns of the enemy if you made it through. Draft dodgers literally headed for the hills—in this case the Carpathian Mountains—or hid in secret rooms and attics until the troops had passed through.

Goldfaden's little assemblage had several men of draft age, and he persuaded a Jewish innkeeper to let them remain in his garret until it was safe to emerge. The days stretched into weeks. Still the soldiers stayed in town. The smuggled food began to taste of despair. But what began as a curse turned out to be a benison: the performers used the downtime to learn their art. As they practiced, Goldfaden, too old for the military, took pen and notebook and went downstairs to the inn.

There he hacked out one of the earliest service comedies, *Recruits,* the tale of a bumbling teenager in uniform. Aware that officials might interpret the play as anti-government, he found places for a patriotic song and an irresistible fife-and-drum-corps march. He brought the manuscript upstairs, and read the cast his new project. It was the next best thing to freedom; they started rehearsing that night. When the coast was clear he booked a large theater, blocked the scenes, and made ready for opening night a week later.

The debut was a smash; just about every adult Jew in Batshan attended *Recruits.* Some of the enthusiasts saw it two and three times, and Goldfaden and his actors were mobbed on the streets. Even so, the supply of willing ticket buyers dwindled fast. After a month it was time for the provincial celebrities to push on.

In England, Queen Victoria was proclaimed empress of India; in America, Alexander Graham Bell sold his newfangled telephone service and Thomas Alva Edison patented his phonograph. But it was still crazy over there, Abraham noticed; the presidential election was in dispute. Did Tilden win, or Hayes? Nobody knew. In Germany, Richard Wagner completed *Parsifal* and began to stake a big claim in classical music. A promising culture, the German one. But there was talk of Wagner's letters condemning Jewish composers. Better to stay in Romania. For the Goldfaden troupe, that country was the focus of the

developed world, and Galantz its epicenter. They journeyed to that
city and settled in.

A signal event occurred in Galantz during the winter of 1877: for
the first time a female performer was hired for a Yiddish production.
From the beginning, Goldfaden had written very minor parts for girls
because, as in Shakespeare's time, juvenile males had to play the roles.
The difference was that in Elizabethan England the Lord Chamber-
lain's Players were forbidden to hire women. The nascent Yiddish
Theater was not held back by law, but by tradition. No respectable Jewish parent would allow a daughter to appear with *any* group of unmar-
ried men—especially one comprised of clowns and musicians.

And yet, in this provincial place a virginal seamstress came to Goldfaden and pleaded for an audition. Astonished, he granted her wish.
Sarah Siegel proved to be an unalloyed delight; she was not only attractive, she had a pure, resonant soprano. He offered her the female lead
in his new operetta. She went home ecstatic—and returned disconsolate: Sarah's mother and father forbade her to join the troupe until she
had a husband. Goldfaden was used to emergencies by now and came
up with an on-the-spot solution. He was already married, and so was
Gradner. But what about the actor he had hired back in Jassy, Sacher
Goldstein? The young man was eighteen, perfect for Sarah. What did
it matter that the two had never met before? Goldfaden argued. This
would hardly be the first arranged marriage in the ghetto. And so it was
done. Sarah Siegel had a husband, the Yiddish Theater had a leading
lady, and now everything was set for the big time: Bucharest.

The capital of Romania provided Goldfaden with more than a fresh
audience. It also supplied him with new talent. In 1877 Bucharest was a
bustling city of manufacturing and middlemen. Scores of Russian Jews
had contracts with the czar's army for uniforms and ordnance, and
they relocated to be near the factories. Several of them attended Goldfaden's show, went backstage, and asked to try out for parts. One of
them, a local choir leader named Sigmund Mogulesko, could not only
sing but do imitations of all the well-known Romanian comedians.
Goldfaden saw a star in the making and signed him up over Gradner's
protest that one leading light was more than enough. At the clown's
debut, the audience went crazy. Gradner exploded. Here was this new-
comer, this *youth,* who mugged, upstaged actors, stole scenes. In a burst
of offended ego, he quit the company, returned to Jassy, and founded
his own troupe of amateurs. Gradner had no original material, but that

hardly mattered. He simply wrote down what he remembered of Gold-faden's dialogue and songs and gave it to the actors. In a place where copyright was almost unknown, every pirate had a license to steal.

Truth to tell, Goldfaden was something of a buccaneer himself. In her account of the early Yiddish Theater, Lulla Adler Rosenfeld observes that in order to beguile his audience, Abraham had to "con-tinually turn out plays, curtain-raisers, and couplets for the divertisse-ments between the acts. He also had to take care of business problems, bribe officials, rehearse the actors and, often as not, jump in and play a part himself." Since Goldfaden was creating a genre with little more than his own energy and conviction, "he may perhaps be forgiven if, along with so much that was original, he borrowed too. It must be admitted that one early operetta opens with a chorus from Wagner's *The Flying Dutchman*."

Other melodies recalled Beethoven and Offenbach. No one seemed to care. The unsophisticated spectators were pleased with any plot they could follow and any tune they could hum. In fact one of their favorites, a lullaby entitled "Raisins and Almonds," has been crooned by mothers ever since. It has never gone out of print:

> *Az du vest vern raykh, Idele*
> *Zolst zikh dermonen in dem lidele,*
> *Ropzhinkes mit mandlen,*
> *Dos vest zayn dayn baruf.*
> *Yidele vet ale handlen.*
> *Shlof zhe, Yidele shlof.*
>
> Beneath your cradle a lamb can be found,
> He'll go to the markets all around.
> Selling raisins and almonds you
> One day will reap.
> From this trade so uncommon do
> Sleep, little one, sleep.

All the while Goldfaden tried to bring his theatergoers along, fold-ing instructions into the comedy. His farces, *The Fanatic* and *Shmendrik*, for example, were elemental. But their subtext concerned the very seri-ous struggle between hyper-Orthodox and enlightened Jewry. In the first play a stuttering pedant, Kuni-Leml, convinces a girl's family that he would make an ideal groom, even though the girl loves another. At the wedding the bride's boyfriend, Max, suddenly appears in the costume of Kuni-Leml, imitating his rival's every gesture. The prospective bridegroom stares open-mouthed.

KUNI-LEML: Reb Kuni-Leml?

MAX: W-what is it now?

KUNI-LEML: I m-meant to ask. . . . If I walk down the street and someone c-calls out to m-me, "Reb K-Kuni-Leml! Reb K-Kuni-Leml!" should I answer or not?

MAX: No, you m-mustn't answer, since you're not K-Kuni-Leml! Now r-run along home!

KUNI-LEML (*Reflecting*): So he r-really is Kuni-Leml, and I am . . . me.

Pandemonium reigns, and amid the confusion true love wins out. But something else prevails as well—the children of the *Haskalah*. They have triumphed over the old-style Judaism of blind obedience and rote scholarship.

In *Shmendrik* the title character is a ponderous *yeshiva* student. With the help of his overprotective mother, he also tries to wed a sweet-faced young woman. She barely manages to evade his clutches by running off with *her* lover. In the end the blockhead is left with a homely girl whose IQ is lower than his. Simple as these narratives were, they spoke directly to the Jewish playgoers of Romania. Before the year was out, "Kuni-Leml" and "Shmendrik" had entered the Yiddish language as synonyms for the kind of dolts who get tangled in their own idiotic schemes.

And then came March 4, 1878—a momentous day for Russia, a catastrophic one for the Yiddish Theater. Outgunned and outmanned, the Ottoman Turks sued for peace. Russian businessmen, enriched by the war and elated by the victory, returned to their homes. Goldfaden's troupe played to smaller and smaller houses, shrank to a few loyalists, and then split up. Their leader refused to give in to circumstance. He spent hours pondering an atlas and asking himself the same question

over and over. Where to go? America? Still out of the question. The
papers spoke of a Lincoln County War in the territory of New Mexico.
Somebody shot an Englishman, a friend of a crook called Billy the Kid.
And then Billy put together a posse to kill the killers. It was crazy over
there. Uncivilized. Wild. Since Russians would not come to him anymore, maybe he should go to the Russians. He would think on it.

CHAPTER THREE

✦

THE FIRST SON

i

AFTER THE RUSSIAN TRIUMPH, a Jewish soldier returned to his home in the port city of Odessa. The angular, high-strung veteran spent his days as a newspaper distributor and his nights at the town's major theater, smitten with an actress. Then again, Jacob Adler was always beguiled by one female or another. He was known in nearly every café, wine cellar, and bordello in Odessa. "And yet," his memoirs note with melodramatic zest, "there was an emptiness. Something was lacking. I was restless, ill at ease, blindly seeking a place where my soul could find peace."

One day as he sat in the paper's editorial offices, Jacob's eye was caught by a story about the Yiddish Theater in Bucharest. "My heart began to beat fast," he recalled; "the blood rushed to my head and I sprang to my feet. I looked again. No, I have not dreamed it. Yiddish Theater! The language is Yiddish, the plays Yiddish, the actors Yiddish. The troupe is under the directorship of the poet Abraham Goldfaden. Gone, my vague longings, my melancholia and malaise! I had a goal, a purpose in life. I was determined to bring the Yiddish Theater to Odessa!" There is no more pregnant sentence in the memoirs of any Yiddish actor. In the years to come, the childless Goldfaden was to have three spiritual sons, and Jacob Adler was to be the greatest of them.

For more than a year Jacob sent the troupe letters full of promises, extolling his fellow Jews, who were "starved" for Yiddish theater. When the war ended, and the audiences trickled back from Romania, two Goldfaden performers sent the word Jacob had been praying for. They were on the way to Odessa. Adler waited for them at the station. As they stepped from the car he was not sure whether to laugh or cry. The hams were identical: "Rosenberg . . . not a hair on his face—a regular priest! Spivakovsky was clean-shaven. The two of them were as alike as two drops of water, both in black-winged capes, high hats, dangling pince-nez, gloves, spats, lacquered boots—a pair of barons!"

At the meeting Rosenberg boomed on about appearances before the king and queen of Romania. "Look at Spivakovsky," he boomed; "all Romania rings with his name." Jacob suspected that boast, like the finery, was all for show. His suspicions were confirmed when the two men asked for a loan. They were down to their last rubles. But not all was lost. Rosenberg turned out to be a practiced confidence man; Spivakovsky, who came from a prominent family, knew many of the local businessmen. Within a few weeks the pair had collected enough money for a first performance. Assembling capable players would be a more complicated matter.

The best candidates Jacob could find were folksingers, bearded, untutored Jews who had never played anything but themselves. He brought them before Rosenberg. The actor erupted: "You look like chimney sweeps, not actors! I need human beings. Do you understand? Go make yourself into human beings!" Excited by the possibility of Yiddish Theater, these amateurs did something no adult male in their families had ever done before. They shaved. Instead of short peasant

coats, heavy pants, and high boots, they assumed frock coats with narrow trousers, white shirts, black ties, silk hats.

Opening night would take place at a restaurant, where rehearsals
began in early June. Passersby peeked in the open windows, gawked at
the players, and asked for a song or two. Rosenberg turned on them:
"We are no wine cellar entertainers, no folksingers and clowns. You
will have to pay money to see us. We are actors—artists!" And pay they
did: 5 rubles for the cheap seats, 10 for places down front.

Two brief sketches began the evening. They were followed by
Recruits, starring Spivakovsky as the clueless soldier-in-training. Jacob
recalled the openers: "The usual business of love. The parents are
against the marriage. The lovers decide to elope. The matchmaker
gives away their secret. Tears—the parents give their blessing—a song,
a dance, the curtain falls." Those appetizers went well, and the entrée
overwhelmed the spectators. Curtain calls were greeted with ovations.
Everyone agreed that Rosenberg had not exaggerated; these Yiddish
speakers were indeed actors—artists, just like the gentile ones in
Moscow.

Several weeks later the group performed at a bigger venue—a real
theater. There they did a string of Goldfaden comedies, including
Shmendrik and *Breindele Cossack,* in which Jacob Adler made his first stage
appearance playing a young soldier. All seemed well; the troupe was
moving from strength to strength. Then, abruptly, bad news arrived.
Goldfaden was on his way to Russia. Jacob made a dire forecast: the
Master will have all the great stars in his company. He will make us look
like the amateurs we are. He will use up all the oxygen in Odessa. We
must get out of town before he arrives. The others sighed like actors
and obeyed like employees. The company booked passage for the
provinces.

But Rosenberg, ever the confidence man, was not content to surrender all that he had won. An idea came to him as they made ready to
leave. "They have a Goldfaden?" he told his colleagues. "We *also* have a
Goldfaden." It happened that Abraham Goldfaden's brother Naphtali
lived in the outskirts of Odessa. He was a watchmaker, but what of
that? Rosenberg dropped in, dangled rubles, and hired him as a non-
acting member of the troupe. Now they, too, could call themselves
"The Goldfaden Company."

Theoretically, this should have given Russian Jews twice the opportunity to see well-done comedy and drama. In fact neither company

was much good. Goldfaden's leading actor was as deaf as a post, "catching cues as a dog catches fleas," says Jacob's memoir. As for his own troupe, the prompter was missing two front teeth, so that when he supplied a line the words were accompanied by unplanned whistles and hisses. It hardly mattered. The Russian Jews *were* starved for theater, and both organizations played to full houses. After a triumphal tour of the major cities, Abraham Goldfaden crossed the Romanian border and charged into Bucharest. As he predicted, the city's Jewish population treated him as a celebrity. Now that the Father had exited Russia, Jacob's pseudo-Goldfaden company had no competition. They confidently booked a theater in Kishinev, where they alternated with a czarist Russian company on tour from Moscow.

At that venue Adler got his first glimpse of big-time backstage life: "The leading tragedian was a great actor but a great drunkard. One night, watching in the wings, I saw him so loaded he could barely be understood when he spoke. Nevertheless, he put on his makeup without even looking in the mirror. He played magnificently, made a marvelous exit, then fell, weeping, into the stage manager's arms, beat his breast, swore he would never drink again, and made his way with a bowed head to his dressing room. The stage manager told me the same scene took place every night."

Jacob also got his first glimpse of a man he would see a great deal in another country, at another time. An eighteen-year-old peddler named David Kessler had fallen in love with the Yiddish Theater. Against the wishes of his deeply observant family he contrived to meet Adler and persuaded him to arrange an audition. Even though some of the actors mocked the bumpkin's manner and delivery, Jacob thought he spotted talent and offered Kessler a job. He might as well have asked for a conversion to Greek Orthodoxy; the senior Kesslers raised such a storm that David backed off. He would not leave home for another two years, when a traveling group of Yiddish players passed through Kishinev. When they departed, he left with them to become, in time, Goldfaden's spiritual third son. David's shocked parents went into mourning. As far as they were concerned, their defiant boy was dead.

ii

IN DANNENBERG the curtain rose on Jacob's troupe—and just as
swiftly rang down. The date was February 28, 1881, and the buzz backstage was that something had happened outside, a street fight perhaps,
or an explosion. A Russian officer took the stage and made an
announcement that drained the blood from everyone's face: Czar
Alexander II had just been murdered. An immediate question rang
out among the actors and the ticket-holders. Were the assassins Jews?

Within weeks all the plotters were rounded up. Several of them confessed and named their fellow conspirators, hoping to save themselves
from the gallows. It happened that all the activists were of Christian
background; during the planning stages, however, they had stayed at
the house of a young Jewish woman. The Russian government, fearful
of radical activities and badly in need of a scapegoat, used that connection to build a case against the Hebrews. They were portrayed as people whose loyalties were suspect, whose rites and temples, whose very
language separated them from the *real* Russians.

With statistics to back him up, Irving Howe characterizes 1881 as "a
turning point in the history of the Jews as decisive as that of 70 A.D.,
when Titus's legions burned the Temple at Jerusalem, or 1492, when
Ferdinand and Isabella decreed the expulsion from Spain." Up until
that year, New York Jewry was largely composed of a few thousand
Ashkenazis from Germany and a smaller number of Sephardics from
Spain and Portugal. They had prospered in the New World, founding
charitable organizations, building the world's largest synagogue, Temple Emanu-El, as well as a major Manhattan hospital, Mount Sinai.
Anti-Semitic incidents were few, and tended to be snobbish rather
than violent (in the novel *Redburn,* for example, Herman Melville
describes a New York City Jew as "a curly-headed little man with a
dark oily face, and a hooked nose, like the pictures of Judas Iscariot").

But from 1881 on, wave upon wave of Hebrews fled Eastern Europe and sailed for the United States. It made no difference that another American president, James Garfield, had just been shot to death. The carnage of war and assassination was now commonplace to Russian Jews; notions of wild Indians and criminal gangs no longer served to intimidate. They had seen worse, and there were more horrors to come.

This mass exodus, some twenty million souls when the final tally was in, was prompted by a series of pogroms—the Russian term for devastations—sponsored by czarist officials. Among the incidents were house burnings, beatings, theft, massacres of men, women, and children. The violence culminated in the May Laws of 1882, restricting Jews from owning land, practicing a profession or craft, or attending schools and universities. The decrees immediately altered the villages and cities of Imperial Russia. Anti-Semitism had been granted official sanction and "spontaneous" riots broke out in carefully selected cities. The Yiddish troupes, fragmented and jittery, scattered in the aftermath of Alexander's murder, waiting for the ax to fall. On August 7 of the following year, it did. A decree was nailed up in every town square. Henceforth, it said, Yiddish Theater was forbidden throughout the land.

Jacob, now married and the father of a young girl, spoke for the actors, designers, directors, and hangers-on. "There was no way around the ukase. It was steel and iron—the law. Nothing remained then but to leave Russia entirely. But where were we to go?" Rosenberg stayed behind in Russia; he saw himself as a crafty loner whose silver tongue and quick hands could get him through any conditions. The others, including Spivakovsky, abandoned theater for other jobs, or toured as street entertainers. To get around the authorities, they called their presentations "German concerts."

Jacob refused to follow their lead. He informed the few remaining members of his company that there was "one piece of light still visible above the flood. London." Privately he had doubts: "Would we survive there? Would Yiddish Theater be possible? Could we play, earn our bread?" There was only one way to find out, and on a cold November day he and his fellow émigrés sailed off to England with little more than the clothes on their backs and the costumes in their trunks.

Aside from a restaurant owner who could feed them for a night or two, Adler knew the name of only one other Englishman. Happily, he was Jacob's distant cousin, Rabbi Nissim Hillel Adler, one of the most influential Jews in the city. The spiritual leader of London's Jewry granted an audience. The clergyman looked down his nose at the actor. Adler remembered that "the very twist of his mouth as he pronounced the word 'Yiddish' told me our beloved language had no place in his heart. And I had come to spread this 'jargon' further, popularize it still more? Worst of all, to do so in a theatre where, God forbid, strangers might come and jeer?"

Faced with such a firm refusal, Jacob had no choice; he put ads in the Jewish papers, asking for financial aid. Some businessmen kicked in enough for several bare-bones productions. He paused, uncertain of how to proceed. The Goldfaden repertoire had always made him uncomfortable—too many bromides, too many fools, too many crowd-pleasing numbers at the expense of character. He wanted to play complex, credible figures, men like himself who spoke from the heart without breaking into song. Yet no one had dared to produce really serious Yiddish Theater, and it could very well be that there was no audience for such dramas. Jacob's ambition had a poignance about it; within him was an uneasy mix of Jewish tradition and *Haskalah* freedom. He knew that the conflict would either tear him apart or help him to bring a new intelligence and art to his chosen profession.

Two plays seemed to fill the bill. Jacob knew very well that *The Beggar of Odessa* was a shameless rewrite of a French play, *The Ragpicker of Paris.* The piece, he was to acknowledge, had "no great literary value. But the role gave so much room for ability, for variation, for the art of mime— in short, I decided that this was an excellent, a truly theatrical play."

Adler's granddaughter described his London accomplishment: "As the Beggar, Jacob sat on the ground drawing from his basket his crazy odds and ends, and his perplexity as he examined these objects was unforgettable." He had a drunken scene that became a tour de force. Pursued, he crawled into his own basket, a contortion that was met with deafening approval. This was followed by a courtroom confrontation, in which the Beggar told his tragic story and pleaded for the troubled daughter he adored. At the final curtain, "when he proclaimed that he stood forever with his own, with the poor, the audience stamped, thundered, shook the walls with their tribute. On a stage so small he could hardly turn about, Jacob Adler had become a great actor."

Two months later he exceeded that performance in the title role in *Uriel Acosta,* based on an authentic historical figure. Acosta was a Portuguese intellectual whose Orthodox family had fled to Holland during the Inquisition. In the play, Uriel concludes that Galileo was right—the earth does move around the sun. This is as sacrilegious to the Jews as it was to the Roman Catholics. Like the Italian astronomer, the Jewish philosopher is forced by the elders in his congregation to recant. But the disavowal is insincere, and only serves to increase his dilemma. The Judaism in which Acosta was raised will not allow him to speak in behalf of science. Science will not allow him to return to an outworn creed. Racked with conflict, he takes his own life.

The operatic plot was made for an actor who enjoyed big moments, and *Uriel Acosta* brimmed with them. For the run of the play, Adler had taken a larger theater and the opening night audience included London's most prominent Jews, including his censorious cousin, in the company of a Rothschild. The crowd's response was terrific; many would not leave the theater until they had a chance to speak to the leading man, press his hands, express their gratitude. Gazing at Jacob's imposing posture and avian profile, one of them bestowed a new title on the star. It was repeated all around, and the sobriquet stuck. Thereafter the actor would be referred to as *Nesher Hagadel*—the Great Eagle.

To top *Uriel Acosta* would have been impossible for most leading men, and even the Great Eagle found it difficult. He finally came up with Friedrich Schiller's *The Robbers,* a good-brother, bad-brother melodrama set in the Middle Ages. Adler was first cast as Franz Moor, the cynical and repellent villain. Then he played Karl Moor, the noble knight who casts his lot with the poor, à la Robin Hood. Finally, he played both roles in the same evening. "Since the brothers never meet in the play," Adler recalled, "I had time between scenes to change my makeup and costume and come on as the other character." He concludes with typical brio, "In one night to play two such parts! Just to throw myself from one into the other cost me whole rivers of sweat. But the satisfaction of it! The achievement!"

Alas, the glorious moment was not to endure. In the winter of 1886 Rivka, the Adlers' three-year-old daughter, died of the croup. Only a few months later his twenty-seven-year-old wife contracted an infection at the birth of their infant son, Abraham. She passed away on the Jewish holiday of Tisha Bov. Jacob saw it as an indecipherable judgment from above. He walked around in a daze for months, barely able to function. Only onstage could he escape his sorrows and recover his spirit. He disappeared into the roles of spectacular heroes and overstated wrongdoers, often assuming their personalities when he went offstage. But the life force was too strong for an extended period of mourning. He had carried on with an emotional young actress, Jennya Kaiser: "Sitting at the play," he remembered, "she found pleasure in weeping whole cups of tears, with never a care that she might injure those beautiful eyes!" A child was born of this union, and Jacob was intent on making it legitimate. Or so he claimed.

Then, in a pattern that was to repeat itself throughout his life, he abruptly announced his engagement to another actress in the company, Dinah Shtettin. Jacob and Jennya ran into each other after the wedding; he said he was still in love with her, she spurned his advances, walked away, and took up with a young Yiddish playwright. Somehow, Adler thought this unfair. To forget his tribulations, he threw himself into project after project, confident that he would build a power base in London, working and living there for years to come. That dream ended on the night of January 18, 1887.

At Smith's theater, located in the East End, Adler scheduled a light entertainment for his followers. *Gypsy Girl,* a full-length operetta in the Viennese style, went very well that evening. Laughter and ovations got more boisterous with each number. The fifth and final act was to close with the spectacular burning of a house, an illusion aided by flames issuing from "Bengal Fire," a mix of potassium nitrate, sulfur, charcoal, and sodium chloride. The harmless effect, well known to magicians, had been in common use for decades. On this night, however, some unwanted sparks floated into the air, and someone in the audience yelled "Fire!" Others took up the shout.

From the stage, cast members looked down at a gathering stampede. The next few moments, Adler recalled in theatrical terms, "was the scene played out whenever men and women cease to be rational beings and give way to blind animal panic. *They* were the actors now, we their helpless, terrified audience." He stepped to the apron of the stage and shouted authoritatively, "There is no fire. There is no danger. Go back to your seats. Nothing has happened. You are all safe!" For a moment all was silent; then came shouts from the rear: "He is lying. Fire! Fire! Fire!" The panic resumed as hundreds pushed and struggled with one another in a frantic effort to get out.

An escapee notified the police, and fifteen minutes later fire wagons pulled up to Smith's theater. They were useless. Adler was right—there had been no conflagration, only mindless hysteria boiling through the narrow corridors. In all, seventeen people were trampled to death that night, among them two children. The city of London officially listed the tragedy as an Act of God. After a decent interval Adler announced that another play was in the planning stages. No one stopped by the box office to ask about the name of the play, or the price of the tickets, or the names of the stars. It was now midwinter, and, the actor wrote, "We moved heaven and earth to get the theater going again. It was useless. Our appeals to the public, our attempts to make them see reason—all to no avail. Talk to the trees and the stones!" Even in flush times the nightly gross had been no more than a few pounds. "How much could we take in now? The theater stayed so cold, dark, and empty you could hunt wolves in the gallery."

Adler considered the alternatives. Russia was out. Eastern Europe seemed to be following the czar's example; there were almost daily reports of pogroms in Poland and Galicia. According to the census, Paris had enough Jews to support a small theater, but every single Yiddish company had failed there. Asked about the City of Light, Jacob condemned it as "a grave." He could see only one open gate. "From America," his memoir states, "we had already received joyful tidings. Maybe too joyful. Experts ourselves in the art of bragging, we had long discounted half the great good fortune reported by our colleagues in that land. But even with half discounted, the other half remained! And one sign we had that erased every doubt: Of all the actors that had gone to America, none had returned."

It was said that a Yiddish troupe was doing business in New York. With what results, no one seemed to know. Letters were sparse, rumors constant. And, Jacob asked his actors, if they did agree to go to the States, how would they find the money? A Yiddish proverb came to mind: *Got vet helfn. Vi helf nor God biz Got vet helfn—God will provide. If only He would provide until He provides.* First Jacob scrounged around London, pleading for a handout; when nothing came of that he announced a farewell performance with high-priced tickets. There was no advance sale. Only one court of appeal was left: Rabbi Adler.

"On that occasion," Jacob noted, "the old man was surprisingly cordial." The reason for the warm response was not hard to discern. "From my first words the Rabbi grasped the all-important fact: I was taking myself and my theater out of London." To get rid of this interloping Yiddishist, the rabbi was willing to dole out £30. The gift amounted to about $150 in American money—not a very generous donation, but enough to take Jacob Adler across the Atlantic, in the company of his son, Abraham (the new Mrs. Adler would stay in London until Jacob established a theater and a home), four performers, and a musical director.

Jacob had heard "confused, uncertain rumors" about Chicago, but they were enough to give him heart. He went down to the waterfront and bought space in steerage at $35 per person. Following the purchase, he wrote letters to a handful of Yiddish actors whose addresses he had in New York City. Early in 1888, along with hundreds of others—Jews, Italians, Slovaks—the little company walked up the gangplank and made ready for a three-week voyage.

The conditions don't have to be imagined; there are plenty of accounts by passengers who made the trip during that period. "Crowds everywhere," wrote one, "ill-smelling bunks, uninviting washrooms—this is steerage. The odors of scattered orange peelings, tobacco, garlic and disinfectants meeting but not blending. On many ships even drinking water is grudgingly given. We literally had to steal water for the steerage from the second cabin and that of course at night. The bread was absolutely unbearable, and was thrown into the water by the irate emigrants."

Another remembered moving from his tiny shelf-bed "with the greatest of caution because I didn't want to be hit with the contents of the stomach being steadily disgorged by my upper neighbor. When I got up and walked by the women's quarters I heard more screaming. Other men were up to help the sick. In a little while our whole state-room was filled with sick and 'nurses.' There was a running to the sailors for water and to the doctor for help and medicine. Instead of water and medicine we received a bawling out for having disturbed their sleep."

Jacob and his colleagues came through the trip thinner and grimmer. Their spirits did not rise until they entered New York Harbor. Ellis Island was only an architect's plan at that time; Adler and company cleared customs in Castle Garden, a drab, hexagonal building in Battery Park, the southernmost part of Manhattan. They sat on the grass outside, waiting for someone, anyone to come down and greet them with a simple *sholem aleichem.* Not one person appeared. "The loneliness! God, what loneliness!" Adler lamented. "They probably feared that with our coming their poor little fishpond on the Bowery would grow even more crowded and muddy." That settled it. He and his colleagues would not spend a single night here. The hell with New York. There was just enough money to take them to Chicago. They caught the train that night.

iii

IN THE GREAT EAGLE'S Ptolemaic worldview, everything centered on Jacob Adler. If people from New York's Yiddish Theater failed to meet the boat, it could only be because they feared competition from a *real* personality. Actually, many factors kept the Yiddish performers away and rivalry was the least of them. The struggle for existence in New York City gave little time for such indulgences as a meeting at Castle Garden, and no spare cash to buy the immigrants so much as a glass of tea.

For a decade after the Civil War, New York City remained a Protestant city. The movers and shakers, whether upright (Episcopal bishop Henry Codman Porter), piratical (J. P. Morgan), or corrupt (Boss William Marcy Tweed), were all WASPs who represented Manhattan's mainstream. But from the 1870s onward, New York's booming economy and large swaths of undeveloped real estate enticed blacks from Dixie and the West Indies, Irish from Hibernia, and Jews from Eastern Europe. The African-Americans gathered in the Tenderloin—an area between Fifth and Eighth Avenues, from 23rd to 57th Streets. The Irish filled up Hell's Kitchen on the far West Side, between Ninth and Twelfth Avenues, from 34th to 57th Streets. That left the Jews with the Lower East Side, from the Bowery to First Avenue, and from 14th Street to well below Canal Street.

The latter area had changed so much since the Reconstruction period that longtime residents felt out of place. The streets above the 60s were still unnamed horse paths, and north Manhattan was covered with scattered woods and several large farms. But each year the city pushed further uptown to accommodate the increasing population. Real estate was booming. More industry was to be expected now that the elevated trains roared over Sixth and Third Avenues. The Brooklyn Bridge was nearing completion. When it was done, laborers as well as executives could commute from their green districts to Manhattan bakeries, railroad yards, and clothing factories.

The wealthy scrambled for new digs, away from the hoi polloi. In Edith Wharton's *The Age of Innocence,* a wellborn old lady complains, "When I was a girl we knew everybody between the Battery and Canal Street; and only the people one knew had carriages. It was perfectly easy to place anyone then; now one can't tell, and I prefer not to try." Bold, upwardly mobile parvenus displaced the gentry without a backward glance. Save for a dwindling group of self-styled aristocrats who attended the opera and gave lavish dinners for one another, background and genealogy ceased to have any significance. John Jacob Astor, a fur trapper, became more important than the descendants of Peter Stuyvesant. Peter Schermerhorn, another sudden millionaire, had been a ship chandler. Frederick and William Rhinelander had been bakers, and Peter Lorillard a tobacco merchant.

The city was full of these scrambling big shots, and downtown ghettoites wanted in on the game. Adam Gimbel and Lyman Bloomingdale rose from salesmen to retail giants. Joseph Seligman, who had started his career by trading cotton for hens, wound up as a leading banker. Citing them as exemplars, Lower East Side merchants worked out several ways to rise from humble beginnings. One was selling; opening small stores and building up a chain. Another, more prevalent, one was manufacturing. Rather than buying ready-made garments to peddle to the city's burgeoning population, they set up factories ("sweatshops" in the argot of the immigrants). There, cloth was sewn and stitched into shape by severely underpaid workers who had no recourse: it was either take the job or starve.

In *How the Other Half Lives* Jacob Riis describes a trip up "flights of dark stairs, three, four, with new smells of cabbage, of onions, of frying fish, on every landing, whirring sewing machines behind closed doors betraying what goes on within, to the door that opens to admit the bundle and the man." He finds "five men and a young woman, two young girls, not fifteen, and a boy who says unasked that he is fifteen, and lies in saying it, are at the machines sewing knickerbockers, 'knee-pants' in the Ludlow Street dialect."

The floor is "littered ankle-deep with half-sewn garments. In the alcove, on a couch of many dozens of 'pants' ready for the finisher, a bare-legged baby with pinched face is asleep. A fence of piled-up clothing keeps him from rolling off on the floor. The faces, hands, and arms to the elbows of everyone in the room are black with the color of the cloth on which they are working."

In this situation the immigrant Jews were victimized by more enter-prising and seasoned co-religionists who had learned the ropes a few years earlier. There was no social safety net for the poor in the 1880s, and precious few charities. In his autobiographical novel, *The Rise of David Levinsky,* Abraham Cahan recalls the protagonist's first day in Manhattan. He and a tailor, whom he had met aboard ship, run into a sweatshop operator on the street. The employer has come down to the Battery to look for cheap labor. The tailor is immediately hired; then comes a question for Levinsky. "And what was your occupation? You have no trade, have you?"

"I read Talmud."

"I see, but that's no business in America."

Out of pity the contractor hands out a quarter and departs. Levinsky is on his own. In a few days he, too, finds piecework in the garment trade.

The oppressed and crowded newcomers sent word back to their rel-atives overseas; America was not quite the Golden Land of their dreams. On the other hand, it wasn't the Pale, either. As David Levin-sky finds, "The sign boards were in English and Yiddish, some of them in Russian. The scurry and hustle of the people were not merely over-whelmingly greater, both in volume and intensity, than in my native town. It was of another sort." The swing and the step of the pedestri-ans, the voices and manner of the street peddlers "seemed to testify to far more self-confidence and energy, to larger ambitions and wider scopes, than did the appearance of the crowds in my birthplace."

Fresh arrivals added to the vitality. They came into the tenements, wave upon wave, until by the end of the nineteenth century the Jewish regions of lower Manhattan were more crowded than the slums of Bombay. If Levinsky and his friends found this perversely heartening, the uptown journalists did not. In the opinion of the *New York Times* the Jewish district had turned downtown into "the eyesore of New York and perhaps the filthiest place on the western continent." The paper's correspondent thought it "impossible for a Christian to live there because he will be driven out, either by blows or the dirt and stench. Cleanliness is an unknown quantity to these people. They cannot be lifted up to a higher plane because they do not want to be."

The *Times* was not alone. "These people" became the bane of New York City reformers. They had a particular distaste for the Eleventh Precinct in Manhattan, the gerrymandered Jewish district. Mother

Mandelbaum was a particular irritant. The 250-pound fence, her husband, Wolfe, and their three children lived at 79 Clinton Street in a
duplex elegantly furnished with furniture and draperies stolen from
the homes of uptown aristocrats. Mother's dry goods were supplied by
a series of colorful burglars, among them Mark Shinburn, who invested
his profits in foreign money orders payable to relatives in Prussia and
then returned to Europe, identifying himself as Baron Shindell of
Monaco.

All this was a source of amusement in the New York ghetto, where
the right kind of outlaw could assume heroic proportions. But outside
that district, the words "criminal" and "Jew" were becoming synonymous. *The Great Metropolis,* first published in 1887 and popular for at
least a dozen years afterward, devoted a long chapter to "New Israel, A
Modern School of Crime."

Strangely enough the author, Frank Moss, displays little of the anti-
Negro bias of his time. The Jews are his main concern, and he notes
that the "colored people who once lived in Baxter Street were a decent
population and were zealous in church going and other religious
duties. They moved away, and the people who took their places were of
such abandoned character that Baxter Street became the vilest and
most dangerous of all the streets."

At first he seems to view the immigrants with sympathy, describing
scores of little factories and garment centers "where men and women
labor far into the night, without holidays or vacations, at the lowest possible wages, barely sustaining life with the utmost expenditure of force
and the most unremitting application." But he quickly discerns the reason why these unfortunates cannot extricate themselves. They exhibit
a "stubborn refusal to yield to American ideas, religious habits and
requirements, clannishness, and hatred and distrust for the Christians."

The dwellers in the New Israel are "addicted to vice, and very many
of their women have no other occupation than prostitution." In this
they are aided by "a fraternity of male vermin (nearly all of them
being Russian or Polish Jews) who are unmatchable for impudence
and bestiality, and who reek with all unmanly and vicious humors.
They are called 'pimps.' " In sum: "The danger of giving these ignorant
and illiterate people the ballot as we do is one that cannot be lightly
considered."

No help was to come from the established Ashkenazis and
Sephardics. In their view, the new arrivals were speaking too loud—

and doing it in Yiddish, a language that grated on the ear. Moreover, the ruffians who were not involved with felonies caused offense in other ways. Hardly had the Eastern Europeans moved in, for example, when some of their leaders began shouting for social justice, complaining about conditions in the places where they lived and worked, calling for a six-day workweek, attempting to keep children out of the shops, forming labor unions.

Why couldn't these agitators keep quiet and go about their business? They seemed to bear a Bible in one hand and *Das Kapital* in the other. The older Jewish families had turned themselves into cosmopolites, pleased to remember that their ancestors once served as advisors to bishops and kings. To them, the Eastern Europeans were nobodies— peasants, proletarians, steeped in poverty and bound to Messianic dreams. The United Hebrew Charities in upstate New York crystallized the old-guard position. Its members, almost all of them of German extraction, told journalists the newcomers were "a bane to the country." The Ashkenazis, they asserted, "have earned an enviable reputation in the United States. This has been undermined by the influx of thousands who are not ripe for the enjoyment of liberty and equal rights, and all who mean well for the Jewish name should prevent them as much as possible from coming here."

Providentially, not all New Yorkers agreed with them. Lincoln Steffens, editor of the muckraking *Commercial Advertiser,* was so taken with the downtowners that he described himself as "almost a Jew." He nailed a *mezuzah* to his office door, attended services on the High Holy Days, and fasted every Yom Kippur. The periodical's star reporter, Hutchins Hapgood, wrote of the city's public schools, "filled with little Jews; the night schools of the East Side are used by practically no other race. Altogether there is an excitement of ideas and an enthusiastic energy for acquiring knowledge which has an interesting analogy to the hopefulness and acquisitive desire of the early Renaissance." Hapgood believed it "a mistake to think that the young Hebrew turns naturally to trade. He turns his energy to whatever offers the best opportunities for broader life and success. Other things besides business are open to him in this country."

The most significant of those things, said Hapgood, was the stage. He described the nascent Yiddish Theater, with showplaces on or close to Second Avenue. The crowds in attendance could be as animated as a crowd at the Elizabethan Globe, or as rapt as children at a pantomime.

Hapgood paid close attention to "the sweatshop woman with her baby, the day-laborer, the small Hester Street shopkeeper, the Russian-Jewish anarchist and socialist, the Ghetto rabbi and scholar, the poet, the journalist." He wrote without mockery about "sincere laughter and tears accompanying the sincere acting," and cheerfully watched "pedlars of soda-water, candy, of fantastic gewgaws of many kinds," as they mixed freely with the audience between the acts. "Conversation during the play is received with strenuous hisses, but the falling of the curtain is the signal for groups of friends to get together and gossip about the play or the affairs of the week." Of greatest interest was a plump young actor who tended to go overboard with his interpretations. In matters of ego, the strutting figure was more than a match for Jacob Adler, and better connected. This was Goldfaden's spiritual second son, although Boris Thomashefsky preferred to bill himself as "America's Darling."

CHAPTER FOUR

✦

THE SECOND SON

i

THE THOMASHEFSKYS, mother, father, and five children, had left Kiev on the wave of anti-Semitism that followed the assassination of Czar Alexander II. The paterfamilias, Pinchas, held strong socialist beliefs. He was painfully aware that every movement was closely watched by the secret police. Just before they closed in, he, his wife, Chaya, and their five children fled to Belgium. From Antwerp, Pinchas booked passage for America. On the first day in New York, he moved the family into an overcrowded rooming house. On the next, he found work in a shirt factory. On the third, his twelve-year-old son, Boris, got a job rolling cigarettes in a tobacco factory. Intimidated at first, the boy soon loosened up and began to sing Russian songs as he worked. One day a young, excitable redhead complained that a number was being rendered incorrectly—"Nyet! Nyet!" he would break in. "It don't go like that!" Abe Golubok offered his own version. It had to be the correct one, he insisted, because he knew from show business. After all, both his brothers were actors. Boris didn't believe him until the day Abe came into the factory with a rolled-up poster, sent from London.

It announced the production, in Yiddish, of Abraham Goldfaden's opera *Witch*, featuring Leon and Myron Golubok. To the cigarette rollers that notice was exhilarating—Yiddish Theater in England, of all places. Abe passed around a recent letter from Leon that was not so heady. It described deteriorating conditions for Jewish performers in London. Productions did take place now and again, Leon reported, but money was scarce. And besides, the chief rabbi discouraged his parishioners from attending. The company needed a new place to show off its wares. What about New York? Was there a chance that some rich American might bring the troupe across the Atlantic?

The ghetto immigrants heard about the uptown theater but never went there. They understood little English, and they were intimidated by the uptown crowds, the men dressed in fine frock coats and bowler hats, the women turned out in furs and feathered boas. The city's great legitimate houses were close to the Lower East Side, but to those who had fled the Pale, they might as well have been on the planet Pluto. A great pity, observed Hutchins Hapgood. The immigrants could have profited from the dramas, and been amused by the lighter fare. Situated not more than a mile from the Barnatos' rooming house, the Union Square Theater offered productions that ranged from Ibsen's *A Doll's House* (retitled *Breaking a Butterfly* for American consumption) to Alexandre Dumas's weepy melodrama *Camille*.

Farther north came the Bijou, the Casino, with its brand-new roof garden, and the Empire, located way up at 42nd Street, in a place that would soon be known as Times Square. Thomas Edison was designing electric lights for the Lyceum. That venue would become the favorite of high society's Four Hundred, who made a point of dressing formally when they went to see a play. New York's elite had made much of Gilbert and Sullivan's new *H.M.S. Pinafore* and of Tom Taylor's *Ticket of Leave Man,* the melodrama of an ex-convict given a "ticket of leave" when he is released from prison, who gets framed by a criminal master-mind and cleared by the detective Hawkshaw.

The immigrants never approached these places, nor did they enter the more raucous vaudeville houses. If the greenhorns were to be entertained, Boris concluded, it would have to be in their own language, spoken onstage by their own *landsmen.* An impossibility, said the other tobacco workers. He didn't think so. For an idea had come to him one afternoon on his way home. Chester A. Arthur now occupied the White House. It was known that this Arthur had once defended a Negro woman in court. She had been insulted and abused on a street-car. It followed that he would make sure America was good to other races as well. And thousands upon thousands of Jews lived in New York in peace and quiet, yes? Well, peace, anyway. It followed that they would be permitted to have their own theater in their own language.

So Boris went out to see Frank Wolf. Here was a man with prime requisites—a big spender with a generous heart. The owner and opera-tor of a major tavern on the corner of Essex and Hester Streets, Wolf liked to show off. He was a fancy dresser; two diamond rings decorated his fingers, and other jewels glittered on his French cuffs. Yet he was an easy mark for charities, and when a poor Jew down on his luck stopped by to cadge a beer, he was always good for a handout. Boris had come to know Wolf well, not from hanging out at the saloon—thirteen-year-old Jewish boys had no place in there—but from the nearby Orthodox syn-agogue. The barman sat on the temple board; the youth sang in the choir on Friday nights.

Boris introduced him to Abe Golubok. Abe did a little Show and Tell with the poster and the letter. Wolf ran his own private poll, ask-ing patrons whether they would pay for tickets to see a local Yiddish Theater. Nine times out of ten he received a positive answer. Wolf, always a betting man, backed up his interest with tickets and $300 for travel expenses. Abe sent them on to his brothers.

The bedraggled Golubok troupe, most of them amateurs from the ghettos of London, arrived a month later. Boris and Pinchas met them at Castle Garden and took them to a cheap rooming house on the Lower East Side. While they unpacked, Boris congratulated himself for playing the role of *shadkhn*—matchmaker—in this arrangement. Never short of *chutzpah,* he argued for renting Turn Hall on 4th Street and for hiring some local talent to fill out the company. Himself, for instance. The Goluboks could hardly refuse; Boris was the reason they were here. With Wolf backing the venture, including costumes and rent, billboards went up, announcing a presentation of Abraham Gold-faden's operetta *Koldunye, or The Sorceress,* featuring the "international star Mirele Krantzfeld." Sure enough, there was Boris's name in the program. He was cast as "Moishe, a pastry vendor."

The group rehearsed at a building on Hester Street. The block, Boris remembered, "was besieged by people shoving to hear the singing. The speculators who had bought all the tickets for the first performance made good money. They didn't even know themselves how much to charge for a ticket, and the public paid whatever they asked." Optimism filled the hall; failure was impossible to contemplate. The euphoria lasted about a week. Then a severe, thick-necked man ("half-Gentile but all Jewish," in Boris's memorable phrase) stomped in. He demanded to see the manager of this Yiddish Theater. The actors looked at Boris. The visitor flashed a badge, wrote out an address, ordered the terrified youth to report to the Immigrant Committee at ten the following morning. He departed without another word.

Along with Leon and Myron Golubok, Boris appeared at the appointed hour. A secretary led them to a room where several older men sat at a long table. The most imperious of them looked the actors over and milked the pause before growling in German-accented Yiddish, "Are you the artists who are going to perform at Turn Hall?"

The trio swallowed hard and nodded.

"Is it true in the play you will perform there is a peddler named Hotzmach, and that this Hotzmach swindles a poor girl who buys needles from him?"

More nods.

"You came to America to portray Jewish thieves, Jewish swindlers? Which of you plays this Hotzmach?"

"I do," Leon admitted.

"Young man, you should be ashamed. And in the same play that you are going to perform there is a scene in which an old Jewish woman, Grandma Yakhne, burns down a house and an entire family is killed. This is true?"

Leon attempted to answer, but the old man banged a hammer and spoke out in the manner of a judge. "You had better not perform your Yiddish play with Hotzmach and Grandma Yakhne. If you do not obey us, know that within twenty-four hours we will send you away from

America on a cattle-boat. We will send you back to where you belong. And now you may go."

Thomashefsky and his friends left in misery. "We were barely able to drag ourselves to Wolf's saloon," his memoir states. "We told Frank the entire story, especially about the threat that they would send us away from America on a boat. The saloon keeper guffawed. And when he told his customers the whole saloon burst into laughter. Only the three of us, poor greenhorns, did not laugh. We stood unhappily with tears in our eyes."

Wolf comforted them. "You should also be laughing. No one can do anything to you here, not even the President of the United States. Keep rehearsing and preparing." A withering smile accompanied his assurances. "Those committee-niks, like last year's snow. Put on your play and be successful!"

Simultaneously abashed and encouraged, the little troupe hired a choir of twenty singers and a twenty-four-piece orchestra. The Lower East Side had never seen, had never even heard of, such theatrical extravagance. *Koldunye* was the talk of the ghetto. On opening night Boris made his way through crowds surrounding Turn Hall. Above the throng were a group of men standing on a wagon—members of the Immigrant Committee. They were shouting and gesticulating angrily. Boris thought he heard his name, paused to get the rest of the sentence, and realized what was being said. The speakers were warning their listeners not to go into the theater. The show was nothing less than *a shanda far yidn*—a scandal for Jews. Boris turned his back on them and pushed into the hall.

Uniformed ushers awaited their final instructions from Frank Wolf, dressed in formal attire and assuming the air of an uptown impresario. Boris informed him of the fuss outside. Wolf dismissed it out of hand. "Thomashefskele," he ordered, "go get dressed and make sure the performance will be good and that group will be about as threatening as the yowls of a cat." People filed in and took their seats as Boris made his way to the dressing room. The first notes of the overture sounded. The actors took their places. Boris routinely counted heads and came up short. Mirele Krantzfeld, the female lead, was missing. He ran to her dressing room. It was dark. He knew that she lived nearby, signaled the orchestra to strike up the overture again, bolted out the door, and ran to her apartment. He found her with a cloth tied around her head.

His memoir describes the next few minutes: " 'Krantzfeld!' I yelled with all my strength. 'What happened? We need to begin the performance—the orchestra is already playing the overture a second time! Why are you sitting there? Come on!' "

With extravagant gestures she wailed of distress—her head throbbed, her teeth hurt, her throat was sore. An appearance onstage was unthinkable; the great Krantzfeld could not go on unless she felt a hundred percent. "I spoke," wrote Boris, "I yelled, I begged, but it didn't do any good. I left her to her headache and her toothache and ran back to the hall." By now the attendees were stamping, whistling, demanding a show or their money back. Boris gave his colleagues the bad news. Before they could react, he bolted into the diva's dressing room, climbed into her clothes, and signaled for the curtain to rise. "The operetta began—the first Yiddish performance in America. I played Mirele's part. In the third act I changed into a boy's outfit and did a solo as Moyshe."

Boris's resourceful debut saved the night, but it did not rescue the company. After witnessing the opening night hysteria, Wolf wanted out of show business. "You may do what you like," he told the actors. "I can't devote myself any more to the theater. My business is a saloon. I wish everyone good luck!"

Without backing, and without Krantzfeld, the troupe folded. Boris considered himself luckier than the rest; he could go back to singing in the synagogue chorus for $5 a week. But even that was to be denied him. The old German from the Immigrant Committee also served on the board of the temple. Over Frank Wolf's objections he argued that such a disrespectful Yiddish *theaternik* would tarnish the Sabbath services. A majority of the committeemen agreed with him, and Boris was fired. As he was to learn from Wolf, this was not all the committee had done to him. Decades later, still embittered, he recalled their treachery. "Krantzfeld had received $300 from the Immigrant Committee not to come perform in the play, and they bought her husband a soda-water stand on the corner of Division and Bowery for having convinced his wife to betray us, *the artists.*"

As irrepressible as he was insolvent, young Thomashefsky scoured the neighborhood for a new angel. He found a well-to-do butcher who adored *Koldunye.* The meat man agreed to take Wolf's place. Boris found a run-down venue, the Bowery Garden, with three important features: an open floor, rows of chairs fastened to one another, and a cheap rent. The owner warmed to the idea of weekend performances, but wanted to negotiate with someone more mature. Never mind, Boris assured him: "The actors trust me. They will do as I say."

It was not an empty boast. So grateful were the performers that they allowed Boris to be impresario, director, and featured player. He let it be known that amateurs were welcome, and soon had all the male walk-ons he needed, then advertised for chorus girls and had his pick of the Lower East Side beauties. All were willing to work for free, as long as they could appear onstage before their friends and families. The one missing component was a resident playwright. This Thomashefsky found in one Israel Barsky, whose ambition ran far ahead of his talent. Barsky had some stage experience in Europe, but in America he made his living in sweatshops. The author's business card said it all:

TAILOR, ACTOR AND
PLAYWRIGHT.

AUTHOR OF *THE SPANISH
INQUISITION.*

PANTS ALTERED AND PRESSED.

The company's first presentation was Barsky's *The Madwoman.* Unlike all the works in the Goldfaden oeuvre, this melodrama took place in America. It set the style for hundreds of plays to follow. An affluent father forbids his daughter to marry an artist. Distraught, she begins talking to herself, sees visions, and is eventually confined to a madhouse. A standard folktale formulation occurs: rich man down, poor man up. The father loses his money and his sight, while the artist gains recognition and becomes a commercial and aesthetic success. He returns to town a wealthy man and marries the girl. She regains her sanity in time to hear her father, now reduced to beggary, singing below her window. She forgives the pitiable figure and allows him to live in her grand house, whereupon his sight returns. Curtain.

As one historian remarks, "*The Madwoman* was not much more absurd

than a half-dozen uptown melodramas on the boards that season."
One Broadway theater presented *Youth,* a play about the shenanigans
of high society. Its best moments, the reviewers agreed, occurred during "the sailing of the troops and the battle scenes." Other hits that
year included the thrillers *The Strangler of Paris* and *Coney Island, or Little
Ethel's Prayer.*

In order to keep his audience interested, Boris had to change his
repertoire frequently. That meant he needed another playwright to
supplement Barsky's journeyman offerings. The nearest and cheapest
one at hand was the elder Thomashefsky. Seated on the aisle, Boris's
father had often griped in a stage whisper, "I can write better stuff than
that." Now Boris asked him to prove it. Pinchas sat down with a pad of
paper and a sharp pencil and found that writing was as easy as talking.
Within the next six months he turned out two plays, *Yankele, Young
Scamp* and *Rothschild's Biography.* In the latter work Boris played Mayer,
the founding Rothschild, first in his humble beginnings, and finally as
the influential dynast. It was his first starring role.

As the youth was to learn, forget, and relearn, his greatest asset—
animal magnetism—was also his severest liability. Now that the company had a place and a repertoire, Boris focused on a very young and
very innocent chorine. Her family soon discovered the affair and raised
such hell that the owner kicked out the troupe in the middle of the
week. They were replaced by Chinese acrobats.

Undiscouraged, Boris went on the road, booking his company into a
Newark, New Jersey, venue. Four people showed up. He moved on to
Philadelphia, where a theater owner took his money but failed to
inform him that the venue was in a neighborhood composed of Germans. The audience found that Yiddish was close to *Deutsch,* but not
close enough. Attendees filed out, grumbling, during the first act.
Thomashefsky and Co. returned to Manhattan and tried to recoup
their fortunes in a hall over a saloon way east on Avenue D. To their
dismay, a whorehouse was doing business on the floor above them; the
words and music were extinguished by the noise of prostitutes and
their enthusiastic clients.

With no money and no place of business, the troupe dispersed.
Boris, who had avoided ordinary labor for so long, was forced to look
for work in a familiar and loathed arena, the tobacco industry. He
found a job in a Sweet Caporal factory on Hudson Street. He also
found the Golubok brothers rolling cigars on the same assembly line.

The three were to stay in place until the spring of 1884. Then, out of nowhere, Boris was reprieved by a message from Michael Yomen, manager of the National Theater. He asked Thomashefsky to "come over and talk business." The business under discussion was Yiddish Vaudeville. Trade had fallen off, summer was coming, and it occurred to him that light entertainment might turn a profit.

Yomen's requirements were rigorous. He demanded a new sketch every week, and it had to contain at least one song and some accompanying choreography. Boris agreed to everything. Thus it was that the National's vaudeville bill included "Parker and His Dogs," "The Bowery Belles," and "Shmendrik's Wedding" the first week, and "Lost in a Pullman" followed by a scene from *Recruits* the next. The summer of 1884 proved to be a golden one for Boris—and for Yomen, who measured the laughter and applause that greeted the Jewish performers. Impressed, he made plans to present full-length Yiddish plays in the fall.

Boris's income allowed the Thomashefsky family to relocate. No sooner had they settled into new digs on Eldridge Street, though, when unsettling news reached them. Something called the Russian Yiddish Opera Company, a team of polished professionals fresh from "a triumphal tour of Europe," had been booked to appear at Turn Hall.

Boris reassured his fellow actors. Manhattan was a big place with more than enough room for two Yiddish troupes, he said. Who knows, maybe even three? But Barsky, the playwright/tailor, knew better than to compete with the real thing. "Pack up, children," he instructed. "You will soon be rolling cigars, pressing shirts." He left them with a final admonition: "Forget theater!"

ii

BARSKY'S WARNING was on the money. Unlike the Thomashefsky bunch, the Russian Yiddish Opera Company disdained ad-libs and made no asides to the audience. They boomed their speeches, smote their foreheads, and beat their breasts in a style calculated to impress the gullible onlookers.

In another scene from his autobiographical novel *The Education of David Levinsky,* Abraham Cahan describes an evening in the Yiddish Theater. The narrator beholds an actress playing a modern Russian girl: "She declaimed her lines, speaking like a prophetess in ancient Israel, and I liked it extremely. I was fully aware that it was unnatural, but that was just why I liked it. I thought it perfectly proper that people on the stage should not talk as they would off the stage. I thought that this unnatural speech was one of the principal things an audience paid for."

At Turn Hall, the leading man, Maurice Heine, and the prima donna, his wife, Sara, played to packed houses every night. The following spring a Yiddish newspaper ran letters from enthusiasts—one demanding that the orchestra be a little more muted, the better to hear the "electrifying voice and speech of Madame Heine." In an unprecedented review, the *New York Sun*'s drama critic journeyed downtown to see *Bar Kochba.* He was overwhelmed by Goldfaden's "richly melodic score." This praise and recognition were more than Boris could endure. "The Heines' success broke my heart," he was to admit, and left town to start again, this time in Philadelphia with his father and a ragtag group of hopefuls. "When I come back," he resolved, "the whole world will listen." He was to make good on that forecast.

Now that the competition had bowed out, the Heines were the only show in town. But in June 1886, it came *their* turn to be rattled by an announcement. The Jewish Operetta Company of Romania had arrived in New York. The director was Sigmund Mogulesko, the clown who had gotten his start in Goldfaden's first company. The Heines reacted quickly, renting the two-thousand-seat Oriental Theater on the Bowery. They assured customers that the refurbished venue had improved seating, good ventilation in the hot weather, and steam heat in the winter. In short, a palace. (These assurances were a requisite: before the Oriental went legitimate it had been a museum, a menagerie, an aquarium, a low-ranking vaudeville house, and a saloon.) In answer, Mogulesko made an in-your-face move, leasing the National Theater right across the street from the Oriental. He renamed it the Romanian Opera House in honor of his country of origin.

Here began the serious rivalries that were to mark the Yiddish Theater throughout its fevered life. At the Romanian, Mogulesko's group played on Friday and Saturday evenings. When the demand for seats increased, Monday and Wednesday evenings were added, and then Sunday nights went on the schedule. The National matched them, night for night, matinee for matinee. Admission prices in both theaters escalated from 25 cents for the back rows, to 35, 50, and 75 cents for seats closer to the stage. Boxes cost $1.00.

In his appreciation of the Lower East Siders, Hutchins Hapgood observed that the Yiddish Theater was now "practically the only amusement of the ghetto Jew." The folks who made $10 a week in the sweatshop bought a balcony seat because they lacked "the loafing and sporting instincts of the poor Christian, and spent their money for theater rather than for drink." But it was not only for the play that the poor Jew attended the performances. It was "to see friends and actors. With these latter, he, and more frequently she, tries in every way to make acquaintance, but commonly is compelled to adore at a distance."

The Romanian opened the 1888 season with an extravagant five-act opera, *Rashi, or the Persecution of the Jews in France.* The dialogue was by Moishe Isaac Hurwitz, one of those extraordinary hustlers who could only have come from Europe, and who could only have flourished in America.

Hurwitz entered the Yiddish Theater in Jassy, Romania, where he saw *Recruits.* After the final curtain, the short, thickset visitor, bearded and dressed *à la mode,* went backstage and wangled an introduction to Goldfaden. He identified himself as the renowned Professor M. I. Hurwitz, specialist in world geography and playwriting.

Something about the man didn't seem kosher, and Goldfaden asked a few questions around town. The "Professor," it turned out, was nothing of the kind. He had once taught Hebrew on the elementary level and was summarily fired from that position. Shortly afterward he converted to Christianity, and was currently a missionary in Bucharest. Confronted with the facts, Hurwitz acknowledged that he had indeed abandoned his old faith. "Hard times," he explained. "I didn't earn much with the old God. The new one brought me 90 francs a month." A man may do what he likes, Goldfaden told him, but there was no way a Jewish audience could accept the work of a Christian missionary.

Hurwitz stomped off into the night. However, the success of Goldfaden's troupe made him think twice about the possibilities of Yiddish Theater. Over the next few weeks he gathered a *minyan.* Before these ten Jewish witnesses he pronounced himself a Hebrew once more, altered his name to Hurwitz-Halevy, hired a bunch of amateur actors, and began to stage his own plays in the back room of a Jassy restaurant. When the Russo-Turkish War emptied the town of its middle-class Jewish population, Hurwitz got out with the rest.

He popped up in London in the mid-1880s, then made his way to New York City, where he contrived to meet Mogulesko. After a tryout, he signed on as the Romanian Opera House playwright. It was a bargain for both men. Over the next several years play after play spilled from Hurwitz's pen, some original, most plagiarized, all crowd pleasers.

To counter the man they referred to as "the sausage machine," the Heines summoned one Joseph Lateiner to the Romanian. This unique figure had been an actor, prompter, and translator in Goldfaden's company, rendering Russian, French, and German plays into Yiddish. In Europe it was his custom, as one scholar put it, "to take a foreign play, squeeze every drop of juice out of it, change the Gentile names to Jewish ones, slap on manly beards and *peyes* (sidelocks) and let them parade across the stage as Jews." He followed exactly the same process in America.

But at least Lateiner tried to adhere to historical truth. His rival Hurwitz had no standards at all; his strength was his speed. The Professor's "history plays," for example, freely mixed the events of two centuries, falsifying events whenever it suited his purpose. Once, in a self-created emergency he cast himself as a sultan in an Oriental drama. The purpose was to save the final act, still incomplete on opening night. "Whatever I say, nod your head," he hissed to the company just before the curtain rose. The playwright came onstage spouting high-sounding phrases for forty-five minutes. It sounded deep; the audience clapped and cheered just as if they knew what was going on.

Lateiner attempted to keep up. At first he celebrated Jewish history; then tried contemporary realism. His most earnest effort was *Tizla Eslar,* the true story of a rabbi recently accused of ritual murder in Hungary. This was supposed to show up Mogulesko's old-fashioned repertoire. But Hurwitz immediately went on the defense. Two weeks later, the Romanian advertised a *two*-play cycle by the rapid Professor. *The Trial at Tisla Eslar,* plus *The Conspiracy at Tisla Eslar,* would be presented on successive nights, a Yiddish Theater first.

Each theater had its fanatical devotees. Some preferred the Oriental, others the Romanian. Each group detested the other, and loudly proclaimed their allegiance. The rivals called themselves *patriotn,* true believers who lauded their chosen author, dressed in the manner of their favorite actors, bought tickets to hated productions so that they could razz the performers and playwrights, out-shouted the theater claques, and engaged in fistfights. No lives were lost in the rivalry between the Oriental and Romanian crowds. But blood was spilled and uptown journalists derided the ghetto's troglodyte behavior.

Ironically, as Nahma Sandrow points out, the harder Lateiner and Hurwitz worked to stress their differences, the more the public linked their names. They became "synonymous with vulgar dramatic baked goods of an uncertain freshness." Both "plunged into the bakery business, until the two were almost continually bent over their respective ovens like cartoon madmen, jerkily kneading and shoveling in play after play after play." The result of that madcap competition was not cheaper prices or a renewed public interest. Audiences came to resent the way Hurwitz rode around town like a Mittel-European prince, driving a phaeton and four horses and looking down on the very people who bought tickets to his fare. They also wearied of the raucous Lateiner supporters. By the late 1880s attendance had fallen off at both the Oriental and Romanian theaters. If those companies were bent on wrecking each other, the patrons asked, why should the public shell out for it? Let the *verdampte* showfolk pay for the demolition themselves.

CHAPTER FIVE

✦

FATHER AND SONS

i

I N THE SUMMER OF 1887 a chorus of cheers went up at Castle Garden. The entire Heine organization had come to welcome the Father himself. They carried Abraham Goldfaden's luggage, looked after his wife, Paulina, conveyed them to a fine hotel, and presented them with a season's pass to the Romanian. That night the troupe played with special panache, a salute to the Father of Yiddish Theater. At a cast party afterward, they begged him to join the company. The word "gratitude" was not in his lexicon. "I must have my *own* company," he replied imperiously. "I can be a part of no other."

At those words, said one of his listeners, "we became as frightened as sheep that see a wolf. The stars saw they would be nothing more than Goldfaden's employees. The supporting actors were used to the old *tsorus* (troubles). They did not want new ones." New *tsorus* was what they got, anyway. It came with the Father.

ii

USING AN AMALGAM of guile and guilt, Goldfaden persuaded the owners of the Romanian to grant him absolute power. Operating directly across the street from the rival Heine troupe, he would have the final say in personnel, set design, costumes, repertory. As a final thumbing of the Father's nose, the theater was renamed the Goldfaden Opera House. *Bar Kochba* was to be their first presentation. This opera, set in the year 137, would relate the tragic and glorious history of the last Jewish revolt against the Roman Empire. It had already been done in Russia, and the New York posters asserted: "This is the finest of the Master's operas, so imposing and provocative that it hastened Czar Alexander III's prohibition of Yiddish Theater." The claim was only a slight exaggeration.

In Romanov Russia, Goldfaden's work had exhibited a scope that was not to be equaled for another forty years, when C. B. DeMille began to direct his celluloid epics. The stage instructions alone gave new meaning to the term Grand Opera. At the finale: "The entire Jewish army comes running across the ramparts. They are met by the Roman forces. The battle begins: swordfights, stabbings, screams. We hear the clanging of swords and the creaking of walls. The Fortress is aflame, and all its towers tumble and break apart. Roman soldiers run to the central gate and rip it open."

In what amounts to a series of close-ups, the gate swings open to reveal three atrocities: "One Roman soldier murders a child in its mother's hands as she kneels, pleading for his life; another Roman holds an old Jew by his hair, raising his sword above him; still another holds a Jew to the ground with his foot, and runs him through with a spear. The entire scene is illuminated by green light from behind the gate and red light from above the ramparts. During the tumult, the curtain falls slowly."

Back in Russia, Jewish audiences knew that Goldfaden had written *Bar Kochba* in code; they were well aware that he was commenting on the czarist pogroms. The trouble was, the Cossacks also knew the code. In the eyes of the government this huge and violent production was meant to inflame the nation's Jewry. It had to go, and with it all other Yiddish Theater works. The prohibition made Abraham a folk hero all across Eastern Europe.

But in America things were different. Here he had to contend with an offstage movement that had been quashed in Russia: socialism. Along the Lower East Side of the 1880s the spirit of revolt was very much alive, kindled by the injustices of the sweatshops. No one quite knew how to organize; the factions were untested, the leadership uncertain. Karl Marx and Friedrich Engels were exotic names to most laborers; their bodies were overworked, their minds ripe for propaganda. A handful of leaders encouraged them to whisper to one another at their machines, meet at night, plan strikes, make demands for an eight-hour day and the abolition of child labor. Organizers reminded them that *they* were the instruments of production, not the bosses. Hadn't the socialists run a candidate for mayor, Henry George? All right, he came in second to Abraham S. Hewitt, but he beat out Theodore Roosevelt, the Republican nominee. The future belonged to the left.

A Jewish firebrand, freshly arrived from Riga, surveyed the scene with a radical friend. At first they were discouraged. "There had been, we knew," wrote Morris Hillquit, "unions of shirt makers, cloak operators and bakery workers at one time or another. We thought them dormant. We found them dead." However, they did locate two unions with a strong pulse, and this was enough to keep them going. The typesetters were men who had always exhibited great pride and solidarity. And the actors in the Yiddish Theater were beginning to show resolve for the first time. At meetings they complained loudly about star treatment given to the few, and the short change doled out to the many. The socialists egged them on: these talented performers were the exemplars of the utopian future. The theater belonged to them; it *was* them. The membership rose to its feet and thrust fists in the air. It was Goldfaden's misfortune to harrumph and strut just as the labor movement started to jell.

The youngest of his performers were still tentative; they needed the work and had enormous respect for the Father. But the more experienced wanted no part of Goldfaden's rigid conditions and they prevailed. A strike was called. Everyone went out. Goldfaden denounced the rebels as ungrateful children and held firm. He discovered that he was powerless; this was one union that could not be replaced by scabs. A month of picketing and refusals went by. When it became obvious that the performers would rather starve than act as vassals, Goldfaden caved in. In a grand gesture he held out a hand to the entire acting community. "There will be no reprisals," he promised. "You will be treated as my equals."

The olive branch was offered too late. For more than thirty days no dramas had been produced, and, consequently, no tickets sold. Debts had mounted up. Strapped for cash, the owners sold their theater out from under Goldfaden and his reconciled company. The new owner had no regard for the past; he wanted to put on shows "in the American language only." Now the Yiddish actors were truly unemployed and Goldfaden had nothing to show for his attitude. Both sides had lost the strike.

Professor Hurwitz came riding to the rescue with an ingenious plan. He dubbed it the Order of David's Harp. For an initiation fee of $1, and a monthly payment of $2, subscribers were promised free admission to certain productions at the Romanian, plus $500 for a dowry when their eldest daughter came of age, plus $500 worth of life insurance. Accompanied by an a cappella chorus singing psalms, Hurwitz toured the neighborhood every evening, speaking persuasively about King David, about Jewish responsibility, about Yiddish Theater.

In a matter of weeks he had addressed just about every Jewish lodge and fraternal organization in the ghetto, and by the end of the summer of 1887, he had signed up some nine hundred customers. With the money Hurwitz leased Poole's Theater at 8th Street and Fourth Avenue and on August 26, 1888, threw himself a big parade from Canal Street to the new showplace. Abraham Cahan, who had Hurwitz's number from the beginning, watched the large demonstration and despaired for his people. "This is what the masses want," he muttered. "Give them Tammany politicians and Hurwitz!"

As the doubters suspected, David's Harp was nothing but a slick

Ponzi scheme. Shortly after the parade, Hurwitz treated himself to a country house and another fancy carriage and four steeds. Only then did he pronounce the insurance plan null and void. It had always depended on exponential growth, and after the initial rush there were no more customers to deceive. Crushed by the results of the strike, and now the bankruptcy of David's Harp, Goldfaden saw no future for himself in America, the place where he had so carefully planned his second act. He took a wistful look at New York and booked passage for the Other Side.

More *tsorus* followed. First, he put together a troupe in Paris. His treasurer absconded with the profits. Weary from the tribulations in America and France, he fell ill, disabled with asthma attacks that left him unable to work. Abraham wrote friends, grumbling about Paulina's expensive shopping expeditions and complaining about his own physical deterioration. "My disease shows how the hardships I have gone through in the Yiddish Theater have affected me," he observed. "I was always of healthy stock, but so be it! Because of my illness, I must not become overexcited or overstrain my nerves."

A year later, still in precarious health, he turned up in Lemberg, Germany. He had in hand the manuscript of a new play, *Times of the Messiah*. It was an autobiographical drama set on the Lower East Side, featuring a long-suffering writer and the actors who didn't understand him. Goldfaden staged that, and some of his old works, with yet another company. That effort ended when the theater demanded a bigger portion of the gate. Rather than face yet another debilitating clash, the old man walked away.

He came to resemble a character in one of his period melodramas, strolling alone and impoverished through the Jewish quarter. One evening he heard his own songs being sung. The melodies issued from the window of an apartment three stories above. In his memoir he speaks of delivering soliloquies in the night, very much like Tevye in Sholem Aleichem's stories: "Don't these Jews know, as they amuse themselves and give their parties, that the composer is wandering about on the streets without even bread to stay his hunger?"

iii

THE NEW YORK CITY that Goldfaden abandoned had become, almost by accident, a world capital. In 1865, when Frédéric-Auguste Bartholdi began working on his immense present to America—a sculpture of a lady with a lamp—he was dismissed as an impractical visionary. Even after the artist won the approval of the French government, he was unable to complete his project in time for the one hundredth anniversary of the United States. Only the statue's raised arm and torch could be shown at the Centennial in Philadelphia. And when the whole thing was finished and paid for by France, the pedestal remained unbuilt. America was supposed to pay for it, but Congress refused to allot the required $100,000. It took the intervention of the press to make the Statue of Liberty a reality. Joseph Pulitzer, a Hungarian immigrant who had fought in the Civil War, married a wealthy woman and bought several newspapers, including the *St. Louis Post-Dispatch* and the *New York World*. Upon hearing that the statue was about to die for lack of funds, he seized his opportunity to make heroes of the public and, not coincidentally, the *World*.

He would accomplish this by asking readers (and potential readers) to send their extra pennies to underwrite the pedestal. Cannily working the ethnic neighborhoods, his writers and editors appealed to the Irish by slamming the British government in editorials, covering the affairs of the Bismarcks for German immigrants, and acknowledging the important Jewish holidays for Lower East Siders. The resultant publicity increased the paper's circulation and gave it, and the city it served, a world-class status. More than $100,000 came in. The massive figure rose in the harbor and was promptly dubbed "Miss Liberty."

As she loomed over New York, other plans took form. Castle Garden was judged inadequate to accommodate the rush of newcomers, and Ellis Island, a larger arena, was readied with new buildings and offices. Ground breaking started for something called a "subway," a rail

system to move people underground from City Hall all the way to
West 145th Street. The elevated steam trains that ran along Sixth
Avenue soon would be replaced by electric cars. The legitimate theater
had expanded from Union Square on 14th Street all the way to 42nd
Street, and to show that the movement north was no fluke, the Metropolitan Opera House had risen up on the southwest corner of Broadway and 41st Street.

Nothing could slake the public appetite for drama and music, not
even the great blizzard of 1888 that buried the city in two feet of snow.
That weekend, the Star Theater had a big draw: the English actors
Henry Irving and Ellen Terry in *Faust*. There was not one empty seat for
the evening or matinee performances. At the same time Daly's Theater
also played to capacity houses: Ada Rehan, a comic star born in Ireland
and educated in Brooklyn schools, led the cast of *A Midsummer Night's
Dream*. An unprecedented ebullience filled the air. Poverty, crime, pol-
lution were all judged to be minor and rectifiable—the United States
could right any wrong. Appraising Dostoevsky in the distinguished
Atlantic Monthly, editor William Dean Howells became the thinking person's cheerleader. He conceded that the Russian had his good points,
but that "our" novelists should "concern themselves with the more
smiling aspects of life, which are the more American."

iv

WORKING OUTSIDE the Manhattan ghetto, Boris Thomashefsky
had been forced to improve his English. In Philadelphia he read the
local papers and learned of New York's popular and financial growth
and longed to return. In the Yiddish papers he saw another reason to
come back to Second Avenue. A young actor named David Kessler had
become the talk of the Yiddish Theater.

The rangy young man had come a long way in every sense. On
the Lower East Side he had come upon a poem by Hugo von Hof-
mannsthal. He understood the lines instantly: "Where is your Self to

be found? In the deepest enchantment you have ever experienced." For Kessler, the Self was to be found onstage.

As a boy David had been dazzled by Yiddish actors moving and speaking in a manner he had seen only in dreams. Originally, the runaway youth knew nothing of mime, music, expression. He knew only that he had to be a performer no matter what the cost, no matter where he had to go. He picked up small acting jobs here and there in Europe; picked up a wife, too, but that venture lasted a very short time. Maurice Heine, good at spotting talent in the rough, finally gave him a break. In Europe, David played walk-ons and filled out crowd scenes. He stood out in any aggregation; the charisma could not be hidden. By the time the troupe sailed for America, he was playing second leads.

As soon as he took center stage, David became the talk of the Lower East Side. The Yiddish papers were full of stories about him; within a year he was a Second Avenue celebrity, the cause of sighs from shopgirls, and of envy from more established performers. None was more envious than Boris, stuck in the City of Brotherly Love with no discernible way out. He decided to see this upstart for himself.

In his memoir, Thomashefsky is painfully honest. "I came out of the House in a trance. I had never even fantasized such an encounter on the Yiddish stage, then still in its infancy, and certainly never confronted such a talent. I remained in New York another few days and saw him in a few more roles. Each time, at each performance, I was more surprised. To my company of young assistants I said, 'Now we have in New York a great actor, a wonderfully worldly artist, who should not be ashamed on any stage in the world, and this is David Kessler.' "

After that experience Philadelphia was impossible—too small, too limiting. Boris *had* to get back to his home city. With that goal in mind, he took his troupe on tour, intending to work his way back to Manhattan. The first stop was Baltimore. When the Thomashefsky troupe arrived there, Bessie Kaufman's parents bought her a matinee ticket. The fourteen-year-old had never seen Yiddish Theater before; she was hypnotized by the performances, led by a diva with a lyric soprano, golden hair, and striking charm. "Her head was piled high with ringlets," Bessie recalled in her memoir, "and she had all this sparkling jewelry. She was the center of attention and flirting and all the men were watching her." No one stopped Bessie when she ventured backstage. There in the dressing room sat the star, chatting away sans wig and costume. The *sheyne meydele* was Boris in drag.

Actor and acolyte talked, one thing led to another, as it often did with Boris, and Bessie was offered a place in the company. After all, the actor purred, she obviously had intelligence and a lovely figure—was she only in her fifteenth year? Wonderful. The company could use an ingénue. He was tired of playing the female parts; she could do them twice as well. The pay was more than Bessie could earn as a seamstress; why not join the Thomashefsky players? She would be completely safe while she learned her craft. Why, his own father would be on the premises at all times.

In the manner of so many Jewish girls of the period, Bessie went home and pleaded with her mother and father. And in the manner of so many Jewish parents, the Kaufmans forbade her to have anything to do with this or any other Yiddish acting company. She was far too young, a mere child, really. And who was this Boris? No doubt a man with dishonorable intentions, a predator. The Thomashefskys left town without her. But the idea of acting took root in her imagination, and her parents couldn't pluck it out. The next time the troupers passed through Baltimore she ran off with them. Boris had a great instinct for talent; Bessie soon inhabited the roles he had outgrown. Two years later, she was happy to show her parents how wrong they were when she and Boris took their marriage vows under a *chuppa,* surrounded by respectable Yiddish actors in dark suits and long dresses.

v

ALL THIS TIME, another actor had also been yearning to come back to New York. Jacob Adler's Midwestern venture had not gone well. The troupe had run out of material early, recycled the fare and watched the audiences dwindle before their eyes. Internecine fights broke out and accusatory questions were asked of the leader. "Why did we come to Illinois, where Jews are as scarce as diamonds?" "Why didn't we take other scripts with us?" "Why weren't we accompanied by a playwright to furnish new material?"

It was time to move on. Jacob left his young son with friends and stopped off in Manhattan. He discovered that he was old news; David Kessler was all anyone talked about. Adler's autobiography spends little ink on this part of his life. "I spent some time looking at the sky between the tall buildings of New York," he writes, "and finally realized it was time to go."

The distraught actor wandered to London, where he saw the wife and child he had abandoned, then pushed off to Warsaw, where there were active Yiddish theaters. He enjoyed a considerable success there; a visiting American had glamour to sell. Once Jacob regained his confidence he returned to London, performing in a start-up company. In self-imposed exile he compiled a thick set of clippings, rave reviews and personality pieces. The best of these he sent on to Maurice Heine in New York.

Heine needed a box office draw; he invited Jacob to join his company, promising star roles and a livable salary. Jacob was not in a position to bargain. In the spring of 1889 he again set foot on the American shore. "A very different arrival in New York this time," he remembered fondly, "and with a very different welcome. If my chariot was not hung with flags and trophies of my triumphs in Europe, it was at least greeted on every side by posters screaming in huge letters that the 'Great Eagle' of the Yiddish stage had flown to the shores of America."

For his comeback Jacob chose *The Beggar of Odessa*. As a rival was pleased to note, "The Eagle was plucked clean." The actor had labored long and hard to establish himself as an interpreter of tragedy; and tender melancholia was what his audience was led to expect. Instead he gave them farce. Silence greeted his punch lines, and scattered catcalls grew into an uproar of hisses. The manager panicked. At intermission he came onstage to complain that it was not his fault; he had never seen Adler before; who knew that this was "a terrible, a third rate" actor?

Jacob tried another trifle later in the week. The public stayed away. "He did not succeed," recalled a supporting player, "until he appeared with his own handsome, naked face, and in the uniform of *The Russian Soldier*. Adler played this role with high melodrama, shouted beyond human strength, and when the curtain fell, the walls shook with applause." The Great Eagle had at last done what Heine expected, and in the ensuing months he was to do much more. That was the trouble. Adler not only tried to attract the general public, he worked to become the heartthrob of any woman who paid attention to his entreaties. One of them was Sara Heine, Maurice's wife. What began as a dalliance was to change the course of many lives.

It was not the only difficulty prompted by Jacob's ego and id. Playing a victimized Jew in *La Juive,* Adler had a series of affecting monologues. They amounted to arias, each one building to a crescendo followed by tears and wild acclaim. Abba Schoenfeld, a handsome actor used to playing leads, was cast in the lesser role of a cardinal. His one moment came late in the play, with the confession that he once fathered a child—a girl condemned for apostasy. After a week of playing second banana, Schoenfeld devised a scheme to give himself the spotlight. In a confrontation with Adler he suddenly improvised a speech: "Do you think it's easy to ask you to forsake your religion? Know then I am a Jew forced to hide his Judaism." From under his red robe he produced the prayer shawl he had been hiding all night, wailed the Jewish prayer, "*Shema Isroel, Adonoy Elohanu!,*" and exited to a deafening ovation. Jacob was genuinely fond of Abba; after the performance he inquired about the ad-lib out of curiosity rather than ire. Schoenfeld replied, "Do you think you will always have the whole delicious goose to yourself? Give *me* for once a taste of the gizzard!"

A more unpleasant occurrence took place the following year, when Jacob and Maurice Heine nearly came to blows over money. Heine had promised his star a sizable portion of the take—too sizable, he now thought. Particularly if those rumors about the Great Eagle and his wife were true . . . The two men started to wrangle early one evening and were still quarreling at curtain time. Jacob refused to go on without a written contract. An understudy was called in. The following week Heine hired David Kessler to play the role.

Jacob's momentum came to an abrupt standstill. He remembered that Boris Thomashefsky had headquarters in Philadelphia and wrote asking for work. As soon as Boris could get free, he traveled to New York. Jacob was holed up at the Occidental Hotel. Thomashefsky recalled the meeting in his memoirs: "It made my heart ache to see the great Adler with his beautiful, clever eyes staying in this rundown place. We sat and joked, his majestic form in a torn silk jacket, his feet in out-of-shape slippers. He made everyone laugh, but in spite of his jokes, I felt his heart was bitter."

The two men got along well and hammered out a contract that day. Adler wanted a good salary; Boris craved respect. The Great Eagle's high-priced agreement to star in *Uriel Acosta* satisfied both parties. The play would open in a large Philadelphia theater mutually agreed upon. There was only one last thing, Adler said. Sara Heine, the actress? She would be ideal for the big part of Judith, Acosta's wife. Thomashefsky, who knew all about the gossip, kept his face straight and agreed to cast Sara in the role.

Uriel Acosta opened at the Standard on South Street and became an overnight smash, attracting Jews from Pennsylvania, New Jersey, and New York. A week later Boris moved it into a larger theater. The production might have played at Dramatic Hall right through the summer of 1890, and perhaps gone over into fall. But Adler lived under the banner "Why have it simple when you can have it complicated?" One day, without warning, his wife, Dinah, came to Philadelphia. The distressed Sara left the cast to avoid a confrontation. Jacob dropped out a day later and headed for parts unknown. The loss of one star would have been difficult; the absence of two stars was impossible to bear. Boris was about to close the show when a letter arrived from Chicago. Jacob had just arrived in the city. Things had changed since he last lived there. The town, he discovered, was now loaded with middle-class Jews in need of entertainment. Boris must come and see for himself.

Boris did go west, with Sara Heine beside him. In town less than a day, she spotted Jacob with another lady and told Boris she had not come all this way to play second fiddle to a Jewish roué. By now Boris had enough *tsorus* without dealing with sexual jealousy between his star players; he booked Sara into a local inn and went off to consult Jacob on business. Surely by now the Great Eagle had at least located a theater and a backer or two. Not a chance. "I thought he was a businessman," Boris lamented. "I found out you could not depend on him. A great artist, tried and tested, who knew every trick of the trade. He liked to tell funny stories, to play practical jokes, to sleep late. In business however—a child!"

Boris hotly confronted Jacob: this whole thing was his fault. Without quite admitting his irresponsibility, the actor offered an idea that might bail out both of them. He knew that Sara owned several expensive bracelets and a valuable ring. These were in her possession right now. If she could be persuaded to pawn the baubles, Boris could borrow the cash, secure a theater, send for his players, and arrange for a Chicago production. The plan defined *chutzpah*—but then, *chutzpah* had brought the Thomashefskys a long way. Why abandon it now?

Boris went to Sara's hotel room and pleaded his case. She was not in a forgiving mood, but he was eloquent and Sara didn't really want to lose Jacob. Anyway, in her mind art was always more valuable than mere sentiment, even when the sentiment was love. She sighed, she remonstrated—and then handed over the jewels. She did have a proviso: her lover must come to the hotel and apologize for his transgression. When Jacob did appear, Sara spoke first: "From you I have had nothing—only trouble and pain." He attempted to defend himself, then gave it up. She had spoken the truth, and he knew it. Two generations later, Adler's own granddaughter Lulla Rosenfeld wrote a damning assessment: "Truly, he was a cause of grief to every woman who loved him." However, he was also the lodestar of every cast who worked with him. Boris used the pawnshop money to rent the place that had always brought the Thomashefskys good luck—the Standard in Philadelphia. In the fall, the Adler-Thomashefsky troupe moved in, delighting the Jewish population of that city. When the lease was up they transferred to another big venue and filled it to overflowing for the rest of the season.

Before they left that venue, the tangle of romantic complications had been resolved to Jacob's satisfaction. The Heines had divorced rancorously, making Sara available, while Dinah and Jacob Adler split amicably. "We remained friends," he stated proudly, "and would appear onstage together." Sara became Jacob's third wife in the fall of 1891; afterward the new husband hosted a champagne supper at the Atlantic Garden, with every consequential Yiddish actor and journalist in attendance.

vi

THAT WINTER Adler grew restless; he needed to get back to New York and show the Yiddish-speaking world that the Great Eagle was ready to soar anew. Boris begged him to stay put, but Jacob wouldn't hear of it. He and Sara left for Manhattan. Boris did not have long to complain; days later he followed the Adlers upon receipt of a telegram: COME IMMEDIATELY. YOU AND ENTIRE FAMILY ENGAGED

AT THE NATIONAL THEATER. It was signed Morris Finkel, director. More would be heard from this gentleman in the near future.

Upon their arrival in New York the Thomashefskys learned the truth. Without warning, David Kessler had left the company, dissatisfied with Finkel's production. Boris was to be his last-minute replacement. The money was good, he allowed, but what were these posters announcing that "America's Favorite" (i.e., Boris) was to appear in Joseph Lateiner's *David ben Jesse*? "I don't know the operetta," he complained. "I've never even seen it! Why have you done this to me? Why didn't you tell me?"

The notices were up, the cast was already in rehearsal. Boris had no choice but to join them. On opening night the trembling star did a lot of stressful throat-clearing and vocalizing. A Yiddish proverb circulated out of his earshot: *Ale Yidn kenem zayn khazonim, ober meystns zaynem zey heyzerik*—Every Jew is a cantor, but he is usually hoarse. Radiating a bogus confidence, Boris hummed in the wings, inwardly praying for a miracle.

It occurred a moment later when he stepped onstage as the young King David, heard the murmurs of approval from young women, recited with fervor, and sang out in a melodic, ringing voice. Numerous curtain calls induced him to come out for bow after bow, and when the uproar subsided he was presented with a harp made of flowers. Thomashefsky seemed to grin with his entire body. He had arrived yet again and this time he was not going away.

By moving into popular theater, Boris proceeded to fill a vacuum. Operettas, comedies, historical spectacles, trashy melodramas, in a word, *shund*—Yiddish for trash—became his specialty. He delighted in the self-designation "America's Darling," and, as far as the shopgirls were concerned, the claim was an instance of truth in advertising. Abraham Cahan's memoir notes that in those days, stage heroes— even biblical ones—wore short jerkins that displayed their legs. "And Thomashefsky's legs were the finest in the Yiddish theater. An operetta at the National would run month after month, while Kessler and Adler had to change their program every week."

The man with shapely limbs relished his new dominance, and taunted rivals with costumes and stage effects. He was to look back with enormous satisfaction on these accomplishments. "A star had to wear slashed doublets, golden crowns, cloaks of satin. All of us did it! Kessler wore a hat with a long feather, bare feet, and a shirt with red patches. Adler, to outdo him, wore a bigger hat with three feathers, a naked throat, a spangled throw over his shoulders, and to make it more realistic, he put on chains, bracelets, and long Turkish earrings."

Boris outshone them both. He assumed a crown, a sword, chains, bracelets, silk hose in three colors, and three cloaks, one on top of the other. "If they had thunder," he crowed, "I had lightning. If Kessler sang the Evening Prayer, I sang the Prayer for the Dead. If they rode in on a real horse, I had a golden chariot drawn by two horses. If they killed an enemy, I killed an *army.*"

But what Boris and the Thomashefskyites relished, his rivals loathed. They all glad-handed each other in public, putting on displays of affection—professionals engaged in the same art with the same need to please a whimsical public. In private, however, the rivalry was intense. To his intimates Kessler complained about the *shund* that he was required to do. He detested the cheap music, the gaudy costumes, the trashy plots. "All day long I am a human being, I speak like a human being, act like a human being. At night I must dress myself up like a turkey, like an idiot! If I went out in the street like this people would throw stones at me for a lunatic. Here they shout bravo!"

Adler had his own dark view of such stuff. In a weak moment, Gold-faden had outlined his formula: "A song, a jig, a quarrel, a kiss." And so it was. No makeup and no costume could change *shund* into art. With a dig at Boris, Jacob wrote, "From my earliest years I have leaned toward those plays where the actor works not with his feet, but with his voice, face, eyes; not with jests and comic antics." The Great Eagle's desire was "not to amuse the public with tumbling, but to awaken in them and in himself the deepest and most powerful emotions."

But who would supply him with the necessary dramas to elicit such passions? Certainly not those twin hacks Hurwitz and Lateiner, or the imitators who had just begun to offer their works to producers. Of course, one could always adapt the work of European writers, but where was the authentic, the serious voice of the Yiddish Theater to be found?

CHAPTER SIX

✦

I WILL WRITE YOU A BETTER
PLAY THAN THIS *HAMLET*

i

JACOB GORDIN CAME TO AMERICA in 1892 at the age of thirty-eight, one jump ahead of the czarist police. Had he stayed in his home another day he would have been caught, jailed, and very likely executed. He was a tall, heavily bearded activist with burning eyes and a censorious attitude. Throughout Russia he was known as a persuasive writer of underground pamphlets. These advanced the cause of socialism and disparaged religious and political orthodoxies.

Vilified by traditional Jewry, attacked by government authorities, he fled to America along with other members of Am Olam—Hebrew for the Eternal People. The Tolstoyan group intended to go back to the land, setting up a socialist farming commune: from each according to his ability, to each according to his need. Like most utopian schemes this one quickly went under, leaving its members penniless.

Gordin forsook the hinterlands for the city and returned to journalism, filing reports and stories for a Russian-language newspaper. Deadlines and piecework did not agree with him, but he made no complaints; there were eight children to support. In order to familiarize himself with the Lower East Side, Gordin dropped in on a Yiddish production at the Union Square Theater. "Everything I saw and heard was far from real Jewish life," he lamented. "All was vulgar, immoderate, false and coarse."

Still, the idea of serious, intellectually provocative drama stayed with him. As Irving Howe points out in *World of Our Fathers,* "Like many half-deracinated Jews of his and later generations, Gordin was mad for culture."

But just what did the word "culture" mean to those strivers? To some it referred to the new European literature they had read (or more likely, read *about*). In France, Emile Zola was inventing the neorealistic novel, unafraid to detail the lives of prostitutes and thieves. At the same time, Paul Verlaine's poetry celebrated decadence, and *la vie de bohème* of drugs and alcohol. Yet it was in the detested Romanov Russia that the most significant work had taken place. The giants, Leo Tolstoy and Fyodor Dostoevsky, threw long shadows over Europe and America. Tolstoy, an aristocrat transfixed with guilt for the seductions and indulgences of his youth, portrayed his entire country, peasants, farmers, nobles, during the Napoleonic era. Still, *War and Peace* was not enough; in his second greatest work the author focused on the angst of one adulterous woman, Anna Karenina, as if to show he could work on a small canvas as well as a panorama.

Unlike his countryman, Dostoevsky could not be bothered with the externals of scenery or the physical descriptions of his characters. His territory was nothing less than the disturbed psyche and its consequences. He was his own favorite subject, whether describing his terrible bouts of epilepsy in *The Idiot,* or his scarifying experiences in prison, a place he called the House of the Dead. Dostoevsky felt on intimate terms with death; as his devotees loved to recount, the author was once sentenced to be executed as a young radical, then spared at the last minute. He remained convinced that his father had been murdered by his serfs, and the subject of assassination haunted his work, from *Crime and Punishment* to *The Brothers Karamazov*. Although both men professed Christian beliefs, and Dostoevsky made no secret of his anti-Semitism, that made little difference to Jewish thinkers in America. From their safe redoubt in the land of the free, they could afford to be above such considerations.

Gordin went them one better. He not only knew the prose works of the European masters, he was also familiar with the new theater emerging overseas and on Broadway. Technically, the big venues were in a class by themselves. Electricity had replaced gaslight, and stages were made deep and high, so that elaborate scenery could be "flown" overhead, out of the audience's sight. As a result, long waits for scenery changes were becoming a thing of the past. Norwegian Henrik Ibsen and the German Gerhardt Hauptmann swept away the romantic excesses of their predecessors with exciting, naturalistic dramas. The works were so controversial they couldn't be shown in commercial theaters, where censors would have neutered the dialogue. Subscription theaters had to be established, private places beyond the reach of official editors where audiences sat openmouthed at the new candor of these plays.

All this was heady stuff to the Jewish intellectual. Wandering along Second Avenue, Gordin dreamed of a new Yiddish Theater, revolutionary, persuasive, modern—the equal of anything overseas or uptown. After all, this was a vibrant and changing city; why shouldn't the Jews be in advance of the change instead of behind it?

He was offended by almost every Second Avenue entertainment. Jacob Adler and David Kessler and Boris Thomashefsky had become familiar names by the time Gordin settled into the city. But to his eyes, all three were hams, strutting in naive and irrelevant dramas and operettas. Yiddish vaudeville was even worse. The music halls displayed the very "tail of the theatrical business, with disgusting shows, demoralizing recitations, vulgar witticisms, emetic beer, and debauchery." Cahan, who had done his own investigations, heartily agreed. He wrote a diatribe entitled "Scandal Has to Be Stopped." It denounced Jewish prostitutes who made every vaudeville venue "a house of assignation," where waiters and doorkeepers acted as pimps. "Since there is a slack season among the pick-pockets, they also qualify for this business." His secular sermon shocked the old—but it did not deter the young. They went to the halls anyway, some to go upstairs with the streetwalkers, but more to get away from their parents for an evening. Amid a clamorous privacy, they could listen to a singer or a baggy-pants comedian, see a one-reel silent film, and, if their luck held, meet someone of the opposite sex as anxious and innocent as they were.

The theatrical community was not unaware of these conditions. The performers and directors searched for a solution. They agreed that a new kind of theater was necessary, a fresh dramatic style. Only that could save the Yiddish Theater from the vulgar and the garish work that pleased the lowest common immigrant. An actor persuaded Gordin to meet Adler and Kessler at a café, along with the man who had become the leading clown of the Yiddish Theater, Sigmund Mogulesko.

Gordin approached the place apprehensively. "I was curious to meet a Yiddish actor," he remembered. "I thought as soon as I told him I wanted to write a play, he would start emoting: wipe his nose on his sleeve, jump on a chair, and recite one of the popular tunes of the day." He was astonished to find "gentlemen with silk hats and handkerchiefs who talked intelligently. In their eyes I even detected a spark of talent."

Gordin's tone of condescension evaporated when Adler dangled the double prospect of money and art. If the Russian would write an original play, the Great Eagle would guarantee a first-class production starring himself, Kessler, and Mogulesko. Jacob was feeling expansive these days; he was getting the best reviews of his career. ("Watching Adler play Sampson," said a typical rave, "the audience sat paralyzed, afraid Samson would destroy the world with his terrible strength.") On the street he enjoyed the kind of celebrity afforded uptown to the likes of Barrymore and Duse. One journalist described a moment on East Broadway, with Adler, "tall, wearing a high hat and long coat and carrying a fancy cane in his hand. I had to stop and watch—not the actor but the people who followed him, their faces shining with adoration and enchantment and awe."

Less than a fortnight after Adler made his proposal, Gordin showed up with a complete four-act drama. He had written the work in a fever of inspiration, he claimed, "like a scribe at work on the holy Torah." Adler read the manuscript and bit his lip. The protagonist of *Siberia* is Reuben Cohen, a man condemned to prison for a misdemeanor. En route to the north he escapes from his chains, rejoins his family, changes his name to Rosenkranz, and assumes another way of life. He prospers and becomes a respectable leader in his community. A rival, jealous of the man's success, discovers his secret and informs the police. Arrest and martyrdom follow.

No one had ever encountered a Yiddish play like this. *Siberia* had none of the long ornamented speeches audiences expected and actors adored. And where was the music? Whoever heard of a production without a tune or two? Without a happy ending or at least a resolution? Gordin considered these objections beneath contempt. He left it to Adler to straighten matters out, and did not return to rehearsals for a week. Upon entering the theater he heard Sigmund Mogulesko trilling two songs. The clown had interpolated them into the dialogue. The second act was more insulting. Sigmund had inserted an entire section of Verdi's grand opera *Ernani*. Gordin erupted, bellowing at the cast, warning them not to tamper with a single word, forbidding the insertion of one unwanted note, stomping out of the theater. Mogulesko riposted, "Anti-Semite!" Gordin boycotted the rest of the rehearsals and refused to attend opening night.

It was just as well. Trained on pageant and song, the audience felt uncomfortable with the plain speaking and unrelieved gloom of *Siberia*. The reaction was so loud and antagonistic the actors could barely hear themselves. Adler could stand no more. During intermission he stepped in front of the curtain. "I stand before you shamed and humiliated." His voice trembled. "If you would open your hearts, if you would open your minds, you wouldn't laugh at this play by the great Russian writer Jacob Mikhailovich Gordin. You must give it your earnest attention." He stood silently for a moment, brushed away tears, and withdrew.

The abashed listeners returned to their seats. One of the actors who had been most hostile to the work acknowledged that "the scene where Adler begged Kessler not to betray him made a strong impression." And at the finale, Mogulesko, playing a servant, spoke the line "Master, we are parting" with such conviction that his voice broke. The audience wept with him. Gordin attended the second night, warmed to the applause and to the intelligent comments he heard in the lobby between acts. Afterward he accepted the apologies of the cast.

But that was the high point of *Siberia*'s run. Subsequent performances drew so poorly that the play had to be taken off the boards. A similar reception greeted Gordin's second effort, *Two Worlds*. His third was called *A Yiddish King Lear*, a reinterpretation of Shakespeare's tragedy, brought into the nineteenth century and furnished with a Russian-Yiddish setting. It featured a wise fool, a successful business-man, his two avaricious *yenta* daughters, his one misunderstood child, and a large supporting cast. "The actors all predicted failure," wrote Adler. They pleaded with him not to play an Orthodox Jew whose chil-dren reject him in old age. He was a leading man; who wanted to see him as a wrinkled geezer? Mogulesko and Kessler left the company, convinced that their colleague had backed a lame horse. Adler refused to budge; the theme of the play reminded him of a song he had heard back in Odessa. That ballad also spoke of a father spurned by his off-spring, and tough old men would mist up when they heard it. If a sim-ple folk tune could elicit such a reaction, he argued, what might be the power of a play on the same subject? And it echoed the Bard, the god of the English stage. What more could they want?

Adler's faith was justified. From the first reading he moved the cast away from cheap laughs and overstated melodrama. Gordin had told him all about the naturalism of the new European drama, and Jacob strove for that kind of intense effect. On opening night, recalled his wife, Sara, "he was not an actor but a force. All of us played with inspi-ration, but the great figure that evening Gordin had given to Adler, and the triumph was his own." Jacob's success seemed to reverberate throughout the city. For the first time, *Harper's* drama critic ventured downtown. Adler, he wrote, "makes the slightest gesture count, and his frequent moments of quiet, one is tempted to say, count most of all. His costumes and makeup were as simple and unobtrusive as the set-ting of his stage; yet, as his clothes grew older and more worn from act to act, and his hair and beard thinner and more thin, the unconscious effect was stupendous."

The Yiddish Theater would never be the same. Gordin's *Lear* had reached the public in a way that no spectacle, no operetta or facile melodrama could possibly have done. From here on, audiences would no longer be content to have a diet composed of nothing but *shund* any more than they would sit still for a dinner composed solely of *kreplach*. Not that the seat holders always met the demands of serious theater. For them, the play seemed indistinguishable from life itself. More than once the Great Eagle was astonished to hear audience members address him during *Lear*. "Come, Yankl!" shouted one man. "Let her choke, that awful woman, your daughter. My wife will give you a won-derful dinner, come to me!"

ii

JUST AS THE YIDDISH THEATER was evolving, so was life on the Lower East Side. Fear of government persecution—city, state, and federal—slowly ebbed away. People encountered anti-Semitism on the streets, but this was local stuff, hostility from one immigrant group, like the Irish or the Italians, to another. This the Jews could handle. They had their own toughs when it came to confrontations, and children quickly learned which neighborhoods to avoid. Denizens of the Lower East Side were heartened by the actions of a man they'd dismissed a few years before. After losing the mayoralty, Theodore Roosevelt had accepted the next-best job: New York City police commissioner. A hate-monger named Rector Ahlwardt came to town, imported by anti-Semites to work up the populace and test the cops. Roosevelt made no open comment, but he saw to it that the rabble-rouser was guarded by a phalanx of forty Jewish patrolmen. The rector got the message and quietly got out of town.

With a new assurance the Lower East Siders inched toward confidence and sophistication, outgrowing the simple formulae of Goldfaden, Hurwitz, and Lateiner. Boris Thomashefsky, Mr. *Shund* himself, commissioned a play from Gordin. He paid the fairly large sum of $60 for *The Pogrom in Russia,* and offered the playwright a part. Gordin was no actor, but he needed to feed his large family and accepted the small role of a Russian policeman for an extra $5 a week.

By now Thomashefsky knew of Gordin's insistence on naturalism, and the playwright was familiar with the actor's flamboyance. During run-throughs they circled each other like boxers in the early rounds. Thomashefsky wanted flashy costumes; Gordin demanded plain peasant clothing, and won. The actors at the Oriental, like the ones at the Union Theater, pleaded for show-stopping melodic interludes. They got a handful of traditional folksongs in a minor key—the kind their characters would have sung in the Russian provinces. Gordin made the mistake of skipping a rehearsal; when he returned a little dance had been inserted in a scene. He slammed his script closed and stomped to the exit. The number was excised.

Authoritative as he was, the playwright let down his guard on opening night. When he came on as the czarist policeman, the reception was overwhelming. People recognized him, applauded and whistled, threw hats in the air, shouted "Hurray, Gordin!" In all the excitement he forgot his own lines. Thomashefsky supplied them, sotto voce. Gordin recovered. In the next act he felt strong enough to criticize a fellow player onstage. Invited into a Jewish home, the Russian officer was presented with a meal. Instead of wishing him good appetite, the actress delivered an aside: "The Cossack should only choke on it." Gordin banged on the table. "That's not in the script!" The audience let out a collective gasp. There were no more improvisations.

Ironically, Gordin's fight for a more elevated theater was given impetus by Thomashefsky's most flamboyant and retrograde spectacle. In the heyday of the new century, Boris could do no wrong. His purring *r*s and liquid *l*s, along with his somewhat *zaftig* good looks, seemed to hypnotize female audiences, who bought tickets to every one of his productions. Nothing could faze him; he was in rehearsal with Hurwitz's operetta *Rouchel* when he learned that his beautiful co-star, Sophia Karp, could not memorize a long monologue. With only two days to go, Boris replaced her speech with a song, cobbling together verses from the 22nd Psalm ("My God, my God, why has Thou forsaken me?"), half in Hebrew, half in Yiddish. The chorus master thereupon set it to music. That number, "Eli, Eli," performed with heartbreaking conviction by Karp, became a hit not only in New York but in every Jewish community in the land.

The cocky young man had become the prince of the Thalia Theater; whatever he wanted to produce was automatically done. Some stage works were ambitious and serious; most were high trash, elegantly presented, enthusiastically acted, empty of content. Boris happily ceded the high ground to Adler and Kessler. While they staged the classics, he gave the Lower East Side the biggest shows it had ever seen, culminating in Hurwitz's grand *Alexander, Crown Prince of Jerusalem,* starring Boris in the title role, wearing his customary tights. Cahan's memoir asks, "Who among the older Jews does not remember how the whole East Side stormed when Thomashefsky played Alexander? He was tall and strong, with a wonderfully sculptured form. A handsomer prince could not be imagined. Shopgirls gave up the necessities of life to buy tickets to this play."

Across the street at his own theater, Adler watched the long lines at the Thalia box office and wondered how he could possibly top his friendly competitor. An inspiration came to him and arrangements were made. One evening, Boris was to recall, the pleasant atmosphere was shattered by an unpleasant bulletin. It came from one of his fans, who had heard a rumor and planted himself in the back row of the Union Square Theater to confirm it. "Adler has just announced from the stage that he will soon produce Shakespeare's world-famous sensational tragedy with music, the greatest work in all of world literature, *Othello.* He said in his speech that Adler will play Othello, that Kessler will play Iago, and they will switch roles every other night."

Equally disturbing was the news that Jacob had insulted Boris from the stage, "saying that with a play like *Othello,* no one will be able to imitate *him,* that you had to be a real actor to be able to play Othello. Othello is no 'Alexander, the little crown prince of Jerusalem.'" Without a plan in mind, Boris improvised his own shocker. Before a full house he declared that he would be the first Yiddish Prince of Denmark. Adler was not the only one disturbed by the news. Hurwitz, fearful for his career, exploded: "Thomashefsky! I will write you a better play than this *Hamlet!*" Boris paid no attention. He had seen the touring Edwin Booth play that role in Philadelphia, and insisted "A Yiddish actor of my stature can bring it off." He commissioned a translation from Moishe Zeifert, a new playwright. "I was called to the Thalia Theater," Zeifert was to remember, "and the company ordered me 'to make Hamlet!'" Save for the salary, the adapter did not find this a happy assignment. He compared it to deconstructing a building. "I took out the foundation, the walls, and the roof. I did it partly out of patriotism—I wanted to take revenge on the 'anti-Semite' Shakespeare; and I believe that up there in seventh heaven the Chairman was also happy with my 'work,' but Shakespeare, poor thing, could only bang his head against the walls of Hell."

To Boris, fidelity to the text was entirely beside the point. If he was overweight for the role, if he could hardly project the Prince's "perturbed spirit," he and his company were well rehearsed. For the star had done something unprecedented on Second Avenue: he hired an outside director, a German who, Boris recalled, "truly put every word in my mouth." Fears of failure tormented him right up to opening night. As he was dressing to go to the theater, his little daughter

Estherl, then five years old, called out, "Papa, you're not going to kiss me good night?"

"I pressed to my heart my child," he wrote, "who was dearer to me than my own life, kissed her, and said good night. The child embraced me with her little white arms and pressed my head to her head, saying, 'Go, Papa, and I'll ask God to give you success.' Tears choked me and I ran out of the house."

The child's prayers were answered. The entire cast performed without a hitch, and played to standees. (Actually Boris could have recited the front page of Hearst's *American* and filled the house, at least with young women. One enthusiast actually started to strip in the aisle, hoping to attract his attention, before she was escorted to the door. And there were always calls for extra bows so that the famous legs could be glimpsed once more.) At the conclusion of *Hamlet,* calls of "Author! Author!" resounded almost every night. Boris didn't have the heart to say that "Shekspir," as the audience called him, had been dead for almost three hundred years. A trouper volunteered to go out, claim authorship, and acknowledge the approbation. In the end, according to Bessie Thomashefsky, "We just used to ask them to forgive us, but Shakespeare lived far away in England, and could not come to see his play."

Othello thrived as well, and the double success gave Adler an idea. He arranged a private meeting with Thomashefsky at the Central Park Casino, far from the prying eyes of the Lower East Siders. There, wrote Boris, Jacob "offered me a three-part combination. Adler-Kessler-Thomashefsky—and we three will tear up America." Negotiations were brief, and the three men signed a contract with much bonhomie and shaking of hands. There would be no egos in this, they all said; lots would be drawn to determine the headliner in any given production. That was the last time they agreed on anything.

iii

BORIS STROVE for popularity and Jacob for art. For his part, David wanted nothing more than to be believed. His personal life was drab—his wife dominated him the way he dominated actors. But onstage the man was electric. "Give me a person, a real person," Kessler would urge erring cast members. He was forever setting them an example. When producers offered him the lead in Offenbach's *La Périchole,* he refused the role and took, instead, the part of an eighty-year-old bandit: "I'd rather play the old thief," he explained. "I sense in him flesh and blood." From his actors he demanded the same flesh and blood, nothing less, at every performance.

Ingénues would burst into tears when he bawled them out for some trivial error; and men were also known to cringe at his tirades. His idea of motivation was rage followed by grudging admiration: "May he burn," he was heard to say after he had put a terrified performer through the wringer. "But the son of a bitch really played that scene."

In another work, an actor underplayed a groom grieving over the bride who had just taken her own life. One of the apprentices watched Kessler pace and grumble in the wings. "When the curtain went down after the last act," he remembered, "Kessler says to the performer in a compassionate tone, 'I have something to tell you. Don't get upset—uh . . .' he wavers, 'your wife, uh . . . don't worry, God forbid it's not terrible, your wife . . .'

"The actor gets desperate and cries fearfully, 'Tell me, Mr. Kessler, what has happened to my wife?' And Kessler turns on him, 'You prima donna, you! Why weren't you so desperate and afraid onstage when they told you that your bride poisoned herself?' "

These manipulations, unkind as they were, evoked strong performances from every cast member, and in the end one of the actors conceded, "He was a tough bastard but he got the best from us. Audiences were always thunderstruck by what we did."

Except for his relentless womanizing, Jacob Adler was a puritan. Supporting actor Boaz Young wrote admiringly, "He never drank, never touched tobacco, never touched cards. Theater!" That dedication to his art could sometimes border on mania. One evening Jacob was in the company of the composer Joseph Rumshinsky. Strolling down Second Avenue, they passed by a Yiddish production in which Adler had starred a few years before. Another actor now had the role, and, says the musician's autobiography, "I wanted to take Jacob to the stage door, but he ran into the lobby. By this time I was convinced he was insane.

"Adler ran down the aisle, stopped in the middle, and shouted in Yiddish, 'I am here, I am with you! We'll play for you, we'll give you good theater!' The curtain descended on the other star. In the dressing room Adler began to apply makeup. He said to me, 'Rumshinsky, my friend, I love theater! But I'm only onstage two or three hours a day, so I have to turn the rest of my life into theater!'

"When he was ready, the curtain rose and the play started again, from the beginning."

In contrast to his colleagues, Boris was the classic lover of wine, women, and song—though surely he loved the mirror more. "His overwhelming masculinity," wrote Lulla Rosenfeld, "was balanced by a softness even more dangerous. He saw himself, the world, and the Jewish destiny as matters of high romance."

At times his intensity carried over from the stage into family life, with consequences that matched anything on the stage. The most melodramatic of them occurred when his adolescent sister acted alongside him. Emma was a comely girl, well developed for her age. Half the men in the company fell in love with her, but she refused their advances. Boris assumed that Emma was saving herself for marriage— and then made a shocking discovery. His sister had been secretly carrying on with Morris Finkel, the director who had brought Boris back to New York. Not only had this middle-aged Romanian émigré been married before, he had a son somewhere in Europe, abandoned at the time of the divorce. The Thomashefsky family descended on Emma and forced her to break off the liaison in a very public manner.

Boris selected an evening when the Thalia Theater was SRO. All 2,700 seats were taken as he stepped before the curtain at the second act intermission. Ticket-holders were advised to stay in place following the finale; there would be a *shvier,* an ancient rite rarely invoked in

America. According to tradition, life-changing vows were to be taken in public before a *minyan,* a gathering of at least ten Jews.

"We have here tonight, ten times ten a *minyan!*" Boris boomed, before exiting to the wings. The audience buzzed; what did the great Thomashefsky need with ten times ten a *minyan*? Some of them guessed correctly—the Lower East Side, after all, was like a small town, where *shandas,* scandals, were the lubricant of life. The others found out soon enough. After the last act, the curtain rose on two Thomashefskys, brother and sister.

The actor played the real scene, as he played all fictive ones, for maximum effect. "Before this audience, before God, do you swear . . . ?" he asked his intimidated sister.

"I swear," she said, trembling before the onlookers.

"That you will never go out with the man named Morris Finkel."

"That I will never go out with the man named Morris Finkel."

"Or ever see him or have any dealings with him again as long as you live?"

She had trouble getting the words out. "Or ever see him or have any dealings with him again . . . as long as I live."

The audience responded with an immense ovation. "Women wept," recalled an admiring witness. "Emma's eyes were dry, but everybody shook her hand. 'It's for the best, Emma child. An old man and a young girl—it never works. You have been saved for some great love which will come to you when you are truly a woman!' "

The public humiliation was too much for young Emma. That night she sought out Finkel and ran off with him. They ended their journey in Philadelphia, where the newlyweds founded a small Yiddish theater.

Over the next decade the Finkels had three children and went about their business. In time Boris grudgingly made an uneasy peace with his brother-in-law, and Emma was invited to appear in her brother's productions. The Finkels relocated to the Lower East Side. Trouble began a year later, when Emma was cast opposite David Levinson, a good-looking, rather withdrawn leading man. If drama was what Boris had wanted, he was about to get it in overplus.

The couple began to meet on the sly. Emma introduced David to her children, and they could not keep the secret from their father. Finkel confronted his wife. She admitted that she had indeed fallen in love. She wanted a divorce. He refused. There was too much at stake here, he reminded her. There must be a cooling-off period, during which

Emma and David would stay far away from each other. Passion must give reason a chance.

She gave in, took the three children to a rented farmhouse in Old Bridge, New Jersey, and resolved to think things out. Several weeks later, during a family outing in the woods, Emma looked up to see her lover impulsively walking up a path. David and Emma embraced, held hands, and strolled in the dappled sunshine. The little boy and his older sisters ran ahead.

A voice rang out behind the couple.

They looked back to see the drunken Morris aiming a pistol at them. He had followed his rival from Manhattan. The trigger was pulled. A bullet whizzed harmlessly by David and split the wood of a nearby tree trunk. Emma gave a galvanic twitch, turning around to see if the children were out of range, just as Morris fired again. The shot intended for the man hit the woman instead. Emma fell, unconscious. Morris, certain that he had slain his wife, turned the gun on himself and fired once more. Death was instantaneous.

The children retained memories of their father's body being carted off. Their mother was also carried away, but the ambulance took her to a hospital, not the morgue. She would never walk again. Misery upon misery followed the shooting.

At first, Levinson moved in with his crippled amour, acting as surrogate father to the trio of bereft children. The Yiddish proverb *Die velt iz a redl un es dreyt zikh*—The world is a wheel and it turns—had special relevance a few years later when the burden proved insupportable. David abandoned Emma for a younger woman.

Boris gave his sister enough money to live on, yet found it impossible to forgive her for breaking that long-ago public vow, and for bringing ruin on herself. But he would not punish the next generation. He found a place in his productions for Emma's prettiest child, Bella Finkel. Early in the rehearsal of a musical the girl was introduced to her leading man. She found him irresistible. Two years later she married Muni Weisenfreund. He would become better known by his stage name, Paul Muni.

iv

GIVEN THE DIFFERENT STYLES, extravagant temperaments, and monumental egos of Jacob, Boris, and David, conflicts were unavoidable. At first these were confined to the rehearsal hall. But the trio's irreconcilable differences soon erupted in public. During a weekend performance Kessler upstaged Thomashefsky, aping the younger man's broad gestures. Boris caught the mockery in the corner of his eye. The scene called for him to break a plate; furious, he smashed two. Staying within character, Kessler, who was not supposed to touch the plates, broke four. Partisans in the audience cheered on their favorite. Adler was playing a mild-mannered rabbi, but he had no intention of missing out on the excitement. He broke some plates himself. The others shattered more crockery. At the end of the play the floor was covered with shards of china. Jacob, David, and Boris were starting in on a table and chairs when the curtain was lowered to prevent further damage.

The debacle was too much for Kessler. He dropped out to seek other opportunities. For all their differences, Adler and Thomashefsky remained partners, tied by contract and, in some strange way, by an emotional bond. For a time they and their families lived at the same address, 85 West 10th Street, Jacob on the second floor, Boris on the third. Adler's morning routine never varied. After ablutions he would stick his head in the dumbwaiter shaft and yell: "Thomashefsky, a black year on your head! Thomashefsky, the devil himself go into your bones!" Only then could he face the day. Boris, amused at this exercise, rarely replied. Let the downstairs neighbor have his little rite; the Thomashefskys were making plans to relocate. They would settle down in the quiet green borough of Brooklyn, away from the Manhattan madness.

Boris's advance in fortunes had come because of a distress sale. The People's Theater, a small Bowery venue, long the home of Irish melodrama, had just declared bankruptcy. The neighborhood had changed; the Hibernian populace had been replaced by Jews and, to a lesser degree, by Italians. Boris seized the real estate opportunity and signed a cheap long-term lease. Settling in, he encouraged playwrights to give him overheated melodramas with big star parts—the kind of *shund* that had made his reputation. Professor Hurwitz came up with an odd play, *Yefestoyer* (A Beautiful Woman), designed for the broad Thomashefsky style. The star played a moonstruck figure who believed that he was about to give birth. "As Hurwitz read us the play," says Boris's memoir, "I feared that the audience would burst out laughing when they heard that a man was going to have a child. I was mistaken. They took it very seriously. Ladies cried, girls sobbed that Thomashefsky, poor thing, had such a misfortune to bear. The play went on for many months with packed houses."

Still, it was not a happy time. It was during this period, Boris lamented, "that I bore a great misfortune in my private life. My beautiful little daughter, my Estherl, the one who had prayed for my Hamlet, became sick with diphtheria and died. She was buried on the same day she took her last breath, and that night I had to play in *Yefestoyer.* In that work a father laments his dead child. I had to play this very scene right after my own child's burial. I broke down on the stage and the curtain was lowered. When they resuscitated me and I went back out on the stage, I did not know what I was doing. I mechanically repeated the prompter's words, which he called out to me from his booth. Naturally the audience noticed this, but they forgave my horrible performance." The tragedy changed Boris; afterward he seemed to aim higher, encouraging the efforts of better dramatists. He took a particular interest in Leon Kobrin, a new writer with a lot to say.

Like his *landsman* Marc Chagall, Kobrin was raised in the little town of Vitebsk, Russia, victimized by anti-Semitism and suffocating czarist decrees. In his early twenties he fled to America. With all the bias Leon had encountered, however, he still regarded Russian as the language of choice. In his opinion, Yiddish was for serving up "simple tales for servant girls and ignoramuses." He clung to that belief while working long hours in Pennsylvania dairy farms, then washing and drying laundry on the Lower East Side—anything to support his wife and infant.

Eventually the surrounding culture got to him, and he started to write stories and novels in Yiddish. These attracted the attention of

Gordin. He took Kobrin on as a protégé, encouraging him to write for the theater. The older man then played good editor–bad editor with the dialogue, alternately flaying the speeches and admiring them, sometimes totally changing plotlines until the original was unrecognizable.

Of all the plays, Gordin thought the best was *Nature, Man and Animal*. He took it to Adler, who saw possibilities—with some changes in the lead role. Up until then, Kobrin thought Gordin the toughest taskmaster imaginable. He was about to learn otherwise. Gordin's main concern, after all, was about the work. Adler's main concern was about Adler. On opening night, having locked Kobrin out of the rehearsals, the actor introduced a new finale of his own devising. "When I confronted him," said the playwright, Adler replied that the fourth act of the original script "had gotten lost; either someone had stolen it or the mice had eaten it." Yet Leon could not find it in his heart to condemn Jacob. "He wrote a new act himself. Still, how marvelously he performed in that play!"

In fact, Kobrin needed all the help he could get. *The Blind Musician,* a drama about immigrant life in America, was typical of his early writings. The play derived from Russian themes, but also showed the increasing (if undigested) influence of Shakespeare on the Yiddish Theater.

The protagonist, composer Yosef Finklestein, is going blind. Consumed with self-pity, he pushes his wife, Rosa, away—but when an acquaintance pays undue attention to Rosa he becomes irate and violent. His tirades become intolerable. Rosa makes a vow: she will stay with the musician until his Carnegie Hall concert; then all will be finished.

In the final act, a storm rages outside the windows, echoing the fury in Yosef's mind. His mother has been staying with them; she lies asleep in another room. Rosa is also undisturbed by the lightning and thunder. The woman's calm only serves to agitate him. He awakens Rosa and begs her to sing the ballad he wrote when they were courting. She obliges, and that sets him off.

"That was created out of self-deception!" he shouts. "I should not have created a love song, but a song about a deluded artist!" He rips up the pages of music, reaches out to Rosa in what seems an embrace, then strangles her. His horrified mother enters. "Yosef, what have you done?" His acidulous response: "You have eyes; you can see. Mama, at least be a mother and strangle me." A patrolman breaks the door open, arrests the blind musician, who slips out of the policeman's hold and falls, sobbing, on the body of Rosa.

Often referred to as the Yiddish *Othello,* this tale of jealousy not only lacked an Iago, it also tended to repeat itself with painful woe-is-me scenes and farcical subplots. Just the same, it struck a nerve; audiences turned out for it, not least because Kobrin had been shrewd enough to introduce the subject of sightlessness. Trachoma is still the leading cause of blindness in the Third World, and in the early years of the century it afflicted the poor of Eastern Europe. The bacterial disease scars the cornea; left untreated it causes irreversible loss of vision. Customs inspectors were instructed to bar all trachoma victims from entry into the United States. As Ronald Sanders points out in his study of Jewish immigration, *Shores of Refuge,* the painful ocular inspection at Castle Garden "was to become a virtual medieval horror in immigrant folklore, all the more so because the possibility of rejection at this point was frighteningly real."

The Blind Musician meant more to audiences than to critics, however. The reviewers thought Kobrin an effective scene writer but a coarse playwright. "There are in the drama a few strong moments," observed one, "a number of psychological insights, a few living characters, and healthy humor in some places." These were not enough. "In short," he concluded, "the Romanticism of Shakespeare's play does a dance with the burlesque jokes of a vaudeville show."

Ultimately, two authors benefited from the popularity of *The Blind Musician:* Kobrin and the Bard. The Yiddish playwright went on to write a series of popular plays about the subject he knew best—the price of Jewish assimilation in the United States. And now that a Yiddishized *King Lear, Othello,* and *Hamlet* had proved commercially viable, a Shakespearean renaissance got under way on the Bowery.

The next few years saw adaptations of at least ten plays in the canon, including *Macbeth, Othello, Romeo and Juliet, Richard III,* and, inevitably, *The Merchant of Venice,* with its complex Jewish centerpiece, Shylock. Of all the productions, none aroused more curiosity than the *Hamlet* played by someone named Kalisch. The Lower East Siders knew who this was; the uptowners learned soon enough that the actor's full name was Bertha Kalisch, and that this Hamlet would be slender, blond, and beautiful.

CHAPTER SEVEN

✦

THE JEW OF THE AGES

i

B ERTHA KALISCH HAD APPEARED in small productions back in her native Lemberg in the Western Ukraine, where she attracted Goldfaden's attention. He hired the dazzling young woman and made her a star in the provinces. But even the Father of Yiddish Theater could not retain her services for long. In 1896, at the age of twenty-four, she came to America and immediately picked up work. Four years later her name sat atop marquees and, unlike Bessie Thomashefsky and Sara Adler, she had climbed there without benefit of an impresario husband. Now she planned to do something no other

Yiddish actress had dared to contemplate. She would follow the lead of
Sarah Bernhardt.

The year before, the great French actress had brought her notorious
production of *Hamlet* to England and America. By playing the title role
she provoked unceasing controversy. (In London, Max Beerbohm sati-
rized her *Hamlet* as a *"tres grande dame"*; stateside, the *North American Review*
found that "the great tragedy has been drained of its dignity, as well as
robbed of its mysterious charm.") The hullabaloo sold tickets and
stimulated feature writers; Bernhardt loved every moment of it.
Kalisch watched enviously, convinced that whatever the actress did in
French and English she could do in Yiddish, and do it better. In 1901
she made up her mind to put on tights and cross the gender line.

ii

THE YIDDISH ACTRESS picked an ideal moment. The twentieth
century's first year had already opened the way for enormous historical
and social changes. In September, at the Pan American Exposition in
Buffalo, New York, a slender twenty-eight-year-old man stepped forward to greet President William McKinley. The disaffected son of Polish immigrants, Leon Czolgosz, had a large white handkerchief in his
right hand. It hid a .32-caliber revolver. Two shots rang out and the
president collapsed, the victim of a lone anarchist. ONLY 20 YEARS
blared the headlines—the time between Garfield's and McKinley's
assassinations. Was the United States becoming the dumping ground
for agitators and revolutionaries? Was it to be the scene of more violence done by foreigners and their children? "Thank God it wasn't a
Jew"—the phrase echoed through the streets of the Lower East Side for
the next week. Ghettoites stayed indoors as much as possible, fearful of
an anti-immigration backlash. Eight days after the attack, McKinley
died of his wounds. The Jewish hope now lay in the new chief executive, former vice president Theodore Roosevelt. Placed on the ticket
to balance the conservative Ohioan, this forty-two-year-old smiling

public man presented an aura of vigorous "trust-busting" Republican-
ism. No one took him seriously. Now he was in charge of the country.

The twenty-sixth president moved to calm the populace. He
reminded the nation that he had not only been the governor of New
York state, but the police chief of New York City. He knew all about
criminals—here and abroad—and how they should be handled. Let no
one doubt his firmness and moral purpose. At the same time, the "new
Americans" should rest assured; all were welcome here, provided that
they join the mainstream and obey the nation's laws.

But other forces had also been put in motion that year, energies
beyond the control of American political power. Queen Victoria died
in 1901. The "grandmamma of Europe," the woman who had a relative
in almost every continental court, had held the throne since 1837.
Britons, their religious beliefs already shaken by Charles Darwin's theory of evolution, began to wonder if the Empire really was as solid and
permanent as Kipling's poems suggested. His "Take up the White
Man's burden . . . To wait in heavy harness/On fluttered folk and
wild—/Your new-caught, sullen peoples,/Half-devil and half-child"
had already become choice material for parodists. Anti-Imperialist
Leagues sprouted up in London and New York. The triumph in Cuba
had established Roosevelt's name when he led a charge up San Juan
Hill. But matters had changed over the next three years. Now American policy was under fire from a new kind of radical, repelled by foreign adventures and racial bias.

Figures of authority slowly began to lose their luster. The royal families of England and Germany, hostile cousins, moved inexorably
toward conflict. Even as far away as Russia, the absolute power of Czar
Nicholas II (another of Victoria's relations by marriage) was secretly
questioned. Unprecedented strikes by students and workers took place
in St. Petersburg, Moscow, Kiev, and Odessa. The czar moved to quell
them, and, yet again, to seek out a scapegoat for the country's economic
and social difficulties.

Against this shifting background, the Jews of the Lower East Side
struggled to define themselves. Appraising the international outlook
and the national psyche, Abraham Cahan grew wary. As America's
Jewish population increased, he wrote, "animosity grows with it.
Nations love only themselves, not strangers. If we get too close to the
Americans with our language and customs, they will be annoyed.
The Americans can't even get along with the Germans, so imagine the

chasm between the shtetl Jews and Yankees—it's like two different worlds. When there are only a few Jews, gentiles go slumming to inspect the novelty. When the Jews fill up the streetcars and parks, we are resented." Others expressed the same radical/conservative view— strive for social justice, but not alone. Move in groups, keep your voice down, don't attract attention.

iii

THE WARNINGS WERE IGNORED. Second Avenue wanted what Broadway had, and the people of the Yiddish Theater had no intention of blending into the scenery. The whole purpose of becoming an actor was to arouse interest and curiosity, wasn't it? Manifestly Bertha Kalisch believed so, and when she defiantly stepped into the part of a Yiddish Hamlet the entire town took notice. The critic for the *New York Morning Journal* happily reported, "There were no airs, there were no frills. There were no poses, no struggles for elusive effect." The female star "got down to the solid bedrock of the idea and hammered at it." As Professor Joel Berkowitz points out in his study *Shakespeare on the American Yiddish Stage,* Bertha Kalisch's Hamlet "was no mere drawing-room experiment. It was popular theater—popular enough not only to remain in her repertoire as long as she remained in the Yiddish Theater, but also to appeal to the 'uptown' critics."

Those critics would come to Second Avenue that year to see the most significant portrayal in Yiddish Theater history. Kalisch's effort was a novelty; Jacob Adler's was art. On reflection, Jacob said that he had once derived enormous pleasure from playing "simple Jews, Jews who were clowns, fools, *shlimazls,* unfortunates." But these characters were as walk-ons, cameos, compared with "the Jew of high intellect, proud convictions, and grand character." That personage was, of course, Shylock. The Adler version of *The Merchant of Venice,* presented at the People's Theater a few months after the female *Hamlet,* was not done to provoke clamor. Indeed, it had only one unusual aspect: a Jewish actor was playing the stage's most infamous Jew. That had never happened before.

Jacob refused to follow the lead of Henry Irving. The English actor had made the Venetian moneylender a resolute gentleman, forced to defend himself against Christian malice. His radical and sympathetic interpretation was well received in the late 1800s; but Adler, who had seen Irving's striking performance in London, wanted no part of it. He saw in Shylock "a patriarch, a higher being. A certain grandeur, the triumph of long patience, intellect, and character has been imparted to him by his teachers: suffering and tradition."

To give Shylock "the prominence he deserved," Adler vigorously edited *The Merchant of Venice,* excising scenes he thought unnecessary and altering the text so that his character remained onstage for more than half of the time. Aided by Joseph Rumshinsky's mood music, Adler redefined Shylock in two pivotal scenes. The first was the shattering discovery that the Jew's daughter, Jessica, has eloped with a Christian.

In the Irving production, Shylock knocked at the door of his house three times, growing louder and more desperate as the curtain lowered. Irving's contemporary, Sir Beerbohm Tree, played the same scene more explicitly, pacing across the stage, crying out in sorrow and covering his head with ashes. Adler opened the front door with an immense key and entered silently. After an almost unbearable pause, he spoke his daughter's name. Silence. He spoke it again, the voice hopelessly booming out "Jessica!" and echoing in a vast and empty room. He came out, bowed down with sorrow, and settled on a bench, his voice quavering with a barely audible Yiddish lament. As the curtain fell he slowly tore his garment—a sign of mourning for the child who has left the faith and thus, in his Orthodox view, life itself.

The court's verdict goes against the Jew in the final scene: he must forsake his gold and convert to Christianity. Shylock's enemy Gratiano sneers, "In christening thou shalt have two godfathers. Had I been judge, thou should'st have had ten more, to bring thee to the gallows, not the font."

In all the other productions, Gratiano pushed Shylock to the ground, where he sat whimpering and defeated, the old Hebrew *in extremis,* victim of his own avarice. In the Adler version, Shylock was also forced to earth, but after a few moments he rose up. From his garment he brushed the dirt of the ground and, symbolically, the stain of anti-Semitism. With an air of moral superiority and innate dignity he made his exit. "Weighty and proud his walk," the star recalled, "calm and conclusive his speech, a man of rich personal and national experience, a man who sees life through the glasses of eternity. So I played him, so I had joy in him, and so I portrayed him."

Jacob's portrait thrilled the Lower East Side—but then, it was supposed to. What Adler could not have predicted was the clamor outside the little world of the Yiddish Theater. The mainstream press embraced his production. In a reference to the prominent English eighteenth-century actor/impresario, *Theater* magazine dubbed Jacob Adler "The Bowery Garrick," and the prominent producer Arthur Hopkins came downtown to make an unprecedented offer. He wanted to present the Adler *Shylock* on Broadway. Jacob refused; he thought his English too heavily accented to recite Shakespeare in the original.

Hopkins had an answer to that: Adler could speak in Yiddish. The other members of the cast, Americans all, would recite their lines in English. The offer seemed bizarre but too flattering to refuse. Adler signed the contract. *Shylock* first tried out in Boston and Washington where patronizing critics described it as gimmicky. Never mind, Hopkins assured his cast; New York would be different.

And so it was. With the original title restored, *The Merchant of Venice* opened at the American Theater in Manhattan on May 24, 1903, and was showered with rave reviews. ADLER SCORES IN SHYLOCK ROLE, said a headline in the *Herald,* and went on to call Jacob's version "that rare dramatic experience on Broadway, the coincidence of a great play and a great actor." The *Evening Journal* proclaimed Jacob a genius who "played the character in a way never seen on the American stage and defying imitation." Shylock was "revealed as the Jew of the ages." And in the judgment of *Theater* magazine, the Jewish actor offered "a striking and original conception, wrought out not only of careful study, but from a racial sympathy, an instinctive appreciation of the deeper motives of this profound and complex character."

It was to be expected that the Jewish press would *qvel* as one of its own received such glowing notices. But surprisingly, most of them paid more attention to the audience than to the actor. The *Yiddish World,* for example, was pleased to find "a deep seriousness on the faces of these Americans. They understood Adler just as well as they did the rest of the actors, and in places even better. They showed this with both the attentiveness and the applause with which they greeted the end of every scene in which he appeared."

As Adler basked in his triumph Goldfaden ended his self-imposed European exile, tiptoeing back to New York City, unnoticed by people in and out of the Yiddish Theater he had invented. Only Jacob was kind enough to drop by occasionally. Out of guilt or gratitude he sent $5 every week so that the old man and his wife, Paulina, could live without starving. Otherwise the star kept his distance. He had become the darling of the establishment press and needed to maintain the image of a modern actor unburdened by the past. After all, it was because of Jacob that critics and reporters urged their readers to take the subway down to the Lower East Side. Even if they couldn't understand a word, they would apprehend the gestures and the themes of "the best theater in New York." The prominent writers George Jean Nathan and Stark Young came to the Yiddish actor's dressing room; so did the matinee idol John Drew.

In the days to follow, the spirit of the ghetto took a galvanic leap. What the public schools taught Jewish children was demonstrably true now: humble beginnings were no bar to achievement in America. Old hands and greenhorns endlessly discussed this in cafés, social clubs, and sweatshops. A Yiddish proverb had new meaning now: *Men ken machn dem kholen gresser vi di nakht,* One can blow up a dream to be bigger than the night.

iv

DURING ITS EARLY YEARS the Yiddish Theater had depended on word of mouth rather than press notices. With good reason. There was no press. There were *attempts* at newspapers, including the penny daily, the *Yiddisher Recorder,* which claimed to have a circulation of over ten thousand—and which collapsed in 1895 after five years of publication. But late in the nineteenth century a true journalistic enterprise had begun. Like the Hearst and Pulitzer papers, the *Forverts*—the *Daily Forward*—dabbled in sensationalism. But the paper had a more earnest purpose than merely titillating its readers. It wanted to educate the masses—to help them get on in the alien culture of America. To do that, the management eventually called upon Abraham Cahan.

The novelist and pamphleteer had helped to found the *Forward,* but left during its first year to seek a wider audience. Cahan, who had entered America at the age of twenty-two, was justifiably proud of his fluency in English, and began to freelance articles to mainstream publications. The *Commercial Advertiser* accepted so many of them that Lincoln Steffens put him on staff. There Cahan proselytized as he wrote. "He was the one," Steffens was to acknowledge, "who brought the spirit of the East Side into our shop and took us, as he got to us, one by one or in groups, in the cafés and Jewish theaters."

In addition to journalism, Cahan wrote a novel, *Yekl: A Tale of the New York Ghetto,* highly praised by *Atlantic Monthly* editor William Dean Howells—the same Howells who had handled Dostoevsky's writings with a pair of tongs. *Yekl* failed to sell, though, and Steffens left the *Advertiser* in 1902. Without his chief backer, and with dim hopes of a literary career, Cahan was forced to look for a position. He found it a year later, when the owners of the *Forward* offered him the job of managing editor.

Cahan was forty-three. For the next four decades he would remain virtually unchanged in appearance and occupation. The thick graying hair, the push-broom mustache, the twinkling pince-nez glasses became as familiar a sight on the Lower East Side as the signs for "Appetizing Delicatessen." His prodigious energy was at last channeled. From the very first weeks he set the *Forward*'s style, championing the rights of labor, exhorting the values of socialism, attempting to make immigrant Jews into real Americans. Early on, the paper awarded a gold fountain pen to the workman who best defined a strikebreaker: "God took the legs of a horse, the head of an ass, the face of a dog, the hair from a hog, the heart of a hare, combined them and out came a scab."

At the same time, the *Forward* advertised a ten-cent Yiddish translation of the Constitution as "The little Torah," and "the high road to citizenship, employment and success." To Cahan, education was just as important as politics—you couldn't have one without the other. When one of his editorials suggested that mothers supply their children with handkerchiefs, he received letters asking what this had to do with socialism. The answer: "And since when has socialism been opposed to clean noses?" And while he was on the subject of table manners, Cahan went on, "not all rules are silly. You would not like my sleeve to dip into your soup as I reach over your plate to get the salt; it is more reasonable for me to ask you to 'pass the salt, please.' "

In *The Downtown Jews,* Ronald Sanders notes that the *Forward* sought to influence the entire Jewish population of New York City and beyond. As Cahan saw it, only one institution stood in his way: the Yiddish Theater. "If the *Forward* was becoming a kind of running Talmudic text for the secular cultural life of the Yiddish-speaking masses, the theaters on the Bowery were serving as that culture's temple." The editor could not write plays, he conceded to staffers, but he had the power to criticize them and perhaps to shape the future of Yiddish drama. Under his aegis the *Forward* ran long and detailed theater reviews. New plays were given the same attention as international news. Writers who agreed with the editor's principles were acclaimed; those who failed to come up to his expectations got panned.

Jacob Gordin was one of those unfortunates. Cahan not only carped about the playwright's work in the pages of the *Forward,* he would go on and on about the man's shortcomings to anyone who would listen. He was particularly hard on Gordin's peasant speeches. In Cahan's opinion they were loaded with highfalutin language—totally unbelievable; common folk must use common words. Gordin got wind of the editor's remarks and his reaction was volcanic. Between acts the playwright stepped onstage to denounce his arrogant critic. Cahan was notified of the incident. He sent word to the theater manager: "Assure Gordin that I won't have any more opinions about forthcoming works of his." Cahan resolved never to sit through another Gordin play, and Gordin resolved never to read another word of Cahan's evaluations.

These were vows made to be broken. But both men bided their time before the moment of total war.

v

FOR A PAPER TO GROW in New York, the prime requisite was a burgeoning audience. But Jewish immigration had slowed down after the first rush, and Yiddish readership had maintained an unpromising status quo. At that moment Russia once again changed the course of American history. In 1903, anti-Semitic feelings ran high in the town of Kishinev. The police chief told town leaders that "it would serve the Jews right if they were driven from the city for encouraging the propaganda of socialism."

A week before Easter Sunday a group of strangers, mostly Albanians, arrived for the specific purpose of wreaking havoc on the Kishinev Jews. On the fateful day, an armed horde gathered. In the words of a reporter from St. Petersburg, the "mob took possession of the approaches to the railway station, where frightful scenes occurred that beggar description. Every Jew who was encountered was beaten until he lost consciousness; one Jew was dragged under a tramcar and crushed to death. The miserable dwellings of the poor were rifled of their contents, which were removed into the street and piled into a heap. Immense clouds of feathers rose into the air."

The violence was a mere prelude. An Irish nationalist, Michael Davitt, was touring Russia at the time. He heard about the pogrom taking place in Kishinev and hurried there, too late to do anything but listen to the survivors. After Easter Sunday, he wrote, "some of the worst outrages were perpetrated. Every Jewish woman and girl the mob could find was raped." One thirteen-year-old was violated and then murdered. The rapists "fought for her body like famished wolves after life was extinct. When found the next morning by her relatives, the body was seen to be literally torn in two." An old grocer, blind in one eye, was attacked. He offered all the money in his possession in exchange for his life. The leader of the men took the money, then said, "Now we want your eye. You will never look upon a Christian woman again," and gouged out his eye with a sharpened stick. Davitt visited another victim, barely alive, in a Kishinev hospital, "whose head had been battered with bludgeons and left for dead. He told me that it was the same gang who killed his mother-in-law, by driving nails through her eyes into the brain."

The next year more than a thousand Jews were massacred in Zhitomir, under the banner of the "Black Hundreds," a violently anti-Semitic organization backed by the czar. Russia's own prime minister wrote in his secret diary, "The aims of the Black Hundreds are usually selfish and of the lowest character. They are typical murderers from dark alleys. Naturally, one's record is still better if he can present evidence of having killed or at least mutilated a few peaceful Yids."

This time the atrocities did not go unheeded by the Western world. The English, French, and German press spoke out. In Russia itself there were grumblings. Tolstoy's denunciation was suppressed by the censor, but his words were leaked to the public. He recognized the czarist government as "the real culprit, which stupefies our people and makes bigots of them." The American president was prevailed upon to make a statement against the Russian violence. Theodore Roosevelt responded with a letter distributed worldwide, expressing "the deep sympathy felt not only by the administration but by all the American people for the unfortunate Jews who have been the victims in the recent appalling massacres and outrages."

At the new embarkation center on Ellis Island, the annual number of Jewish arrivals rose from 57,000 in 1902 to 76,000 in 1903. The influx was too much for bureaucrats to handle. Thousands of immigrants were held back, complaints got out, and that fall the president made a personal visit to the island. Roosevelt "inspected every part of the work," said an official report, "and held an impromptu examination into the case of a Jewish woman, detained since July with her four children." Her husband was supposed to have called for the family, but he had been too sick to make the trip. The president intervened and got the family admitted. The next year, 1904, some 106,000 Jewish immigrants were welcomed to the New World.

In his novel *The Storm*, Sholem Aleichem portrayed his fellow immigrants at that time, fleeing from the continuing Russian pogroms "with valises, sacks, packages, and pillows, pillows, pillows! Their faces were terrified, their eyes darting about in every direction. They trembled when they heard a shout or even a whistle. . . . The word 'America' had for them a special magnetism, a kind of magical meaning. It stood for an ideal of which many, many had long dreamed. They imagined America to be a kind of heaven, a sort of Paradise. 'We hope, God Almighty, they will let us in and not, God forbid, send us back.' "

The Russian exodus was to bring new vigor to the Lower East Side. All boats seemed to rise on the tide; uptown, Longacre Square was renamed Times Square in honor of the newspaper, and the *Forward* enjoyed a corresponding prestige in its own neighborhood. The Yiddish Theater prepared new programs to entice the fresh wave of culture-hungry arrivals. Producers anticipated good times without end. No one bothered to heed a prophetic warning from the social philosopher Max Nordau. In Paris, he was interviewed by a journalist who asked him about the new congestion in Manhattan. "America saves the man, not the Jew," he observed. "Jews in America should live in groups to preserve their character and their ideals. Influenced by foreign surroundings, Jews lose their identity." Such a loss seemed inconceivable by 1906. The Lower East Side was enjoying a second renaissance, and thanks to the newfangled telephone and wireless telegraph, the world was learning all about it.

vi

ON A PLEASANT JUNE evening that year, Manhattan's original odd couple strolled down Second Avenue. The tall man with black beard and dark, deep-set eyes was Jacob Gordin, now a dominant presence on the Lower East Side. With loud voice and spirited gestures, the Russian immigrant went on about his adaptations of Shakespeare and his interpretations of Tolstoy's thought.

Gordin's American companion, back in the United States after an absence of twenty years, was a dedicated author, master of nuance, life-long bachelor, apolitical, bald, clean-shaven in recent years, tentative in style and speech, as gentile in his way as the other was Jewish. The playwright led the way and chattered on; Henry James did the gawking. He had followed the news of pogroms in Russia and of the ensuing torrent of immigrants spilling into downtown Manhattan. Ever curious, he demanded to see the phenomenon for himself. A friend had arranged the meeting between the novelist and the playwright, who grandly took his guest in tow.

What James apprehended did not seem encouraging. All around him was the pulse of cultural life, the voracious appetite for technical knowledge and dramatic art—the very art at which he had failed so publicly in London. But the great observer failed to see what was spread out before him. His delicate senses were besieged and affronted. It seemed to him that these people bred like animals. The fire escapes that ran down every tenement were reminiscent of "a little world of bars and perches and swings for human squirrels and monkeys."

And there were those offensive accents. At the Royal, a favorite hangout for Jewish performers, foreign intonations turned the café into a "torture-room of the living idiom." This "Hebrew conquest of New York," James predicted, would permanently maim the language. In the future, "whatever we will know it for, certainly we shall not know it for English."

Gordin thought a comedy might be the best choice for Mr. James's first downtown experience. He bought two tickets, and they entered the Liberty Theater. The fare turned out to be even more cringe-making than the world outside the stage door. The guest excused himself after the first act, not because it was incomprehensible but because the audience offended. Ticket buyers emanated "a scent, literally, not further to be followed."

Appalled, James concluded, "There is no swarming like that of Israel, when once Israel has got a start, and the scene here bristled, at every step, with the signs and sounds, immitigable, of a Jewry that had burst all bounds." This was an elegantly expressed variation of Henry Adams's letter to his brother. "God tried drowning out the world once," wrote this grandson of President John Quincy Adams, "but it did no kind of good, and there are said to be four-hundred-and-fifty-thousand Jews now doing kosher in New York alone. God himself owned failure." They were doing a lot more than kosher. The swarm that had burst all bounds was slowly—too slowly for the likes of Adams and James—learning the ways of the New World.

With this second influx of Eastern European refugees, New York was serving yet again as a microcosm for both kinds of Jewish fervor:

the passionately religious, and the purely ethnic. If the old orthodoxies were not persecuted, neither were they welcomed. The secular components of Judaism, on the other hand—adaptability, a pursuit of knowledge and opportunity, a high regard for artistic endeavor, an obsession with social justice, a heightened, almost melodramatic sense of life— were encouraged and rewarded in the Promised City.

Every immigrant group had its heroes and heroines, and many a business giant, sports figure, and politician was looked up to. But for the Jews on the Lower East Side, the artists of the theater were held in special regard. As journalist Harry Golden points out, during these years of struggle and assimilation, "the immigrants had not yet learned about Christy Mathewson or Ty Cobb . . . the folk heroes of the ghetto were the actors, the journalists, the cantors, the critics, the playwrights, and the composers; but mostly the actors."

Ignored by the general public, Abraham Goldfaden wanted a piece of this hero worship. He ached to be recognized not only as the Father of Yiddish Theater but as a still viable playwright. But the indifferent responses of the producers told him that he had become irrelevant, an antique from another era. There was even a rumor, he learned, that the Father was repeating himself, retreating into senescence. As a desperate gesture he took his old work *Ben-Ami* to Boris Thomashefsky and begged for a professional reading with experienced actors. Boris could not refuse—and much to his surprise found that the play was met with considerable enthusiasm. He agreed to direct it. Goldfaden told his wife that he now had but one ambition: to see *Ben-Ami* become popular once more. He could then die happy.

In December 1907, his dearest wish came true. *Ben-Ami* opened to a roar of applause, encores, the awarding of flowers, and, finally, a speech by the grateful playwright. He walked down Second Avenue to his apartment clutching the bouquet. Swinging open the door of the flat, he shouted: "Paulina, Paulina, they gave me laurel wreaths! I'm not senile, Paulina, I'm not senile!" The moment was so sweet he insisted on savoring it for the next five nights. At each performance he laughed and cried and took bows from his box seat. On the fifth evening he experienced some discomfort and pain in the chest. He walked home slowly. That night he died in his sleep. No one, not even Goldfaden himself, could have written a more emotionally satisfying finale.

Boris, a connoisseur of melodrama, reveled in the moment. Having rescued the deceased from oblivion, he insisted on the last word. The truth was that he had planned to take *Ben-Ami* off the boards after a couple of weeks. Now, in the wake of renewed interest, he saw an opportunity to extend the run—and to make a speech. En route to the cemetery he addressed the mourners. "If not for our old father Goldfaden," he intoned, "we none of us would have become tragedians or comedians, prima donnas, soubrettes, playwrights. If not for Goldfaden, we'd be plain and simple Jews, choir singers, folk singers, clothes peddlers, machine sewers, cigarette makers. . . .

"Goldfaden went out like a light in his dark room while we, his children, ride in carriages, own our own houses, are hung with diamonds. Union members, club members, pinochle players, decision makers, managers, sports—we're nice and warm, all of us. But our father was cold."

It was a fine lamentation, and better business. *Ben-Ami* played to full houses for the rest of the season. But there was no Goldfaden revival. Audiences were being exhorted to "better" theater, and with this one exception, the drama critics looked down upon the good old days when the Yiddish Theater was young. Contemporary plays were what they were looking for, written by freethinking playwrights. The trouble was, everyone had a different definition of freethinking. Case in point: the enduring quarrel between Jacob Gordin and Abraham Cahan. Having sworn never to see or read each other's work again, they promptly ignored their promises and engaged in yet another battle of egos.

Gordin's drama *The Purity of Family Life* had just opened. In the *Forward,* Cahan complained that "the leading feminine role was not a role at all, but a collection of propagandistic speeches. Madame Keni Liptzin, in this part, had nothing to play. Instead of an actress, she had to be a speechmaker." As for the supporting players, they were "of the variety-stage type that we are used to seeing from the pen of Mr. Lateiner—not one jot better."

The comparison to a notorious hack was the final, unendurable insult. In *Dramatische Velt* (Drama World) Gordin wrote of Cahan: "Whatever I build he tears down. It's clear that we are working for the sake of the selfsame people. But I want to lead them forward, and he drags them backward through the *Forward.*"

Cahan returned fire, aware that his opponent had an extra weapon in his arsenal. After all, Cahan could only write prose; Gordin could create dialogue to make his point. Although the playwright regarded himself as a socialist, he was not blind to the faults of the left. In *The Russian Jew in America,* the author created a duplicitous labor leader, clothed, mustached, and bespectacled in the unmistakable Cahan style. At the finale, the man betrays his followers and becomes a boss. "Everything would be fine," he booms, "if not for the union." Those words pushed Cahan over the edge. He stood up in the darkened theater and yelled in Russian, "*Eto lozh!*" (It's a lie!)

Battle lines were drawn, and the crossfire grew intense. Neither side knew that the war between Gordin and his enemies was drawing to a close. For the playwright, a lifelong smoker, had been diagnosed with throat cancer. Suddenly internecine battles no longer seemed important to him. A bigger matter intervened: who would see to his large family when he was gone? He traveled overseas, hoping to secure royalties for the plays that had been pirated. The trip did little good. He returned to the United States and wrote a mordant comedy, *Dementia Americana,* satirizing the immigrants who had jettisoned their background and ethics for the Almighty Dollar. During rehearsals the author's suffering was evident, and an actress tried to console him: "Don't worry. After all, this is not your first play." "No," replied Gordin. "But it will be my last."

Dementia received a cold response from critics and public alike. Worse still, the *Forward* ran several pieces accusing Gordin of plagiarism for articles he had written many years before. This was to be the ultimate showdown between rivals. The series started in early April of 1909; by the end of the month Gordin was dead at the age of fifty-eight. Cahan backtracked; the paper ran a black-bordered obituary and a reporter duly exclaimed, "What a personality this was! What an example to all men! We hardly dared speak of him. Of Jacob Gordin one always expected something great. One could do no less, and he expected it of himself!"

Leon Kobrin summoned up an image of the deceased: "His eyes like two fires, sharp as knives; in his right hand, a stick, and in the left—one of his plays. He passes, and the actors tremble when they catch sight of him. People who know him say, 'There goes Gordin,' and those who don't know him look after him and say, 'What a good-looking man.'" Jacob Adler added a greater compliment. Gordin was not only an important playwright, he was "My rescuer, my Messiah! Without him I would have no life in the theater."

Gordin had no such romantic notions about himself or his work.

His last writing was not a play; it was a posthumously distributed fable about the narrator, his wife, Jehudith, who represents the Jewish people in general, and his stepdaughter, "a neglected, sick child growing up in squalor and dirt"—obviously the people of the downtown ghetto.

"I took this child as my own, gave gifts to her. Perhaps my gifts were of little value, but they were the best I had. And for all this, the mother hated me. She hated the gifts I had given the girl. Nevertheless, I continue to love the child. And although today Jehudith and I have nothing to give each other, we still remain one body and one soul. She doesn't pay me much attention, yet in spite of it all I still love her. I know that when I fall, her friends, bought for a few coins, will dance on my corpse and she will look on, unconcerned. The day I die is the day she will forget me."

If this was the self-pity of a dying man, it was also an accurate forecast. No plaque commemorates Gordin's name; his plays go unrevived. As historian Lulla Rosenfeld sadly notes, "No man of genius has ever been more brutally consigned to oblivion, no writer so idolized in his lifetime so totally neglected after his death than Gordin." She is particularly hard on Cahan: " 'Realism' was the catchword of the day, and like all catchwords it made wise men foolish."

CHAPTER EIGHT

✦

MOISHE THE INSATIABLE

i

I N 1910, some wag labeled New York City the nation's thyroid
gland. It was both a put-down and a compliment. Since Manhattan could not grow out, it had grown up and become a completely
vertical borough. Subways reached beyond midtown, allowing the poor
and lower middle class to commute from the outer boroughs to jobs all
over the city. The new president, William Howard Taft, brought with
him a shining optimism about the country's future. He had been
administrator of the Panama Canal, and boomed the virtues of "dollar
diplomacy," trading not only with Europe but with Central and South

America. In New York the word "imports" not only denoted furniture and rugs, bananas and sugar, tea and coffee. It was also understood to mean streams of humanity taking over the downtown streets. In the dilapidated buildings south of Washington Square, immigrants nurtured the cuisine and the street life of Italy. Chinatown, between Pell and Mott Streets, was a place where visitors could see old men in native costume and pigtails. Below that neighborhood a Greek colony thrived. Turks and Arabs settled near the Battery, where they set up trading bazaars reminiscent of those along the Levant. Little Germany was north of the Bowery, Little Hungary nearby, with restaurants and shops that catered to Old World taste.

"To explore these quarters of the city," observes historian Lloyd Morris, "was an adventure on foreign soil. Only the facades of the buildings persuaded you that you were actually on Manhattan Island, reminded you that nowhere else could you become an alien so abruptly and diversely." Within those quarters, no area seemed as insulated from uptown life as the Lower East Side. But the effect was illusory. To be sure, the ordinary folk still bore the scars of their experience in the Pale. They talked among themselves, read the Yiddish papers, and went to the Yiddish Theater rather than the palaces uptown. But it was no longer possible to screen out the happenings of the world beyond the ghetto.

The emergence of feminism, for example, first signaled by Bernhardt and Kalisch, could be seen and heard in the new demonstrations for women's suffrage. In Washington state, women had just been given the vote. The number of females attending college had increased 150 percent since the beginning of the century. And the first large suffrage parade took place on Fifth Avenue, organized by the outspoken Women's Political Union.

The telephone, not yet within reach of the poor, was nonetheless a potent factor in communications. The transatlantic cable brought news from Europe, translated by Morse code operators the instant it arrived. What Winston Churchill was to call the "old world at its sunset" could be seen at the funeral of Edward VII when the crowned heads of more than twenty countries met for the last time. Death had brought them together. In a matter of four years, war, thicker than blood and stronger than thrones, would cruelly and permanently separate them.

Seven English-language newspapers were published every morning in New York City, and another seven in the afternoon. In addition there were Greek and Italian and Russian and Chinese newspapers, as well as eight Yiddish dailies. Many of the journals were sensational in nature, but all demanded a basic literacy from a news-mad readership. The horse-drawn broughams, carriages, and carts were giving way to the automobile. Electric lights, which had turned the uptown theater district into the Great White Way, were coming to the Yiddish Theater as well.

They would need them. For only a few blocks from Hester Street a new form of entertainment beckoned to passersby. "Nickelodeons," owned by William Fox, a former garment worker, and Marcus Loew, once a fur cutter, offered flickering movies to patrons for only 5 cents. A new craze got under way when professional broadcasters offered free music and news over the airwaves. Radios became a part of the living room furniture of the middle class; poorer people constructed receivers out of Quaker Oats boxes, wire coils, tiny crystals, and cat's whiskers.

Young Jewish entertainers, who might have made their mark in the theater, instead tried their hands at singing, dancing, and comedy in vaudeville. The Lower East Side's most richly gifted youth, little dark-eyed Israel Baline, changed his name to Irving Berlin and started working for a midtown song publisher. Like all tyros, he started by commenting on what he knew, and what he knew best were the sounds and attitudes of ghetto theater. These he augmented with inventive situations, bordering on caricature and even anti-Semitism:

> *Yiddle in the middle of your fiddle, play some ragtime*
> *Get busy, I'm dizzy, I'm feeling two years young . . .*

And

> *Come and hear the Yiddish professor,*
> *Mr. Abie Cohen, Mr. Abie Cohen,*
> *Come and hear him tickling the piano*
> *In a first-class Yiddisha tone.*
> *I would never kiss him on the lips,*
> *But I'd kiss him on the fingertips . . .*

And

Your automobile is burning, Abie—
What shall I do, What shall I do?
I know that it's insured for twice as much as it cost;
In another minute I'm afraid it will be lost.
What's that? You want me to keep talking,
And you'll pay for the telephone call.
Well, how's da Mamma, How's da Mamma?
Better get the fire insurance papers from her,
For your automobile is burning, Abie—
Congratulations, goodbye . . .

A street singer and pop-eyed clown, Edward Israel Iskowitz, orphaned at the age of three, took his act to the vaudeville circuits and, as Eddie Cantor, made his way to the big time. A cantor's son, Asa Yoelson, later Al Jolson, entered the same venues in blackface. So did the imposing Sophia Kalish. When she dropped the burnt cork and acknowledged her ethnicity, the singer was rewarded with a number written in her honor: "The Yiddisha Rag," whose colorful song sheet read "Respectfully dedicated to Miss Sophie Tucker." The lady they called "The Last of the Red Hot Mamas" stayed a headliner for the next fifty years. These performers were followed by scores of other Lower East Siders with kinetic energy and a kind of demonic ambition.

Yet the Yiddish Theater kept going, thanks to the czar. The pogroms continued in Russia. A group of Bolsheviks, some of them Jewish, robbed a train in the Urals, and a wave of student strikes took place in several cities to protest the treatment of Jews. The government's reprisals were swift and harsh. At the same time, a spellbinding monk, Gregory Rasputin, worked his way into the confidence of the Romanovs. He encouraged Czar Nicholas II to make even more repressive moves against non-Christians of all kinds. Russian Jews continued to flee by the thousands, headed for the port of New York.

The spillover from Eastern Europe filled the venues and furnished new talents for the city's Yiddish theatrical companies. The trouble was, these new refugees turned out to be as unsophisticated as the old ones—perhaps more so. Generations of life in provincial *shtetls*, followed by years of intimidation and brutality, had kept them innocent of art. Now that they had reached the astonishing safety of America, they wanted melody, farce, melodrama played without subtlety or complication. The managers gave it to them. Keni Liptzin, the leading actress in so many of Gordin's plays, lamented the situation. *Shund* had come back in fashion "because the post-Gordin dramatists are weak, and the managers are afraid of literary drama. Even when it is a money-maker, they find other reasons for its success." Her *kvetch* included the Yiddish press. Drama critics were "not honest, and besides, they were insulting," their language "suitable for fishwives."

David Kessler had worse to say. He was performing in a play called *The Ironmaster* when he heard hisses and laughter. "I was struck dumb," he remembered. "I knew that I ought to continue, but was absolutely unable to do so." He appealed to the audience. "Was there a rip in my clothes? Had I forgotten to button my doublet? I was very angry, and I spoke with passion, and the crowd became silent, but the play did not continue." The next night he changed his tactics. "I made a burlesque of the part. I did not play it with truthfulness. I waved my hands and I stamped my feet. I had eight curtain calls. It is useless to act well with some people."

A line about a Second Avenue ham made the rounds: "He used to be a good actor, poor fellow, but now he's just a star." Damned if that will ever be said about me, declared Jacob Adler. He had come too far to turn back, and at the Thalia his company made one last attempt to honor their favorite Yiddish playwright, Jacob Gordin.

From across the street at the People's Theater, Bessie Thomashefsky watched them fail. Her memoir is filled with schadenfreude. "Well," she notes, "they had made their reputations with Gordin, so who could blame them? But at the People's Thomashefsky and I were coining money. Very soon the Thalia began to envy our full houses. We delivered the goods to the faceless audiences we called by the single name of 'Moishe,'—the great almighty public."

The Thomashefskys consumed every penny of their box office receipts. Their luxurious house in Brooklyn was deemed too hot for the summer and they acquired a grand dacha in the Catskills. The young son of Rudolph Schildkraut, Vienna's most celebrated actor, was invited to the twenty-acre estate. To him it appeared to be "the domain of a millionaire. Not even the great German director Max Reinhardt had achieved this style of living." Best of all, "a part of the grounds had been set aside for an open-air theater. During the summer Father starred here in a one-act play that Thomashefsky staged just for the entertainment of his colleagues."

Boris's son Harry recalled a gray afternoon when no live performance was scheduled. A silent film unreeled on an outdoor screen, featuring Thomashefsky in an experimental role. "Father hated his work in the movie. There were plenty of rocks on the ground and he pelted his image with stones. Then he had the film run again and threw more things until the screen was in shreds. Back in New York City people thought he was smitten with himself. On stage, definitely. On screen, no."

Meanwhile, as Bessie stated, the Adlers maintained their loyalty to Gordin long after the public lost its appetite for his searing dramas. Sara starred in Gordin's adaptation of the Tolstoy novel *Resurrection,* playing a pure, self-sacrificing peasant girl. She followed it with *The Homeless,* Gordin's bleak portrait of immigrant life in New York. Once again she portrayed a guileless, self-abnegating soul—Mrs. Bathsheba Rifkin, a middle-aged woman whose husband comes to find her an embarrassing relic of their life in Eastern Europe. He takes up with a modern woman, an intellectual who supplies what Bathsheba cannot: a connection with the vibrant social and intellectual life outside the Rifkins' confining flat. After he leaves her, she becomes one of the ironically titled homeless, an immigrant with a place to lay her head, but with no position and no future in the New World. Bathsheba winds up in a mental institution.

Upon release, she finds her husband remarried and her son estranged. All that remains are memories of Russia, now gilded in her fretful mind. Looking out the window at falling snow she begins to babble. Too late her neighbors summon an ambulance. She has descended into madness for the last time. Dancing and clapping her hands, she chortles in a childlike manner, "I am going home! I am going home!" as the lights dim. Lulla Rosenfeld notes, "Keni Liptzin produced her own version of *Resurrection* some years later. But no actress, no matter how gifted or ambitious, ever dared to follow Sara Adler as the simple Jewish housewife of Jacob Gordin's *Homeless.*"

These works were respectfully but not fully attended. The Adlers found themselves in the red. Rosenfeld recalls the day Jacob finally surrendered to Moishe, presenting a lachrymose tragedy called *The Living Orphans.* On opening night there were ovations and calls of "Author! Author!" Jacob brought the playwright onstage and made the shortest curtain speech of his career: "You and this man," he informed the audience, "are ruining the theater!" There was a becoming blush from "this man"; after all, an insult from the Great Eagle was worth more than praise from lesser celebrities. Besides, he knew that *Orphans* would run for weeks and weeks, and that no producer ever sneered at box office receipts.

Nevertheless, Jacob never made his peace with substandard theater, dealing with his professional discomfort by turning *shund* into a family joke. He circulated true stories of the egomaniacal actress who insisted on top billing, renaming Shakespeare's play *Juliet and Romeo*. And of the tragedy that featured a mother crying over her stricken child: a doctor enters, shaking his head. She entreats him to sing a final lullaby. He strolls to the footlights, instructs the orchestra leader, "OK, professor! Shoot!" and then sings the up-tempo "A Mother Is the Best of All Things."

He also told of a white slavery drama that took place in Chinatown. One of the Yiddish actors who doubled as father and villain was taking some sun on the theater roof. He had fallen asleep when the stage manager roused him. Bolting onstage, he realized that he was wearing two conflicting pieces of makeup, a long white beard and a pigtail. To rescue the moment he addressed the onlookers: "You think because of my beard I am a Jew. But in my heart"—here he abruptly pulled off his whiskers—"I am a Chinaman!" Two generations later the line was still alive; anyone in the Adler family who misbehaved was told, "In your heart you are a Chinaman!"

ii

SEEN TOO CLOSE, the Yiddish Theater appeared to be going in reverse. David Pinski took a longer view. Born in Russia, educated at Columbia University, he made his argument in a book, *The Jewish Drama*, widely distributed in 1910. His story of the Yiddish Theater amounted to a play in three acts, all of them dominated by writers rather than performers.

Act one centered on the groundbreaking Abraham Goldfaden and his immediate followers, especially the commercial vulgarians, Hurwitz and Lateiner.

Act two was the story of Boris Thomashefsky's commercial achievements and Jacob Adler's artistic ones. They were followed by Jacob Gordin and the Gordinites, who created a higher form of theater, but whose achievements were short-lived.

Act three would reinvent the Yiddish Theater, filling it with significant artistic fare—by Pinski, of course, but also by other high-minded playwrights.

The author set out to prove his own theory. Early experiments turned out poorly, but they led to *The Treasure,* a drama that attracted the attention of Max Reinhardt. He produced the play in Germany in 1910, where it created a small sensation and this, in turn, caused New York to take notice.

Pinski's drama was hardly a groundbreaker. The subject matter—the corrupting power of money—had been addressed by a dozen playwrights before him. What separated *The Treasure* from the other works was its bold fusion of reality and symbolism. A Russian *shtetl* is shaken by a rumor: the town grave digger has come upon gold coins in a burial plot. A day later, the poorest of the poor becomes the most flattered man in town. Marriage brokers vie for his daughter's hand; snobs and politicians seek his company.

The more he denies the gossip, the more the townspeople are convinced that he has hidden the money. This causes smiles to stop, threats to begin, and the cemetery to be desecrated in a futile search for treasure. Too late, the townsfolk learn that the man was telling the truth after all—there are no buried riches. There never had been. An epilogue takes place in the graveyard, where souls rise from the earth, take over the stage, and scatter their comments:

THE DEAD (*Shrouded, they walk among the graves whispering their words*):
I thought we would not come out today at all.
The dead fear the breath of the living.
We fear them more than they do us.
The distinguished and the wealthy must surely have had a bad day.
It fairly smelled of money and they had to lie with the worms.
Don't flatter yourself. We would have been no better. We *were* no
    better.

Elemental, stark, poignant, rueful, *The Treasure* reached past Second Avenue to the corridors of Harvard. For the first time, the work of a

Yiddish playwright was praised by Professor George Pierce Baker, soon to become the teacher of Eugene O'Neill, George Abbott, and other Broadway luminaries. He read the play in translation and compared it to the work of Ben Jonson. If Pinski's dialogue "lacks the poetic expression of *Volpone*," wrote Baker, "it has a finer truth of characterization."

Baker's judgment was shown to Jacob Adler. He reacted with pleasure—and a vital competitive spirit. Using his own savings, he bought the rights to Leo Tolstoy's last play, *Redemption,* the study of a Russian nobleman on his way down. In November 1911, a staff writer for *Theater* magazine journeyed to Second Avenue. "A number of Broadway notables," said his opening night report, watched the drama "which Jacob P. Adler had the courage to present. Throughout his admirable impersonation, and throughout Protasoff's fall from revelry to penury, Mr. Adler kept burning that spark of nobility that was finally to end the noble's pitiful existence."

Also in attendance that night was Leon Kobrin, whose recollection gives a rare glimpse of the Adlerian technique: "Not one loud cry! How softly and dreamily he told his drinking companions the story of how he became a living corpse! In every move, every turn, you saw the Russian aristocrat! And in the courtroom scene, when he met his aristocratic wife, now married to another, how he looked at her! How his eyes begged her to forgive him! What a silent mute play this was, how full of soul! Even his suicide did not break the quiet of his performance. Silent as a shadow he took himself off, and then offstage—the shot!"

iii

WHILE ADLER WAS SAVING New York's Yiddish stage from its basest self, the world of the Russian Jews suffered yet another blow. In the spring of 1911, the body of a twelve-year-old boy was found in a cave near Kiev. The victim had been stabbed more than forty times. Since the killing had occurred at the Passover season, the ancient charge of blood libel was raised against the Jews in the area. Only a few such Hebrews actually dwelt in and around Kiev, and a mass of evidence pointed to a Russian criminal, a gentile involved with contraband and smuggling. Nevertheless, the anti-Semites managed to find a likely candidate. Mendel Beilis was the foreman of a brickyard, and his alibi could be backed only by his family. He provided the government with an ideal candidate for framing. The police arrested Beilis and kept him locked up until trial. All intellectuals were banned from serving on the jury because it was thought that such men might be sympathetic to Jews. The jurors saw a stream of pseudo-witnesses provided by the government. Well rehearsed as they were, their evidence did not hold up under cross-examination. All along, the instruments of publicity—the wireless and the newspaper—kept the world informed of Beilis's ordeal.

Naturally, the Jews of New York followed the trial on a daily basis. But the personnel of the Yiddish Theater did something more. "It seems," said the *Forward,* "that we can expect a theatrical Mendel Beilis epidemic. One small theater has already made a 'play' out of the trial in Kiev, and others plan to do so as well. This is a shame. The small theaters have often committed the sin of trying to take in a few dollars by putting people and events on the stage that should not yet be dramatized, but these theaters were not then taken seriously."

Boris Thomashefsky swiftly got in on the act. Posters proclaimed: "Next week! Great, astonishing news! The true Mendel Beilis in Thomashefsky's Theater. Mendel Beilis in the great historical blood-libel trial." David Kessler was not one to sit idly by; his posters advertised "A dramatization of the Mendel Beilis trial specially sent from Russia for David Kessler's theater." Even Jacob Adler played Beilis in his own production. This time the critics were not kind to him. One review lamented, "It pained the hearts of the old friends of Adler to behold the level to which he has sunk. . . . Adler of the great Gordin roles is no longer what he was. Another Adler has taken his place." A second journalist observed that the play about the Russian Jew was "not written with a pen, but swept together with a broom. . . . Crying, moaning, groaning, and yelping. And voilà! A brand-new drama for Moishe's enjoyment."

In the end, despite every effort of the czarists, the jury voted six to two to acquit Beilis—a verdict of not guilty in Imperial Russia. News of the verdict spread almost as fast as the Yiddish hacks could scrawl. A lot of Lower East Side greenhorns considered these plays nothing less than three-dimensional newsreels. Asked about the headlines, a new immigrant could not understand the commotion. A reporter was within earshot when she was informed:

"Mendel Beilis is free! Have you ever heard such news?"

The young woman waved her arm dismissively. "I knew that last Saturday night."

"What do you mean?"

"With my own eyes I saw Mendel Beilis released at the Metropolitan Theater."

iv

IN CONTRAST TO SECOND AVENUE, which was feeding off contemporary world events, the Yiddish theaters of Europe seemed to be caught in a time warp. In Scandinavia, Strindberg was attempting new forms of expression, and Ibsen was wrangling with once verboten subject matter. English and French theaters offered the kind of experimental works that George Bernard Shaw described as "the 19th century hating itself." For the Moscow Art Theater, Anton Chekhov wrote strange new comedies of mood and misdirection, breaking the heart as they mocked Russia's hopeless dreamers. All this caused a buzz in the cafés of New York. But overseas, where such experiments might be expected to be a powerful influence, Yiddish Theater went on as if it were still 1880. Not that this was displeasing to ticket buyers, among them that most revolutionary Jewish intellect, the twenty-something Franz Kafka.

He had become a habitué of the Café Savoy, Prague's Yiddish venue. His presence was well known even then. In Isaac Bashevis Singer's 1970 short story "A Friend of Kafka," an old Yiddish actor recalls his friendship with the Czech author: "In the theater I saw all the defects that Kafka saw in literature, and that brought us together. But, oddly enough, when it came to judging the theater Kafka was completely blind. He praised our cheap Yiddish plays to heaven. He fell madly in love with a ham actress. When I think that Kafka loved this creature, dreamed about her, I am ashamed for the man and his illusions. Well, immortality is not choosy."

An entry in Kafka's notebook shows the validity of Singer's fiction. The diarist may have gone to mock, but he stayed to admire: "Day before yesterday among the Jews in Café Savoy. *The First Evening of Passover* by the playwright Feinmann. At times (at the moment the consciousness of this pierced me) we did not interfere in the plot only because we were too moved, not because we were mere spectators."

Kafka felt that assimilated Jewish actors—Rudolph Schildkraut, for instance—served as intermediaries, "enlarging the horizons of non-Jews, without illuminating the existence of the Jews themselves." That radiance could only come from "the poor Jewish actors who act for Jews in Yiddish. By their art they sweep away the deposits of an alien culture from the life of the Jews, and display the hidden Jewish face which is sinking into oblivion, and so give them an anchor in the troubles of our time."

In her study *Kafka and the Yiddish Theater,* Evelyn Torton Beck notes, "The tiny stage of the shabby Café Savoy, its simple sets and extravagant costumes, the exaggerated acting style, the fusion of the comic with the tragic, and the use of stage devices as visions and tableaux" were salient features of the Prague troupe. It is these characteristics that reappear in Kafka's work. "The simple settings of many of his narratives, particularly those directly following the theater experience ('The Judgement' and 'The Metamorphosis'), bear a close resemblance to the atmosphere and setting of the Yiddish Theater."

Indeed, when a friend objected to the Savoy's overstated stage effects, Kafka's reply might have issued from an American immigrant witnessing a Second Avenue production for the first time: "So it should be. To create the desired effect their emotions and actions must be larger than the feelings and actions of their audience. If the theater is to affect life, it must be stronger, more intense than ordinary life. That is the law of gravity. In shooting one must aim higher than the mark."

v

WHILE KAFKA WAS MAKING his observations, the Yiddish Theater in New York again lurched forward, though not without objections, jealousies, and recriminations. In May of 1911, the Schildkrauts
of Vienna were back in New York, where Rudolph offered his own
interpretation of *The Merchant of Venice*. A cartoon in a Yiddish paper
seized this occasion to play up the rivalry between this Shylock and the
previous one. Jacob Adler is caricatured in a box seat at the theater, as
he warily peers at his onstage competitor. The actor's thoughts send up
the Merchant's most famous speech: "Am I not a human being, as he is?
If the actors union hands me its demands, do I not cry? And if I am
sued for breach of contract, do I not laugh? And if I cut a fresh porter-
house steak, do I not draw blood? So why can he act better than I?"

Schildkraut's production turned out to be legendary, but for the
wrong reasons. Years later hardly anyone could recall his interpretation, but thousands swore they were there for a certain matinee. The
star's reputation as a womanizer was on a par with Boris Thomashefsky's. One Wednesday afternoon the audience was filled with sighing
young housewives, many of them with infants in tow. The babies were
left in their carriages, parked in the lobby under the supervision of a
doorman, who charged 10 cents per pram. As the court scene began, a
yowling could be heard at the back of the theater. The doorman burst
in: "Baby's crying!" Schildkraut froze. He resumed, taking the speech
from the top. He halted once more. Two dozen mothers had dashed
out, each assuming her child was the offender. Schildkraut began
where he had left off, only to be interrupted by the rush of women
returning to their seats. One had her baby with her. It was still cater-
wauling. The seat holders loudly shushed the pair and the mother
desperately opened her blouse and offered the baby her breast. Schildkraut's son recorded the next few moments: "At last there was silence.
But in a minute the wailing started again, topped by the high-pitched

voice of the frantic woman: 'Hush, hush, darling! Take it, take it, quick! If you don't take it, I'll give to Schildkraut!'

"Theater was never like this in Berlin."

Later that season newspaper cartoonists depicted a second rivalry, this one between two Yiddish divas. *Mirele Efros,* one of the few Jacob Gordin dramas still in the Second Avenue repertory, was known informally as "the Yiddish Queen Lear." The story—a resolute and powerful woman betrayed by her greedy sons—had not lost its appeal since the first performances in 1896, with Keni Liptzin in the title role. She had been playing that part, off and on, for more than fifteen years, and the notion of anyone else as Mrs. Efros was unthinkable. Then came the visit of Esther Rokhl-Kaminska—mother of the twentieth-century star Ida Kaminska. A celebrated actress in the Polish Yiddish Theater, Esther considered herself the equal of any English luminary and, with a nod to the great English actress, preferred to be billed as "The Yiddish Eleanora Duse."

When the imperious star brought her production of *Mirele Efros* to New York, a newspaper drawing showed Liptzin and Kaminska similarly costumed in voluminous black dresses and shawls. Liptzin points to her rival and wails to an appalled onlooker, "Look who is coming to take my place!"

Madame Liptzin was not so easily dislodged. Reviewers acknowledged Madame Kaminska's "more modern, more realistic" Queen Lear, but nearly all of them preferred their local heroine. Cahan took it upon himself to speak for the Lower East Siders. Unlike Kaminska, "Mme. Liptzin did not go about the stage like a rich housewife of Grodna or Berditchev, but like a queen. Melodrama was the core of her *Mirele Efros.* Whatever one may say about the faults of her playing, her *Mirele* was among the outstanding interpretations created on the Yiddish stage."

Kaminska realized that her understated style had no chance against the extravagant Second Avenue style. She confided to colleagues, "I can't explain it, but I could never act the way they do." She preferred the audiences out of town—particularly in Philadelphia, where she drew large crowds and more appreciative reviewers. Another Yiddish Theater production was taking place when she arrived in that city, and she bought a ticket. She saw a young Jewish actor. Maurice Schwartz seemed to possess an unusual combination of energy, native intelligence, and ambition—everything but control. She resolved to change his life. In the process, she changed the Yiddish Theater itself.

CHAPTER NINE

✦

WITH GOD'S HELP,
I STARVED TO DEATH

i

I N 1912, Manhattan was still reeling from the shock of the Triangle Fire in Greenwich Village. Young women of Jewish and Italian
extraction, 146 in all, had perished either in the flames or, more
horribly, by jumping out of windows to their death. A United Press
reporter happened to be in Washington Square on March 25, 1911. He
called in the story: "Thud—dead, thud—dead, thud—dead. Sixty-two

thud—dead. . . . There was plenty of chance to watch them as they came down. The height was eighty feet. . . . Then came love amid the flames. A young man brought a girl to the window. Those who were looking saw her put her arms around him and kiss him. Then he held her out into space and dropped her. But quick as a flash he was on the window sill himself. His coat fluttered upward—the air filled his trouser legs. I could see that he wore tan shoes and hose. His hat remained on his head. Thud—dead, thud—dead—together they went into eternity. I saw his face before they covered it. You could see in it that he was a real man. He had done his best."

The doomed workers had been locked in by owners who wanted to keep their employees from going out on long breaks. The tragedy, overdue given the horrifying conditions in so many lofts, reverberated long after the bodies were interred. Angry at the inhumane treatment from the bosses, protesters demanded justice. The court refused it; owners were fined a mere $75 per casualty. But the International Ladies Garment Workers Union, joined by the Arbeiter Ring (Workmen's Circle) and the *Forward,* would not be turned away. They collected money for the victims' families and kept up a barrage of protest in rallies and editorials. Labor unions gathered strength, not only in local negotiations but in national politics.

A contretemps between Teddy Roosevelt and his handpicked successor, William Howard Taft, split the Republican Party into the regulars and the Roosevelt "Bull Moose" outsiders. The newly invigorated Democratic Party, strengthened by union members and progressives, nominated Woodrow Wilson, an intellectual who headed Princeton University. He won a convincing victory and began a series of sweeping governmental reforms. The aura of change was everywhere. *New Masses,* a magazine dedicated to political and aesthetic radicalism, advocated revolution not only in Russia but in America, and its editorials were quoted all over the land.

The latest instance of feminism on the march, Margaret Sanger, a former nurse and advocate of birth control, began writing a column for the *New York Call.* It was daringly entitled "What Every Girl Should Know," and dealt with such taboo subjects as sex and venereal disease.

A year later came the Armory Show. Held at the 69th Regiment Armory building on East 26th Street, it introduced Americans to nonobjective art. Marcel Duchamp's *Nude Descending a Staircase* seemed emblematic of an exhibition designed to disturb and infuriate. A *New York Times* article was headed "Cubists and Futurists Are Making Insanity Pay," and most readers agreed with the paper's assessment.

It was a heady time to be in town, and Maurice Schwartz's head was filled with big plans. He knew all about Strindberg and Ibsen and Chekhov. He would take these Slavic hicks, these untutored settlers, and introduce them to a new kind of theater, a theater of symbolism and innovation. He would be a secular rabbi, instructing with nuance and example.

For that, a man would need an ego as big as the Flatiron Building, and Schwartz was well qualified for the role. But he had something more than self-confidence. He nourished the same ambition for his people that he had seen in Jacob Adler and David Kessler and Boris Thomashefsky—a yearning to make the stage a part of the immigrant experience, to elevate the Jews of New York, to bring art into the lives of common laborers and their families. More inspired actors may have worked on the Yiddish stage at that time, but none had a nobler ideal.

The grain merchant's son was born in the Ukraine in 1890, traveled to England with his parents, and planned to sail to America with them. According to his memoirs, the budget did not allow for the whole family to emigrate, and he was stranded in Liverpool at the age of eleven. With unusual self-assurance for a boy his age, he made his way to London, got a job as a child laborer in a rag factory, fell ill from overwork, and drifted into a kind of Dickensian vagrancy until his parents rescued him and brought the youth to the United States in 1903. By then he was fluent in English as well as Yiddish. Bilingualism was to be a great asset in the coming years.

As a youth in New York, Maurice attended every Yiddish play he could afford, indiscriminately joining with random groups of *patriotn* claquing for Mogulesko, Thomashefsky, Adler, Kessler. In his eyes they were all masters, and he resolved that somehow he would work his way into their company. Even to paint scenery or move a spotlight would have seemed a heavenly assignment. But the way to the big time was blocked by experienced professionals, and he was forced to find work out of town. A small troupe in Bridgeport, Connecticut, gave Schwartz a walk-on in a Yiddish play. It ran one night. He came home enthralled, only to be mocked by his parents for wasting his time. Much like Kessler before him, he exploded in rage and moved out.

Hanging around the Yiddish Rialto he heard that a troupe in

Cincinnati needed an actor to play small roles. The young man auditioned, won the $8-a-week job—and earned an extra dollar for assuming the duties of stage manager. As Schwartz remembered it, for that additional money he spent nearly every evening "shoving furniture and scenery around, packing and unpacking before and after the show, and helping the extras with their makeup." Before long he got the break he had been hoping for.

His boss in Cincinnati was a temperamental impresario/actress who quickly became infatuated with her actor/stage manager. He reciprocated—or pretended to, no one was ever sure. In any case, she fired the company's director and replaced him with Maurice. To justify her faith in him, he spent $30 of his own money on klieg lights, and began experimenting with them. These were used to great effect on tour. When the troupe reached Philadelphia, they became the talk of the city. It was then that the Czech actress Esther Rokhl-Kaminska came to town and dropped in at a matinee. She planned to stay for five minutes. She remained until the final curtain. After the audience had left the theater, she went backstage to meet the young man whose production had so impressed her. Just before she returned to Europe, she mentioned Maurice's name to David Kessler, one of the few New York actors who had won her respect. A month later David came down to Philadelphia and offered Maurice the small part of a lawyer in the Yiddish adaptation of *Madame X,* a popular French drama of adultery, prostitution, and murder. Schwartz quit the company and headed for Manhattan that night.

Energized by the new New York, he appeared onstage in several plays during the 1912 season. Things came to a halt when someone at the Hebrew Actors Union discovered that this upstart had not auditioned for the guild members. The union had established a rigid policy about performing on Second Avenue: any actor, no matter how big his out-of-town reputation, was required to audition before a group of union members. Failure to please them meant a blacklisting throughout the city. Confident, poised, Schwartz appeared and read some lines. The committee turned him down.

Perhaps, Maurice reflected, he had been too arrogant. He avidly prepared for his next shot, and this time presented himself humbly, and read his lines with close attention to detail. Again they rejected him.

Maurice was frantic. A three-strikes-and-out policy was in effect; one more rebuff and he would be kaput. Other actors who had been

similarly treated rarely passed their third audition; crushed, they usually left the city, hoping to catch on with some regional organization.
But Schwartz was made of sterner stuff. Even then he could pick up the
scent of power wherever it resided. On the Lower East Side, the *Forward* was a font of influence, and Abraham Cahan *was* the *Forward*.
Schwartz obtained a private audience with the great one, and in the
offices of the paper staged his own private audition. Cahan was
impressed enough to intervene on Schwartz's behalf. On the third try,
the union gave its approval. Maurice was on the wing.

ii

OF ALL WRITERS whose works were staged by the Yiddish Theater
in New York, none was more beloved than Sholem Aleichem. Perhaps
that was his trouble.

Born in the Ukraine in 1859, Sholem Rabinowitz simultaneously
pursued careers in finance and literature. Shortly after the turn of the
century he made a clean break from the stock market. From then on
he earned a living—often precarious—as the pseudonymous Sholem
Aleichem ("Peace be with you" in Yiddish), writer of stories, novels, and
sketches. In time he was drawn to the theater, as were many of his fellow
Zionists. Theodore Herzl, the founder of Zionism, wrote plays; so did
the existentialist philosopher Martin Buber and Israel Zangwill, the
first person to describe America as "the Melting Pot."

Aleichem's early plays displayed the author's distinctive touch—a bit
of comedy suddenly brought up short by a revelation. In *Mentshn* (People), Fanitshke, a servant girl, leaves a family, then pops up years later,
overdressed, Frenchified, and bursting with forced laughter:

RIKL: I think she's a little too happy.

HERTS: I'm afraid she's had a few too many.

FANITSHKE: *Ce n'est pas vrai.* I don't drink! I don't drink liquors, I drink wine! Champagne, *parole d'honneur.*

HERTS: So you have a fiancé already, Fanitshke?

FANITSHKE: What "Fanitshke"? No more "Fanitshke"! Fania Yefimovana. All the officers—and the generals—know only Fania Yefimovana. *Et basta!* Two students beat each other up over Fania Yefimovana, *parole d'honneur!* They beat me up, too, see? (*Rolls up her sleeve, shows a blue mark, and laughs hysterically.*)

In Yiddish writing, Aleichem became known as a sprinter rather than a distance runner. The one-acters tended to outshine the full-length dramas; the short stories rang truer than the novels—and they had a longer life. Issued in book form, the newspaper pieces sold phenomenally well. Especially the ones about a recurring character called Tevye. The public couldn't get enough of the simple milkman working his route, speaking about his five daughters ("Girls have a bad habit of eating during the day and growing at night"), giving his customers a précis of his past life ("With God's help, I starved to death"), all the while addressing the Almighty with a pungent, weary tone ("A Jew must hope, keep hoping, and if in the meantime his life is full of grief and disaster, well, that is what we Jews are for, chosen from all the people in the world, all of them envying us").

Tevye's popularity reached beyond the bounds of Eastern Europe, and as New York's Jewish residents learned of Aleichem, so he learned of them. With a combination of fulsome praise and an odd candor, the playwright sent an appeal to the Yiddish Theater's leading light. "Incomparable Master!" began his letter to Jacob Adler. "I send you a play which I have composed from several works written by me. Great Maestro . . . only an artist like yourself is capable of creating and showing the soul of this character."

The flattery continued, followed by a sales pitch. "Great Master of the Stage! In my play you will find none of the effects on which the Jewish public has for so many years been nourished. You will find no soul-tearing scenes, no corpses in cribs, no demented women, no patriotic songs or nationalist speeches, no transient boarders seducing innocent maidens, and no vulgar jokes. You will find only a simple Jew,

father of five daughters, an honest, clean, wholesome, and greatly suffering character who, with all his misfortunes, will make the public
laugh from beginning to end."

No patriotic songs, no vulgar jokes—this was fine with Adler. It was
probably the lack of soul-tearing scenes that put him off. In any case,
after due consideration he concluded that the story of Tevye the Dairyman was not his glass of tea and passed on it. Aleichem came to New
York anyway, and hardly had he set foot on American shores when he
was invited to a banquet of prominent Manhattan citizens. Elegantly
turned out in a continental suit and pince-nez glasses, he was introduced as "the Jewish Mark Twain." (Samuel Clemens, the other star
guest, cheerfully responded by identifying himself as "the American
Sholem Aleichem.")

When Adler learned of that celebration he changed his mind and
openly expressed an interest in the work of this gifted writer. Boris
Thomashefsky followed suit. Each requested a private audience; each
asked for a full-length play. Anything Aleichem handed them—anything at all, they assured him—would be guaranteed a first-class production. The author responded warily; he was disinclined to show
projects that had already been turned down, and claimed that he had
nothing on hand. However, he did suggest that some of his *books* might
be adapted for the stage . . .

Thomashefsky moved fast; he bought the rights to *Stempenyu,* Aleichem's first novel, for a thousand dollars—a sum equal to the average
annual salary for American workers. The book seemed a natural for
shund. A blithe violin virtuoso plays with women's hearts—until he falls
in love with the unhappily married Rokheleh and the complications
and fireworks begin. Adler would not be outdone; for a thousand dollars he took an option on another Aleichem novel, *Samuel Pasternak, or
The Scoundrel,* a portrait of naive speculators involved in a stock market
they can neither afford nor understand. Adler knew that most of his
audience had no idea how such a market operated. But he also knew
they were pro-labor, anti-plutocrat. *Pasternak* would give them a chance
to laugh at a Ukrainian version of Wall Street opportunists.

The two impresarios raced each other to the finish line, each anxious to open his own project before the other could complete
rehearsals. In the Goldfaden tradition, Thomashefsky ordered tunes to
be inserted into the text. He paid Joseph Rumshinsky to put Aleichem's rhymes to music. On closer examination, though, Boris decided

that the author's verse was not good enough for the notes. He inserted couplets of his own devising and tacked on a few of his own melodies. By the time the songs were edited and adorned, Rumshinsky wrote, the special Sholem Aleichem charm had vanished. "New words were added, so-called lyrics, and new bits of melody injected, which drowned the folk quality. The entire piece was inundated with cheap theatrical effects."

Across the street Adler kept urging his cast to learn their lines quickly so that they could open before Thomashefsky's troupe. Matters had reached the point of hysteria when friends of Aleichem intervened—the widely advertised competition was no way to treat an author of such standing. Resistant at first, both Thomashefsky and Adler ultimately agreed to a truce. Both shows would open on the same evening.

In her biography, Aleichem's daughter, Marie Waife-Goldberg, refers to that opening night. The family had temporarily settled in Geneva, en route to the New World, and the playwright sent them an account. "I had to split up in two," he reported. "I attended two acts in one theater and two acts in the other." Audiences in both places called for the author as soon as the curtain was lowered—at the intermission of one and the finale of the other. "*Stempenyu* made an impression of something poetic and patriarchal. *The Scoundrel,* on the other hand, compelled the audience to keep its mouth open and laugh all through the performance."

In Second Avenue cafeterias, the author affected an indifference to reviewers. To his family he was nowhere near as dispassionate. One communiqué gives an accurate summary of the situation facing playwrights in the Yiddish Theater. "I am confident about the non-Jewish press, since it is more honest than the Yiddish; the Yiddish is partial, and I expect nothing good from it. But that's not worth a farthing—the main thing is the public, the masses."

Aleichem's intuition about the Yiddish press was on the money. Notices in the middle-class newspapers were favorable. One paper assured its readership that with these two new plays "Sholem Aleichem opened a new world for the theater public." Another stated that "The hopes that Aleichem would bring a new spirit into the Jewish theater of America have been fulfilled." Here at last was "the work of a real artist," a true original and not an imitator of Shakespeare or Tolstoy or even Gordin.

It was the left-leaning press that did him in. Disappointed that the playwright took no political stance, Cahan panned *Pasternak* in the *Forward.* The production was too long, too frivolous—more of a vaudeville than a genuine play. The Lower East Side's radical newspaper, the *Warheit,* greeted Aleichem with a one-two punch. First came the editor, who told readers that he had exited at intermission despite the evident skill of the star, Jacob P. Adler. The coup de grâce was delivered by the paper's official critic. He condemned this as the worst play ever produced in the history of the Yiddish Theater.

Back and forth the reviewers went, some for, some against. Aleichem dared to hope that the controversy would provoke interest and stimulate ticket-buying. It was not to be. After two weeks of public indifference, both plays folded. The writer, ever resilient, completed another work and gave it to a representative. The script was brought to Jacob Adler. "A new play by Sholem Aleichem!" he gushed. "Father in heaven, quick, quick, let me see it, let me hear it!" Turning the pages, he could barely contain his zeal. "The dear hand of Sholem Aleichem! What a golden hand! What a golden language! How he writes! How his characters talk!"

Jacob's effusions should have been a warning signal; as he read, Adler marked up the script, changing the "golden language." In the end, he turned down the play—there were simply not enough turns for a leading man. The Jewish Mark Twain sat down at his desk yet again. Conquering New York was never an easy task. Was it impossible? Was the author behind his time, or ahead of it? He refused to believe either alternative.

iii

EVEN IN THE BEST of seasons, Yiddish Theater audiences were distracted by business and familial obligations. Now came new competitors for their attention. Movies were getting longer; *Quo Vadis?* ran for nine reels—about two hours. Thomas Edison perfected disk recording; the ungainly cylinders were on their way out. And then there were the topics of politics and paranoia. These often took precedence over everything else, including neighborhood gossip.

In 1913, a Jew in Atlanta, Georgia, was accused of murdering a teenaged Christian girl. So pervasive were the feelings of anti-Semitism in that state that the testimony of a black man was permitted in the courtroom. This witness was in fact the killer, who admitted as much to an attorney. His confession was suppressed; the jury turned in a guilty verdict and the judge sentenced Leo Frank to death.

The *Atlanta Journal* wanted no part of the kangaroo court. The condemned man, said an editorial, "has not been fairly convicted, and his death without a fair trial and legal conviction will amount to judicial murder." The paper had some influence; so did leading business and political figures. The governor commuted Frank's sentence. Before any legal procedures could take place, a mob stormed the prison and spirited the condemned man away. They hanged him from a tree. Newly emboldened, members of the Ku Klux Klan openly distributed photographs of the corpse dangling from a branch. Pro forma investigations took place. The investigators turned up nothing and no one was indicted.

The Leo Frank lynching made the front pages of mainstream newspapers everywhere. Naturally it had the greatest impact on Jewish readers. Yiddish papers interpreted the murder as a New World pogrom. There was talk of making it into a stage drama à la Mendel Beilis. But by then Adler, Thomashefsky, and Kessler had learned their lesson and knew to stay away from dramatizations of an authentic American tragedy. They left matters to an aggressive new organization, the Anti-Defamation League of the B'nai B'rith, to combat anti-Semitism. Some of the well-established German Jews protested; they thought such a group would only arouse hostility, calling attention to something best left alone. Why make a big *megillah* out of something that would be solved by education and assimilation? Internecine arguments rang out over the next several years. They only stopped when the rising tide of anti-Semitism could no longer be denied or ignored.

The new history of the Jews began on the morning of June 28, 1914. Archduke Franz Ferdinand, heir to the Austro-Hungarian Empire, was killed by a Serbian nationalist. By the end of summer, Austria-Hungary had declared war on Serbia, drawing in other nations as the fighting began. Soon nearly every major power was involved. On one side were the Allies, Britain, France, and Russia; on the other was a coalition of

Central Powers, Austria-Hungary, Germany, and Turkey. For the Jews of Eastern and Western Europe, the start of the Great War signaled the end of one sort of misery—and the beginning of a new and infinitely worse kind.

Immigration to America effectively ended; borders were closed and all able-bodied men ordered to serve in the armies of their host countries. As an official report put it, at the time of the hostilities, "One-half the Jewish population of the world was trapped in a corner of Eastern Europe that was absolutely shut off from all neutral lands and from the sea." On the one hand, those thousands of Jews knew no other home; on the other hand, they despised what had been done to them by Imperial Russia. Loyalties were in collision, and played themselves out on the international stage.

In America, Jewish sentiments first leaned toward isolationism despite the fate of their co-religionists. Irving Berlin, a reliable barometer of public taste, was writing songs like "Hurry Back to My Bamboo Shack" and "In Florida Among the Palms" in the prewar period. The following year he urged, "Let's all be Americans now—Lincoln, Grant and Washington/They were peaceful men, each one/Still they took the sword and gun." The year after that he appeared in the uniform of a U.S. Army private to sing "Oh, How I Hate to Get Up in the Morning."

Lower East Siders leaned toward Germany, principally because it was fighting the czar's hordes. (Indeed, a large group of German-Jewish intellectuals got behind Kaiser Wilhelm; Albert Einstein was one of the few who would not sign a petition supporting the Fatherland's war.) But in Europe there were no Jewish battalions as such. Hebrews fought in every army—including the Russian one. Only a handful of Russian Jews, acting on principle, joined Polish legions rallying in Austria to combat the czar's troops.

What emerged from all this was a horrific slaughter of fairly evenly matched armies, until, in 1917, America entered the war and Old Russia completely collapsed. The Bolsheviks took over, annihilated Nicholas and his entire family, and announced the formation of a new and progressive Soviet Russia. The Jews of the region, and far beyond it, were ecstatic. One of the earliest signs of enlightenment affected the Yiddish Theater. Leon Trotsky, the Red Army strategist, placed his sister in charge of a new Arts Department, overseeing just about every aspect of creativity. This newly formed bureau would not only allow Yiddish Theater, it would *subsidize* it. The stepchild of Russian drama, always impoverished, forever operating under the shadow of a whimsical and brutal state, had been rescued by the Bolshevik revolution. What was more, V. I. Lenin himself made a record demanding an end to anti-Semitism. His message was broadcast on loudspeakers in every Russian city. It was almost impossible to conceive of such circumstances taking place in the country that had invented the word "pogrom."

The Lower East Side was even more delirious than the rest of America by the time the Armistice was signed. JEWISH TROUBLES AT AN END, read one banner headline in the Forward. Another stated FULL RIGHTS FOR ALL OPPRESSED NATIONALITIES. NEW LIGHT RISES OVER RUSSIA. Abraham Cahan contributed a personal note: "Mazel Tov to Our Jewish People; Mazel Tov to the World." It was a glorious moment, spoiled only by an occasional bitter observation. The writer Isaac Babel, riding with the Red Army Cossacks, wrote in his diary: "Same old story. The Jews expected the Soviet regime to liberate them, and suddenly there were shrieks, whips cracking, shouts of 'Dirty Yid.' "

Other complaints followed. But surely, it was argued, this was the voice of the rabble, not the new men. Once discipline was established, all the residue of hate would vanish. It was only logical. This, after all, was the twentieth century. Deliverance had arrived.

iv

THE RESCUE HAD COME too late for two Second Avenue celebrities, one established, one struggling. Sigmund Mogulesko, the little clown celebrated by Hutchins Hapgood as the Yiddish Theater's one true "genius of comedy," had suffered from a sore throat that would not heal. Every recitation became an exercise in agony, always concealed from the public. His fellow performers marveled as he broke up the audience and then wept in the wings. Finally, early in 1914, he could no longer speak. Leon Kobrin remembered those last days. "The Yiddish comic spirit loves a peppery joke. Mogulesko delivered such jokes with an air so natural, so innocent, as to make them irresistible. His illness could not destroy his spirit. The creative power so alive in him found, in spite of everything, a way to express itself. When his throat choked, Mogulesko sang with his face, with his movements. When his last strength was gone, one foot moved—and laughed!"

For Sholem Aleichem, the war years were no better. The death of his youngest son was a blow that sapped the author of energy and will. No new ideas came to him. He unearthed one of his old dramas, *The Big Winner,* and shopped it around. No one responded. Aleichem condemned the theater managers as "louts who treated playwrights with the sensitivity of cattle drovers."

In the winter of 1916 he was felled by influenza. Spring brought no relief. He invited friends to drop by, but even these brief visits were exhausting. The last one occurred at the end of April, when Aleichem played host to a small group including the rising dramatist Peretz Hirschbein. Gathered in Aleichem's living room, the group listened to Hirschbein tell a favorite Yiddish Theater story.

A *shund* tragedy described the downfall of a Jewish shoemaker. Down to his last ruble, he fashioned a new pair of boots for a landowner. The trouble was, the rich man bought only on credit. In the last act he entered, tried on a boot, and found it too small. The shoemaker saw ruin ahead; the money would not be paid and the villagers would say that he had lost his skill. As the landowner continued to struggle with the misfit, a wail came from the balcony. Was this a deus ex machina? No, only the voice of a neighborhood cobbler who had gotten too involved in the play: "Powder!" he boomed. "Sprinkle some powder into the boot!"

Hirschbein told the story well, and the small crowd broke up at the punch line. Not Aleichem. As the others laughed he rose, excused himself, and went to his room. He never left it again. Two weeks later he died there at the age of fifty-seven. More than 100,000 mourners turned out for one of the largest funerals in the history of New York City. The deceased was praised downtown and uptown; shops were closed, and that evening the Yiddish theaters went dark in his honor. But no Sholem Aleichem plays were to be presented in any of them for years to come. It was a matter of timing, as it always is in the theater. Goldfaden had gotten offstage at exactly the right moment. Hurwitz and Lateiner had overstayed their welcome. Jacob Gordin departed too soon. So did Aleichem, who entered—and exited—before New Yorkers were prepared for the truths he had to tell. They would not be ready for another fifty years.

CHAPTER TEN

✦

LUFTMENSCHN AND

SCHNORRERS

i

THE YIDDISH SATIRICAL JOURNAL *Der Groyser Kundes* (The Big Stick) ran a cartoon that neatly encapsulated the Yiddish Theater in middle age. Under the title "If Shakespeare Had to Sell a Play Today," four progressive panels showed the playwright in conversation with Jacob Adler, David Kessler, and the Thomashefskys, Bessie and Boris. All four reject his work because it lacks "punch," "national fervor," or some other vital component.

A satiric newspaper article made the same point. A journalist interviews Shakespeare's ghost and dispenses sage advice. The Yiddish Theater is different nowadays, he points out. If the Bard would make his mark on Second Avenue, his efforts must feature "some kind of girl, you understand; and bastards; and someone should say Kaddish in the third act; and some pale woman, you understand, should carry 'the fruit of love under her heart.' "

There should follow "a little duet with the comedian, and in the last act the lover should fall back in love with his beloved." Plus it wouldn't hurt if "the music should come in with a happy melody and it should thunder and snow and a torrential rain should fall, and two suns with five giant moons should shine through the window and—" But Shakespeare refuses to hear any more. He withdraws to his tomb.

More than a dozen Yiddish theaters were in operation, all of them large, airy, equipped with plush seats, well lit with electric bulbs and high places to fly the scenery. Classic plays could have been handsomely staged there, but producers were not interested in taking a chance on high culture—unless the texts were heavily amended. (Ibsen's *A Doll's House,* for example, was supplied with a fourth act in which Nora and her husband happily reconciled.)

Uptown, a few strivers aimed high on Broadway. Eugene O'Neill's first full-length play, *Beyond the Horizon,* won an audience and a Pulitzer Prize. But it was a rare exception to the standard fare. Soubrette Marilyn Miller enjoyed her greatest triumph with *Sally,* the story of a girl who rises from dishwasher to ballerina. The musical had a score by Jerome Kern ("Look for the Silver Lining" became an instant standard) as well as a ballet by Victor Herbert. The *Ziegfeld Follies* and George White's imitative *Scandals* packed them in every night. In vaudeville, "olios" set the style: a parade of magicians, animal acts, and patriotic tableaux, ranging from the feats of Houdini to "Freak Acts" like Evelyn Nesbitt, America's first sex kitten, whose financier husband had shot her lover, architect Stanford White.

Dr. Frank Crane, one of the first analysts of popular culture, spoke out against an amusement tax. Theater, he commented, was vital to the American people *because* it was frivolous: "The stage is not a nation's weakness, extravagance or undoing, but it is a nation's deep refreshment that gives to the hearts and minds of a great people that spirit of courage and light and adventure that is needed to achieve success."

Since the uptown crowd was going for pure diversion, Second

Avenue producers asked, why should the Yiddish Theater be any different? Almost all "serious" actors withered in this new climate. The case of Keni Liptzin was an example of the times, a real-life drama that might have been written by Jacob Gordin. Ten years before, the tragedienne's long-running role as "Queen Lear" had been so impressive a theater was named for her. But she never was one for the light touch, and in the modern era became almost unemployable. Her adoring husband got into the act, backing any producer who would give Keni a starring role.

To come up with the money he sold off their various real estate holdings and jewelry. When there was nothing left to pawn he signed promissory notes to theater men. One night he toted up all he owed, concluded that he was bankrupt, and shot himself. His wife found the body. Instead of going mad, she kept acting on, playing gratis for the producers to whom she was indebted. They were not fond of serious plays, but since that was all the diva could do, and since she was working for free, they took her on. Eventually she paid back every one of them, and at that point they shut the door. She never took another role. "Now I am alone and homeless," Liptzin lamented. "My only consolation, my only happiness, is the stage, but I sit idly weeks and months because my theater has been taken away from me." Taken away from her, and given to a new generation of actresses willing to appear in anything that brought in the paying customers, no matter how shallow or inconsequential.

To be fair, if the producers were venal, they were also realistic. What they felt instinctively, Margaret Mead had codified in her study of the second-generation American. When the son leaves home, she wrote, "he throws himself with an intensity which his children will not know into the American way of life; he eats American, talks American, dresses American. He will be American or nothing.

"In making his way of life consistent, he inevitably makes it thin; the overtones of a family meal on which strange, delicious, rejected European dishes were set, and about which low words in a foreign tongue wove the atmosphere of home, must all be dropped out.

"His speech has a certain emptiness; he rejects the roots of words—roots lead back, and he is going forward."

For the first time in a decade, backers were forced to think about the going forward, and the rejection of a language and a way of life. Suppose no more wretched refuse came to New York? Suppose assimilation continued to drain the ghetto of newcomers? Forget the classics and the experiments, said the smart money; fill the seats while you can, stage the crowd-pleasers that guarantee full houses. Because, who knows? Over the next few years the Yiddish-speaking audience just might disappear altogether.

ii

AT THE DAWN of the postwar period, Maurice Schwartz made his move. The moment could not have been more propitious. David Kessler had made the mistake of going into business with his stepson, Max Wilner. They had argued continually over salaries and repertory, and one day David walked out of his own office.

The superstar put an announcement in the Yiddish press. "During the entirety of my long career, I have never suffered so and never had to struggle so for my art and my existence as I have since entering this partnership. The end has come. I can remain no longer. I have not received a cent in wages for the entire last season. Having put $25,000 of my own money in this theater, I am left, as they say, with the shirt on my back, but I am content. I will not get lost. Although it carries my name, I have no connection to Kessler's Second Avenue Theater. I don't know, and I don't want to know, what is going on there." His next move was a barnstorming tour of Yiddish theaters in Montreal and Toronto.

As this transpired, Boris Thomashefsky announced a new schedule—his customary mix of the commercial and serious, with a heavy accent on *shund*. Adler had cut back, but was still active enough to star in a new Russian-Jewish play called *The Governor*. In Brooklyn, two theaters offered all-Yiddish programs. Here was the opportunity Maurice had fantasized about for more than five years.

With golden tongue and relentless charm, he persuaded investors to lease the elegant, low-priced, Irving Place Theater. Once upon an era, that venue had offered German productions. But in recent years sauerkraut had been renamed Liberty Cabbage, and baseball players with

Teutonic names were called "Dutch." The language of the hated kaiser had faded into the background.

The place had been empty since America entered the war. True, it was located some twenty blocks north of the Yiddish Rialto, but the neighborhood of Irving Place had a reputation for safety and cleanliness, and the immigrants had lately shown a willingness to leave their own neighborhoods in search of diversion. Schwartz settled in, issued casting calls, and put an ad in the *Forward* announcing his intentions. The headline asked: CAN A BETTER YIDDISH THEATER SURVIVE IN NEW YORK?

The question was purely rhetorical, posed by one of the cockiest young men in the city. He followed it with a defining statement. "For the past two years I have been going around with a plan to put together a troupe that will devote itself to playing good literary works, an honor to the Yiddish Theater."

Schwartz went on about the theater managers who considered him "a madman, a dreamer, because the opinion reigns that such high theater cannot exist." Ever mindful of public relations, he excused them: they weren't villains, they were victims, trapped in big theaters too large for noble experiments. In those caverns, a serious play had no chance. "A little gesture with the eye is too little. If you want to show you have temperament, you eat the scenery."

This would not be the case at the Irving Place locale. Schwartz enumerated the reasons why. His theater was intended as "a sort of holy place, where a festive and artistic atmosphere will always reign." In it, "a company of artists who love beauty" would "strive to bring the Yiddish Theater to a beautiful fulfillment."

Those who thought he was going highbrow on them could relax. He would also put on "comedies, worthy farces, and nice operettas." Melodramas would also find a place, as long as they had "interest and logic." Finally, there came an appeal to organized labor: "If the theater unions give us the support we need, I am sure the Irving Place Theater will be the pride of our Jews in New York."

iii

LIKE MAURICE SCHWARTZ, the actor Jacob Ben-Ami turned twenty-nine in 1919, and, like Schwartz, saw himself as the avatar of a new Yiddish Theater. He, too, had paid his dues as a Jewish youth in Russia. The farmer's son sang in a synagogue choir and acted in amateur productions. He was handsome, and his skills so evident that talent scouts came around with an offer—convert to Christianity and you can study acting at a Moscow academy. He refused. Keenly aware that he had no future in Russia, he headed west.

The ambitious youth was hired to do walk-ons with London companies and presently made a name for himself. When one of the troupes set sail for New York, Ben-Ami was invited to come along. Before his thirtieth birthday he was directing plays, insisting on the naturalistic approach he had seen in pre-Revolutionary Moscow.

Everything that rises must converge; it was inevitable that Schwartz and Ben-Ami would run into each other. When they did, Schwartz got onto the subject of the Irving Place Theater. The two men were identical in their yearning for a better Yiddish Theater. So what if their styles differed? Why not work together for the common good? Ben-Ami agreed to come aboard for $75 a week—on one condition. No matter what happened during the rest of the week, one night must offer a "literary" production. Schwartz smiled and extended his hand.

And so the two pillars of the Yiddish Theater, rivalry and nepotism, were put in place yet again. The network of interlocking relations included Ben-Ami's boyhood friend Lazar Freed, who specialized in the roles of *luftmenschn,* men who would rather dream than do. Freed's wife, Celia Adler—Jacob's daughter—joined the group. In addition there was Celia's brother-in-law Ludwig Satz, who specialized in Jewish Pagliaccis, alternately making the audience laugh freely or sob uncontrollably. Schwartz also hired a young, pretty actress named Bertha Gersten, whom he was later to marry.

The first season opened with *Man and His Shadow.* Like many of Schwartz's productions, it was a melodrama more notable for the performances than for the writing. At a cast party, an actor's wife gushed to an unknown guest, "You must go see my husband in the new production." The author pretended ignorance: "In whose play does he appear?" She was nonplussed: "Who knows?" A *Forward* story remarked that in Schwartz's theater the actor was everything. "What is the result? The dramatist is the fifth wheel on the theater cart."

Ben-Ami set out to restore the balance. He told Schwartz that a verbal contract carried with it exactly the same obligations as a written one. A literary play must be staged *one evening per week.* But Maurice had since changed his mind. He wanted nothing to do with projects that had "deficit" written all over them.

Ben-Ami was adamant; grant him his night or lose him forever. Schwartz argued: he had scheduled works by Schiller and Tolstoy. Weren't they enough? Who needed some new, untried, and probably pretentious Yiddish author? Worn down, Ben-Ami consented to a $5-a-week pay cut—if he could stage the play of his choice. Schwartz agreed, but in the end refused to allocate money for sets and costumes.

Ben-Ami went ahead anyway, casting himself and Celia Adler as the principals of *A Secluded Nook,* a Chekhovian work by Peretz Hirschbein. Schwartz watched an early rehearsal. A girl was arguing with her lover in a rural garden. He departed angrily; she pined silently. The village madwoman walked through, singing and muttering to herself. The girl's mother entered and pulled her daughter into their little cottage, fearful that the lunatic had put the *kenahorah*—the evil eye—on them. No one was left on the stage. From the wings came the cracked voice of the madwoman, still singing. The lights faded.

Schwartz turned to the prompter.

"That's it?" he inquired. "That's a curtain?"

"Well," the prompter said with a shrug, indicating Ben-Ami, "that's literature."

Schwartz was unsurprised when a handful of enthusiasts showed up on opening night. Affectation would always have admiring pseudo-intellectuals. This particular claque was composed of highbrows who gave themselves the tongue-in-cheek title of *Schnorrers* (freeloaders). They were vociferous in their appreciation, and they returned the following Wednesday, bringing friends with them. Those friends brought others. Could it be that Ben-Ami was right? That you could have art and arty on the same roster? He rejiggered the Irving Place schedule, allowing performances of the Hirschbein play to take place on the weekends. Two months later he pushed the leading man aside and stepped into his role.

iv

THE NEXT YEAR Ben-Ami and his associates made good on their threat, breaking away to their own place. The Garden Theater in Madison Square was just as luxurious as Schwartz's Irving Place Theater. Ben-Ami could afford the lease because he had found an angel, Louis Schnitzer.

The financier's story was as old as Broadway: his wife was an actress. Henrietta Schnitzer had appeared in many roles at the Neighborhood Playhouse. These failed to satisfy her. She wanted to be more than a performer; she wanted to be a Name. And she convinced her husband that Ben-Ami was the man to make it happen.

Now that he was in funds, Ben-Ami hired an entire company and put up a proclamation to rival Schwartz's. In the new Jewish Art Theater, clearly modeled after the Moscow Art Theater, there would be no stars. No actor could refuse a role. The leading man in one play must appear in a minor role in the next production. All publicity must mention the names of the cast alphabetically, in the same size font. And no director could act in a play he was directing (a daring break with the Moscow Art Theater policy, then considered the most progressive in the world—Konstantin Stanislavsky had no compunction about acting in the plays he directed).

As Ben-Ami was the first to acknowledge, theater is not judged by what it intends, but on what it delivers. To give his words substance, he hired an outsider as principal director of the Jewish Art Theater. This, too, was a break with tradition. Only on rare occasions did Yiddish troupes scout talent west of Second Avenue. And Emanuel Reicher was as outside as they came. Decades before, the German had abandoned performance for direction, making his reputation in Berlin as an interpreter of ultramodern works. A series of artistic coups brought recognition without remuneration, forcing him to look for jobs outside Germany. Reicher thought to try his luck in America, where his reputation had preceded him. Ben-Ami sought out the director and offered a contract.

The actors soon learned they were in the hands of a very different sort of artiste. Customarily, Yiddish Theater directors gave line readings, stepping and strutting around the stage to demonstrate what they wanted. Not Reicher. Celia Adler fondly remembered his technique: "He was able to draw out from an actor exactly what was expected from a role without exhibitionism on the part of the director; he never showed an actor how to do it, he would quietly discuss and explain the role and what should be the effect of the scene. He never specified what the actor should do; he presented the overall concept of the scene."

The Jewish Art Theater's first production, Hirschbein's *The Idle Inn,* won favor not only from the Yiddish press but from mainstream periodicals and books. In his clothbound overview of New York theater, *In the Garrett,* critic Carl Van Vechten called Reicher's the finest production he had ever seen onstage. *Theater* magazine said the direction was "so subtle that even to those who do not understand the language there is an effect of naturalness which is the height of great art." Ben-Ami was singled out for tribute: "His passion has rarely been equaled for intensity on the stage in America. Every moment that he is on, the stage is surcharged with dramatic vitality." By the end of the season, *The Nation* named the Jewish Art Theater "The noblest theatrical enterprise among us. It stands aloof from all the pressures of commerce and popularity."

In yet another ghetto irony, this cheering squad was to bring down what it had so assiduously praised. *Theater* magazine lauded Reicher's direction for imparting "a swing of rhythm and an exquisite command of detail." Broadway producers took note and lucrative offers poured in. Reicher intended to finish the season, and perhaps stay on after that—until Henrietta Schnitzer's ego forced the issue.

Next up that season was Gerhardt Hauptmann's *Lonely People,* with an important female role, a part coveted by Celia Adler. Mrs. Schnitzer wanted it as well, and because her husband was the chief backer of the Jewish Art Theater she got the role. To Celia's immense satisfaction, the production of *Lonely People* did not meet with the expected approval. Abraham Cahan went out of his way to pan it. "Despite her beautiful figure," he wrote, "Mme Schnitzer's performance was not good enough for the role she played." Undiscouraged, the Madame continued to behave like a diva from the old days. She flouted the strict bylaws of the Hebrew Actors Union, declining to audition for major roles and refusing to appear in crowd scenes.

Out of the Schnitzers' earshot Celia sneeringly referred to Henrietta as the *balabuste,* literally a bossy woman, but meant in this case to signify the boss's wife. Most of the troupe agreed with Celia. Ben-Ami felt compelled to state their case to the money man. As long as things went Louis's way the rich man was all smiles; when they turned against him he reverted to the vulgarian he had always been. Ben-Ami was to remember that his financial partner "showed me the 'fig' [a crude hand gesture], saying, 'The lease is in my name.' " Emanuel Reicher heard about the confrontation and wasted no time. A few weeks later he took a better-paying and more influential position with the Theater Guild on Broadway.

Ben-Ami followed the director out the door. His English was almost unaccented by now, and he confidently auditioned for all the uptown producers. Several parts were available; he opted for a key role in the splashy Broadway production of *Samson and Delilah.* A review in *The Nation* indicated the general opinion: the play was "tawdry," and therefore "the chief circumstance attending this production is the transference of Mr. Ben-Ami from the Yiddish to the English stage. He has given us this season of his youth and art."

Less than two years after its promising start, the Jewish Art Theater went out of business. Maurice Schwartz wasted no time. He moved his troupe out of Irving Place and into the Garden, operating under the title of the Yiddish Art Theater. Great plays of almost all kinds would find a home here, from Shaw and Strindberg, to Pinski and I. L. Peretz. But there would be no Shakespeare. When someone suggested that Schwartz do his own interpretation of Shylock, the refusal was firm and permanent. "It's an anti-Semitic play," he concluded. Upon witnessing a previous production, he "realized why they had the Kishinev pogroms."

To the press and public, Schwartz presented himself as a bold new impresario. In fact, from the earliest days he was as cautious as he was canny. One of the Yiddish Art Theater's most durable plays found a home in his theater only after it had made its mark in Europe.

The Dybbuk was the creation of Shloyme-Zanvl Rappoport, a one-time Hasid, activist, poet, emergency aid worker, and ethnographer—an encapsulation of the Jewish experience in Eastern Europe. Born in Lithuania, Rappoport wrote under the nom de plume of S. Ansky. He lived just long enough to see the Revolution take place. On his deathbed he urged a Vilna troupe of Yiddish performers to stage his Jewish ghost story, and they honored the request. A modest reception was expected; *The Dybbuk* turned into the sensation of the year.

It also ignited a furious counterattack. One critic wrote an entire book about the "pseudo-art" of a man who had the gall to invent a folk-tale and pass it off as authentic. He went on to excoriate the play's "philistine audience and its deluded admirers." Defenders rose to praise Ansky, and the ensuing debate attracted more publicity. The Yiddish papers had carried item after item about the storm provoked by *The Dybbuk* in Red Russia, and a great curiosity ran through the Lower East Side. With maximum fanfare the Yiddish Art Theater announced that the play would open the company's 1921–22 season. At last Yiddish-speaking New Yorkers could see what all the fuss was about.

v

THE DYBBUK (subtitled *Between Two Worlds*) reflected Ansky's belief that Judaic tradition had grown irrelevant. He predicted that it would soon be forgotten, covered over by current events. Ritual, liturgy, worship on the High Holy Days were no longer enough; art was the key to Jewish survival in the twentieth century.

The play's most awkward device was a celestial Messenger, a last-minute insertion suggested by Konstantin Stanislavsky when he was considering the play for his Moscow Art Theater. In the end the Master chose not to stage *The Dybbuk,* but Ansky took the idea and ran with it. The Messenger begins act one by stating the theme in an anecdote:

Once a rich but stingy Hasid visited the rabbi. Taking him by the hand the rabbi led him to the window and asked him to describe what he saw through the pane. "I see people in the street," the Hasid said. Then the rabbi took his hand again and led him to a mirror. "Now what do you see?" he asked. "I see myself," the Hasid answered. "Do you understand? Both the window and the mirror are made of glass; but as soon as you cover the glass with a small amount of silver you no longer see others but only yourself."

The plot is rudimentary. Khonon, an impoverished *yeshiva* student, has fallen in love with Leah. Her father, Sender, disapproves of the liaison, and arranges for Leah to wed another. Khonon experiments with the mystical Kabala, hoping to thwart the old man's scheme. A supernatural messenger appears with bad tidings. The Kabalistic rites were ineffective; the wedding will take place as planned.

Upon hearing the news, Khonon collapses. But as he crumples to the earth, the expression on his face changes from despair to ecstasy. "The twice-proclaimed name is revealed to me!" he says with his dying breath. "I . . . see it! I . . . I . . . I have won!" The words seem empty, the boast meaningless. But at her wedding Leah abruptly falls to the ground. When congregants lift her up, she speaks in a voice not her own—the voice of a man. A dybbuk has entered the body of the bride and she speaks with Khonon's voice: "You have buried me! But I have returned to my promised one and will not leave her!"

There is only one course to take now; there must be an exorcism. The rabbi in attendance calls for men in white robes, equipped with rams' horns and candles. "With the power of the almighty God and with the authority of the holy Torah," intones the rabbi, "I sever all the threads that bind you to the world of the living and to the body and to the very soul of the maiden Leah. . . . I banish you from the community of Israel."

The threat of excommunication is too much for the still religious dybbuk. Khonon surrenders and agrees to leave the body of his beloved. Leah returns to her normal state, assured by friends and elders that she's free from the evil eye and ready to enter life as a married woman. They encourage her to nap before the ceremony. When she awakens, she is alone. Or is she?

LEAH: Who is here making such a sad sound? I can hear your voice, but I cannot see you.

KHONON'S VOICE: You are set apart from me.

LEAH: Your voice is as sweet to me as that of a violin on a silent night. Tell me who you are.

VOICE: I have forgotten. I can remember only if you remember me.

LEAH: It's coming back to me now. Once, not long ago, my heart was drawn to a bright star. In the deep of night I shed sweet tears, and someone appeared in my dreams. Was it you?

VOICE: It was.

LEAH: Ah, I remember. You had delicate hair and sad eyes. You had pale hands with long, slender fingers, and thoughts of you haunted me. Why did you leave me?

VOICE: They placed so many walls between us. I tried to climb the barriers, but they were too high. My opponents trampled out my flame in you. I departed from your body so that I could come to your soul.

LEAH: Return to me, my true bridegroom, my true husband, I will carry you in my heart, and in the still of the night you will come to me in my dreams and together we will rock our unborn baby to sleep.... (*Wedding march sounds in the background*) They are about to lead me to the wedding canopy to marry a stranger. Come to me, my bridegroom!

VOICE: I am coming, this time for your soul. (*Materializes against the wall in white*)

LEAH: Must it be like this? If it must, why am I afraid?

VOICE: Don't be fearful of love. Come to me. (*Suddenly in command*) Come to me!

(*Leah removes her black cloak and obeys, speaking in a faraway voice*)

LEAH: He is light and I am flame and we join into Holy fire and rise . . . and rise . . . and rise. . . .

(*Khonon lowers her body to the floor, then takes a flame from her breast, straightens up and holds it aloft. He and her spirit fade away.*)

RABBI: Too late . . . we are too late. What comfort can I give the father now? Or were we wrong all along? How can I know? (*To the messenger*) Go now. And tell Him no matter how we are thwarted, our faith will remain undiminished. We cannot understand Him, but we will seek Him, if only to complain.

MESSENGER: Blessed be the true judge. May they rest in Paradise.

For decades, the cafés resounded with heated discussions of *The Dybbuk*. Even detractors admitted the enchantment Ansky had produced with images of floating lovers, the *shtetl* in phosphorescent twilight, the God-haunted life of peasant Jewry. But what was its meaning? Was Ansky saying that true love was more important than material goods? All very well in the world to come, but try getting along in this world without cash.

Was he glorifying the Almighty? In that case, why did the young couple have to suffer and die?

Was this just a collection of folktales with a frisson? Or was it a meditation on history, an interpretation of Thomas Mann's words about the Jews of the Bible: "Deep is the well of the past. Shall we not say it is bottomless?"

CHAPTER ELEVEN

✦

AN AMALGAM OF
FRANKENSTEIN AND MARX

i

IN 1921, the year of *The Dybbuk* in New York, two giants stumbled. Jacob Adler leased a summer cottage in Pine Hill, a resort town in the Catskill Mountains. His children and grandchildren stayed there for days at a time; colleagues from the Yiddish stage made frequent visits. They prevailed on the paterfamilias to return as Shylock—so many young people had not been around when he astonished the city with his interpretation, inaugurating the Shakespeare revival on Second Avenue.

Adler told them he would consider it. Did he do that to humor them? Or did he have a genuine desire to make, once more, the famous demand for a Venetian's pound of flesh? No one ever found out.

For on a hot day in July, as the sixty-five-year-old swung in a hammock, chatting away, his voice grew indistinct, and he suddenly seemed disoriented. Family members took him inside, away from the heat of the day. An hour later, the grandchildren were told to keep quiet; Grandpa Jacob was in pain. Within the house could be heard cries and sobs. Children were tearfully instructed to pray for their zayde—he was very ill. The following day the Yiddish headlines had the story: JACOB ADLER FELLED BY PARALYTIC STROKE.

Two months later David Kessler was rehearsing a play in Brooklyn when he doubled over in pain. Violent cramps forced him to cancel the run-through for that day. In a matter of twenty-four hours he shook off the pain and called for another session. The leading man spoke and strode with his customary vigor until the last act. At that point the cramps recurred. He passed out. Sirens blaring, an ambulance rushed him to a local hospital. The next day he was wheeled to the emergency room, where surgeons attempted to remove an intestinal blockage. The big, dominating figure, invulnerable for four decades, died on the operating table.

In a backhanded valedictory, Abraham Cahan observed that when David Kessler began his career he would declaim in the style of the day. Later, however, "In Gordin's plays Kessler began to *speak* on stage for the first time. This came *from* him, but the role had brought it *to* him. It ignited his powers of imagination. He got used to the role, sensing himself as a living human being, and the real-life tone came naturally to him. What was lacking in the words the actor put in with his performance. Kessler did not know this at first. Intelligent theater-goers explained it to him, and I was one of them."

Kessler left no memoir, no instructions, no disciples. His only legacy was the instinctive naturalism that had eluded Yiddish players for so long. Widely imitated, it drove them on, and enabled some of them to make the crossover to mainstream theater. But that was not enough to sustain his name. If anyone ever needed proof that the actor's life and art are writ on water, David Kessler stands as the prime exemplar—the most obscure celebrity ever to occupy center stage.

By the time of Kessler's death Adler had begun a slow and incomplete recovery. After much concern and consultation, the family told him what had happened. His reaction was so distressing that from then on, Jacob's granddaughter Lulla recalled, "all bad news was kept from him." The following summer, "newspapers were hidden when Caruso died." The suicide of an admirer was also concealed, and one night Adler startled his family by asking why this friend was not there. Somebody found a hasty explanation, and a short uneasy silence followed.

"I suppose he is already under the earth," Adler said. Nobody contradicted him.

The bent, white-haired figure had planned to write his memoirs; now he was forced to dictate them in his Riverside Drive apartment. Adler's tone suggested the lament of Ishmael: "Where are they now, the true ones of yesterday? Where is Goldfaden, my rabbi, my teacher? Where is Mogulesko, the young companion whose career flowered together with my own? Where is Gordin . . . where is David Kessler— though we were competitors we loved one another. Better than any one he understood and appreciated my art, and knew, too, that better than anyone, I understood and appreciated his. Where are they all? The dark undertaker has laid them all away and left me here alone, the last of my generation."

Money had never meant very much to Jacob, but it took on a crucial significance during his decline. Even with the help of his children he needed funds for daily assistance. The situation was not very different from the way Bertha Kalisch would deal with old age. Almost blind, she was led onstage for a series of "Farewells," and they produced enough cash to pay her medical bills. A similar benefit was staged for Jacob at the Manhattan Opera House, advertised as "The final appearance on any stage of Jacob P. Adler." The sold-out house watched a variety program peopled with celebrities, among them the vaudevillians Al Jolson, who sang and whistled, and Will Rogers, who cracked jokes and spun a rope. A Metropolitan Opera tenor concluded the tribute with "Pack Up Your Troubles."

Adler himself appeared. He read from the first act of Gordin's *A Yiddish King Lear,* unable to stand, but vigorous of voice. The profits of the night—$15,000—went to the honoree. Heartened, the family scheduled a series of "Final Appearances." The last occurred at Kessler's Second Avenue Theater, where Jacob went through a scene from Gordin's *The Stranger,* typecast as a stricken old man. Wiping their eyes, audience members made repeated requests for yet another bow. Adler's wife, Sara, kept track; there were eighteen curtain calls. In his dressing room, she spoke in wonder. "You made them cry as they never cried before." The old man's head was not so easily turned. "It was not my art that made them cry."

One morning he read that the great Russian director Konstantin Stanislavsky was in town with the Moscow Art Theater. Jacob demanded an audience. He was frail, but two of his eight children, the actors Luther and Julia, got Jacob up in his best suit and drove him to the Russian's hotel. As the car pulled up, their father abruptly changed his mind; he felt too ill to get out of the car. Word was sent upstairs. A few moments later Stanislavsky showed up in bathrobe and slippers. He had heard much about the work of Jacob Adler. Climbing in back, he embraced the actor. The two men spoke effusively in Russian, embraced, wept, and said their farewells.

"Lonely as I am," Adler related to his stenographer, "I have my memories of the Yiddish Theater, memories I must set down so that, dipped in blood, lit with the tears of a living witness, the world may know how we built, out of the dark realities of Jewish life, with our blood, with our nerves, with the tears of our sleepless nights, the theater that stands today as a testament to our people."

Jacob was not as forsaken as he wanted the reader to believe. Three of his grown children were starring on Broadway: Luther in *Humoresque*, playing opposite the popular actress Laurette Taylor; Julia, as Jessica to David Warfield's Shylock in *The Merchant of Venice*; Stella as the lead in Karel Capek's drama *The World We Live In*. All of them acknowledged his influence. Yet this was not enough: Jacob Adler needed time and attention, and above all he needed to organize his memory, to provide a coda to his career. Shortly after his seventieth birthday, he dictated ruefully, "I am now at the time, the poet tells us, when the soldiers, the hands, begin to tremble, and the watchmen, the feet, begin to falter. The sun is growing darker. Clouds begin to cover the moon. What was deepest, most satisfying, most beautiful in my rich life is every day fading."

On he went, talking and mourning and writing, completing his memoir just before he was gripped by a grand mal seizure. Jacob Adler died on March 31, 1926. For a moment, the heart of the Yiddish Theater stopped beating. The actor was certainly not fault-free; he could be self-centered to the point of solipsism. Yet he was also aesthetically ambitious; he chose to appear in plays of stature even when it meant diminished profits, and he was the first to show the English-speaking world that a ghetto actor could have the power and glamour of a Barrymore. Other Yiddish performers had taken up his fallen banner and run with it. They did so with equal courage and more polished skills. But they operated in a postwar world. The stage was shifting under their feet.

The administration of President Calvin Coolidge had set down roots, and callous immigration policies had gone into effect. Working-class immigrants were no longer welcome in the United States. The Jews who did manage the high hurdles of Ellis Island were skilled tradesmen and professionals, equipped to enter the middle class as rapidly as possible. These people already had a smattering of English and wanted more. They had little interest in immuring themselves in the Lower East Side, and less in watching ghetto stage productions.

The bleak future of the Yiddish Theater was Topic A at the Hebrew Actors Union on East 7th Street, as Adler's colleagues gathered to speak about his contributions, and to mourn his loss. A *New York Times* obituary had just called Jacob "the world's leading exponent of the Yiddish drama." In a rare follow-up piece, the paper had added, "Thirty years ago the folk of the east side 'Ghetto,' for the most part immigrants lately arrived, lived in the cultural atmosphere of Middle Europe.

"In the technique of the theater they were Victorian, but in nature and spirit Elizabethan. They argued and wept and cheered, not only unashamed, but with joy and pride in their emotions. To this folk Adler brought a drama as primitive as themselves, touched with a broadly human sympathy and illumined by moods of nobility." Sad to say, "with Jacob Adler passes the heroic age of the Yiddish Theater. Whether or not his King Lear ranked with the Hamlet of Edwin Booth, it unquestionably belonged to the same great school." In one judgment the paper was inaccurate. Adapting to survive was second nature for American Jews; the Yiddish theater was down but not out. In fact, it was about to enjoy a powerful resurgence. Even as Jacob Adler was laid to rest, the rescuers were entering from stage left.

ii

NOTIONS OF A FINAL SOLUTION were given added fervor by the humiliation of Alfred Dreyfus, framed as a spy by a group of anti-Semitic officers in 1878. More agitation against the Jews came after the ravings of the czar's minions, anxious to convert, deport, or kill the Russian Hebrews during the early part of the century. But the most powerful impetus for the Holocaust rose from the mud of Verdun and the trenches of the Marne.

A cease-fire took effect eleven minutes after the eleventh hour of November 11, 1918. A day later, the statisticians went to work. When their ghastly arithmetic was finished, they calculated that ten million lay dead in the soil of the battling nations. Another twenty million had been maimed, the victors limping home to an empty celebration, the losers to an intolerable humiliation. The Great War, the war to end all wars, had actually laid the foundation for a new and unimaginably atrocious one. Because of the global conflict, Europe's balance of power had been wrecked, a rising generation of potential leaders had been slaughtered, and the economies of practically every nation lay in disarray.

Someone had to be blamed for this international catastrophe. The generals and the elected officials pointed away from themselves, and the novelists and poets whose colleagues had died in the war had their say as well. "The glory of combat," once a phrase that stirred millions, no longer had any meaning. The new catchphrases were "moral fatigue" and "international malaise." A search for scapegoats got under way, as it did after every war. Leading the literary pack, T. S. Eliot found a specific group to blame, deliberately placing them in lower case:

> *The rats are underneath the piles*
> *The jew is underneath the lot*

ABOVE: *Producer/actor Boris Thomashefsky billed himself as "America's Darling" at the turn of the century.*
BELOW: *Boris as the Yiddish Theater's first Hamlet*
RIGHT: *Boris's rival Jacob P. Adler in his greatest role as Shylock*

ABOVE: *Playwright and composer Abraham Goldfaden, the legitimate father of the Yiddish Theater*

LEFT: *David Kessler, a fierce competitor and one of the earliest proponents of naturalistic acting*

ABOVE: *Charlie Chaplin visits Maurice Schwartz
backstage at the Yiddish Art Theater.*
BELOW: *Schwartz, left, in costume, directs a scene from the 1939 film*
Tevye der Milkhiker (Tevye the Milkman).

LEFT: *Bertha Kalsich, one of the Yiddish Theater's greatest divas, playing "The Light from St. Agnes" in vaudeville*
BELOW: *The dashing Jacob Ben-Ami in costume*

RIGHT: *Crossover comedienne Molly Picon at the Second Avenue Theater in 1930*
BELOW: *Marlon Brando and Yiddish Theater veterans Paul Muni and Celia Adler in the 1946 proto-Zionist drama,* A Flag Is Born

די זעלבע אידען אין אן ענגלישען טהעאטער.   אידען אין א אידישען טהעאטער.

FACING PAGE, CLOCKWISE FROM TOP LEFT: *Yiddish Vaudeville on the Lower East Side; the Moorish-style Irving Place Theater "uptown" at 15th Street; Jacob P. Adler's Grand Theater, at the Bowery and Grand Street; Max Reinhardt's striking production of* At the Gate *for the communist ARTEF company*
ABOVE: *Groyser Kundes (The Big Stick), a comic periodical, depicts a mannerly Broadway audience—in contrast to the crowd at a Yiddish Theater production, who yell, hiss, and read newspapers during the onstage drama.*
BELOW: *The Orchard Street Market ca. 1898, when an influx of Jewish refugees from Eastern Europe eventually made the Lower East side more crowded than Calcutta*

ABOVE: *In 1909 Boris Thomashefsky's Arch Street Theatre Company in Philadelphia outspent and outperformed productions in New York and Europe.*

BELOW: *From a 1916 issue of* Groyser Kundes: *"If Shakespeare Had to Sell a Play Today" shows the Bard being rejected by Kessler and Adler, as well as by the impresarios Bessie and Boris Thomashefsky.*

The wrong people seemed to have money in the postwar period, and without much warning, portraits of the beaky Hebrew predator came back into fashion. There was Meyer Wolfsheim, for example, the conniving gangster of *The Great Gatsby:* "He's the man who fixed the World Series." "Why isn't he in jail?" "They can't get him, old sport. He's a smart man."

There was Robert Cohn, the rich and unlikable Princetonian of *The Sun Also Rises,* who had been overmatched in a boxing ring. "It gave him a certain satisfaction of a strange sort, and it certainly improved his nose."

E. E. Cummings, who had been in a concentration camp during the war, could not shake the prejudices of his youth:

> *beware of folks with missions*
> *to turn us into rissions*
> *and blokes with ammunicions*
> *who tend to make incitions*
>
> *and pity the fool who cright*
> *god help me it aint no ews*
> *eye like the steak all ried*
> *but eye certainly hate the juse*

The result of all this was something George Orwell was later to define as doublethink: the ability to weld two false ideas in a way that defied all systems of logic. During the postwar period, the specter of the wily Jew was raised yet again in international consciousness. He and his kind were supposed to have caused the war in order to fatten their coffers. When the profits ran out they ended the conflict, thus stabbing Germany in the back. That was Adolf Hitler's charge, and he would maintain it until his dying day.

Unmentioned in his autobiographical *Mein Kampf* was the fact that a Jewish officer had awarded him the Iron Cross. Or that the German troops had mutinied all by themselves, refusing to follow Kaiser Wilhelm (who had saved his own skin by slinking away to a safe Netherlands exile). Or that Alfred Krupp, Germany's principal merchant of death, was in fact a well-known anti-Semite.

The wartime profiteer was but one aspersion cast upon the character of the Jew. Another, diametrically opposite, pictured the Bolshevik Hebrew as manipulative and half mad, an advocate of free love who would despoil Christian women, who called religion the opiate of the people, who stole from the treasuries of the world in order to fund godless communism. Unmentioned was the fact that Karl Marx, co-author of *The Communist Manifesto,* warned the world against Judaism. Born of a Jewish mother converted to Lutheranism, he wrote a very specific caveat: "Let us not seek the secret of the Jew in his religion, but let us seek the secret of the religion in the real Jew. What is the profane basis of Judaism? Practical need, self-interest. What is the worldly cult of the Jew? Huckstering. What is his worldly god? Money.

"Very well: then, in emancipating itself from huckstering and money, and thus from real and practical Judaism, our age would emancipate itself."

To the paranoid spirit of the Germans, and to many of their neighbors, to be both an ur-capitalist *and* a Bolshevik at the same time was beyond the talents of any people on the planet—except of course the Jews. This mind-set was not exclusive to Europe; it infected America as well. Russian Jews were never more than 5 percent of the general population, but they were disproportionately represented in the new government. Leon Trotsky had become chief of Soviet foreign affairs; Yakov Sverdlov was chairman of the Executive Committee; Grigori Zinoviev led the Communist International. U.S. anti-Semites were thus furnished with new material. More was to come on the heels of the Revolution.

In 1920 Prohibition took effect. The passage of the Eighteenth Amendment gave rise to a new criminal class of distillers and importers—as well as the spread of speakeasies, illegally serving booze to patrons anxious to flout the law. Two of the biggest bootleggers were Canadian Jews, Sam Bronfman and Louis Rosenstiel, and much was made of their ethnicity. This was coupled with the Red Scare, exacerbated by Woodrow Wilson's attorney general, A. Mitchell Palmer. The most prominent of the president's cabinet appointees, Palmer pointed to a series of warning signs from the left. Bombs had been detonated in eight cities, including Washington, D.C., where Palmer's own home had been damaged by an explosive device. In addition, a series of violent strikes had taken place in the early postwar period, led by communist and socialist agitators. Palmer also looked disapprovingly at the rising divorce rate and the feverish Negro music and abbreviated clothing made popular by a new generation coming of age. These, too, he blamed on communism.

In a widely quoted essay he wrote that the Bolshevist movement was "eating its way into the homes of the American workman," and "tongues of revolutionary heat were licking the altars of the churches, leaping into the belfry of the school bell, crawling into the sacred corners of American homes, seeking to replace marriage vows with libertine laws, burning up the foundations of society."

Egged on by a group of agitated congressmen, Palmer and his special assistant, J. Edgar Hoover, began a series of raids, targeting "radicals" of every persuasion. Thousands were arrested and held without trial. In December 1919, the raids were capped by the deportation of 249 aliens, put aboard the USS *Buford* and shipped off to the Soviet Union. Jewish names were of particular interest to Palmer's agents, and Hoover expressed a singular pleasure after the arrest of Emma Goldman, a high-profile deportee whose views about free love and birth control were a favorite subject of the tabloids.

The times hardly seemed right for a radical Jewish theater group— especially one whose purpose was to stage a new kind of Yiddish Theater. Yet that was exactly what the avant-garde had in mind as its members gathered in clandestine meeting places, operating under a variety of false names. In his study *The Jew and Communism,* Melech Epstein describes a typical "club" in New York City, occupying a floor in an office or apartment building. "The inner walls were taken out, and a stage built on one side. The walls were painted and decorated with posters and placards, and the ceiling was festooned with colorful crepe paper. Facing the stage was a buffet for sandwiches and hot and cold drinks, served by the girls." The organizations with sufficient membership "also maintained dramatic groups, dance groups, mandolin bands, sport sections, libraries, and the inevitable *samizdat*—wall newspaper—brought over from Russia."

Things eased up a bit in the early 1920s, when Woodrow Wilson was displaced by the new president. Warren G. Harding wanted nothing to do with controversy—and very little to do with politics. The Red Scare diminished in a period the Republican president defined as "Less government in business and more business in government." Scandals quickly undid him, however, when it was revealed that several of his associates had used their official positions to line their own pockets.

Depressed and unnerved, Harding went on a tour of the West in 1923, accompanied by his untainted secretary of commerce, Herbert Hoover. The president confessed in a quiet moment, "My friends—they're the ones that keep me walking the floors nights!" and asked Hoover, "If you knew of a great scandal in our administration, would you for the good of the country and the party expose it publicly or would you bury it?" Hoover urged the president to go public as soon as possible, to save the GOP. Whether Harding planned to take Hoover's advice would always remain a mystery; in August 1923, he died in San Francisco of a heart attack. Vice President Coolidge replaced him, assuring the country that prosperity, not partisanship, was his main concern.

That summer a group of clubs felt secure enough to found the Folks Farband far Kunst Teater (The People's Association for Art Theater), a mix of communists and socialists. At first, the *Forward* socialists maneuvered the communists out of the executive committee. In a show of strength, they wrote an official declaration, honoring the memory of Samuel Gompers, founder of the American Federation of Labor. The communists wanted no part of it. They argued that Gompers had been against immigration, that he had opposed teaching the working class any language but English, that he had been far too conciliatory to management in union negotiations.

A vitriolic debate followed. In the end, the socialists walked out, leaving the communists in full control of the Farband. No longer was it an umbrella organization representing the entire gamut of Jewish labor. The hard left had won. Once in the hands of the communists, the Folks Farband became the Arbeter Teater Farband (Workers Theater Alliance), which went by its acronym, Artef. The group determined to go against the zeitgeist.

Wherever the personnel of the Artef looked, it seemed that Americans sought to avoid reality. Frivolity was the main theme of Broadway shows, crystallized in Ira Gershwin's verse:

> *Old Man Trouble*
> *I don't mind him—*
> *You won't find him*
> *'Round my door*

Men were only too happy to flout the laws against liquor by drinking in speakeasies; women impudently mocked conventions by wearing short hair and abbreviated skirts. It was, as John Updike points out, "a light-hearted era" in which Buster Keaton and Harold Lloyd could dominate the silent screen, and Dorothy Parker could encapsulate an era in a quatrain:

> *Drink and dance and laugh and lie,*
> *Love, the reeling midnight through,*
> *For tomorrow we shall die!*
> *(But, alas, we never do.)*

Against the national tendency toward ridicule and derision, Artef made its stand. The irony was that this innovative group could defy any convention and any leader, save for one who lived six thousand miles from New York. The anti-Semitism of the Soviet leader, Joseph Stalin, was no secret even then. But whenever the subject was raised, the true believers confronted doubters with two essential facts: a) the Soviet Union had promoted many men and women with Jewish names. And b) Yiddish theaters flourished in Minsk, Odessa, Kiev, and some smaller cities.

So how bad could it be for the Jews of Russia? What sane Hebrew would choose a return to the days of the Romanovs? The Soviet Yiddish Theater had rubles to work with, directors, lighting, and set designers. Why, there was even a star, Shlomo Mikhoels.

iii

IN 1925 Artef leased an office in Union Square, the heart of radical life in New York. Incorporated, the group began a fund-raising drive, selling $5 bonds to member organizations. In statements to the community, members exhorted New York's Jewry to abandon the "bygone idylls, Hasidic legends, all kinds of tall tales," and to forget "the notion of bourgeois life, family drama and romantic complications." Inserted in a Goldfaden play, two lines crystallized their new aesthetic. As a funeral procession passed by, an onlooker inquired, "Dead? Who died?" The enthusiastic answer: "The old Yiddish Theater!"

But Maurice Schwartz refused to be elbowed aside by the leftists. He staged dramas with political content (although carefully set in the past), among them *Danton,* Romain Rolland's portrait of the French revolutionary, and Ernst Toller's *Machine Wreckers,* based on the Luddite anti-industrial riots in England. The communists condemned these productions as "insincere and hollow." Nathaniel Buchwald, a propagandist for the communist monthly *Der Hammer,* predicted that the commercial Yiddish Theater would return to "dybbuks, domestic dramas and shtetl idylls." He was correct. The socially conscious plays failed to draw, and Schwartz quickly reverted to his standard fare.

In response, the Artef set up its own theater in 1926, the year of Jacob Adler's demise. Actors were recruited and taught by Jacob Mestel, a director/theorist who had toured with Ben-Ami and written about the theater for various periodicals. Mestel believed that his co-religionists had a knack for vocal mimicry and physical gesture, and that this talent was responsible for the abundance of great character actors on the Yiddish stage. On the other hand, Jewish performers spoke a low-class jargon, a language that had changed very little since the Goldfaden days. A drama studio was set up on East Eleventh Street, where young Yiddish actors would learn "speech melody and collective language instrumentation; how to forge out of the old pathos and the modern tempo a rhythm suited to our times."

When they were fully schooled, the actors went public. Three projects were produced, one right after the other. The Artef debuted with an immense, booming pageant entitled *Mass, Play and Ballet of the Russian Revolution.* The work took place not in some ordinary clubhouse or middle-sized theater; it was presented in Madison Square Garden, before an audience of twenty thousand. Led by their ballet teacher, the classically trained Russian émigré Michael Fokine, the troupe depicted the oppressed czarist nation, the upheaval, and life in the new nation improved a hundredfold under the Bolsheviks.

Well received, this naive spectacle led to a second production, attended by two thousand people at the Central Opera House in Manhattan. *Strike,* a stark Yiddish melodrama written by Buchwald, had been workshopped the previous summer at the communist Camp Nitgedayget. It featured a "Machine Dance" with oppressed laborers and symbolic figures of the workers' enemies: the Union Bureaucrat, the Capitalist, the Militarist, and the Priest.

Their third production, *Red, Yellow and Black,* presented the history of the American Jewish labor movement in four scenes. Once again it was staged at Madison Square Garden. Once again its message was conveyed with choreography, dance, and aggressive songs in Yiddish, punctuated by fund-raising speeches and a final singing of the "Internationale," the communist anthem.

Not until the early 1930s did the Artef awaken to a central fact: weighty symbolism and agitprop were not the ingredients of a satisfying theatrical experience. The studio alertly battened on to the late Sholem Aleichem. The beloved and apolitical author, who had once been a stockbroker, was enlisted in the fight against bourgeois capitalism. Aleichem's interest in Zionism, frowned on by the communists, went unmentioned in their presentations.

The first production of his work was staged at Carnegie Hall. Usually presented in monologue form, *Kasrilover Hoteln* (The Hotels of Kassirovka) was done as a group recitation, the comrades delivering their lines by popping their faces out in large placards. Later, they went at Aleichem again, turning a children's story into a turgid ballet-pantomime entitled *Lag Boymer* (Springtime).

That evening was rescued by Boris Aronson's outstanding set and costumes. The man who would ultimately receive worldwide fame as the designer for a very different kind of Aleichem work, *Fiddler on the Roof,* had come of age just as the Revolution began. He wanted nothing to do with the fashionable realism of the day; for the young artist, Stanislavsky already seemed passé. He went on to Germany, published two books of his bold paintings and designs, then came to America, where he immediately found work in the Yiddish Theater.

Aronson's initial efforts, done for Schwartz, were undistinguished. It was not until he worked with Artef that he hit his stride. *Lag Boymer* featured dancers costumed as trees, and cubistic symbols that represented the cutting edge of theater design, far bolder and more inventive than anything on Broadway. A choir of raves greeted the production, capped by *Theater Arts Monthly*'s appraisal: Aronson's work was "the bravest experiment in scenic design that the season has disclosed."

Backstage, however, the designer met with unexpected hostility. Schwartz, intrigued by the Artef when he thought he could control it, turned against Aronson's aggressive designs and the company's stark

performances. His memoir ridicules the troupers as an arty and posturing crowd, basically "afraid to do a realistic play." Under Artef's
aegis, he claimed, "actors began making peculiar motions with their
hands speaking in squeaky tones, rolling their eyes, sighing at the
moon, began to speak the way people are going to speak in the future,
millions of years from now . . . everything the reverse of natural: point-
ing at walls and furniture, holding a walking stick upside down, jumping instead of walking, and instead of natural human faces, backward
noses and crooked cheeks."

Schwartz's was a minority view—until Jewish settlements in Palestine suddenly came under attack from Arab militants in 1929. Dozens
of unarmed *yeshiva* students were murdered. A great mourning took
place on the Lower East Side. But the Yiddish-speaking communists
refused to participate in the general grief. The *Morgyn Freiheit*, their
unofficial organ, originally blasted the Palestinian incidents as a Middle Eastern pogrom. Orders soon came down to reverse engines and
denounce their former position as "counterrevolutionary." The next
day the headline read ZIONIST-FASCISTS HAVE PROVOKED THE
ARAB UPRISING. The article went on to explain, "The roots of the
revolt of the Arabian masses are to be found in the economic exploita-
tion of the Arab peasantry, whose land has been appropriated by
British imperialism through reactionary Jewish Zionism."

The *Freiheit* was not forgiven for calling the Middle Eastern troubles
a "Zion orgy." For five days, Jewish-owned newsstands refused to carry
the paper. "Red" journalists were expelled from the Yiddish Writers
Union for anti-Jewish activities, and the Hebrew Actors Union distributed a blanket condemnation of the communist newspaper. Members
of the Artef found themselves similarly condemned or marginalized.
They pressed on regardless, opening the 1931 season at the Princess
Theater on West 39th Street.

By then the Depression had taken root, but the communists viewed
this as a ratification of their core beliefs: harsh economic conditions
served to reveal the sham of capitalism, thereby hastening a second
American Revolution. An official statement quashed all competitors:
"The bourgeois Yiddish Theater, without any exceptions, is saturated
with national chauvinism, with hatred for the working man and with
respect and sympathy for the wealthy and clerics." That kind of fare
"injects ideological poison into the hearts and minds of the working
Jewish masses."

Given Artef's refusal to depart from Bolshevik sloganeering, the company might well have become a hackwork assembly line. Oddly enough, that was not the case. Two productions showed unusual imagination for that season: *Jim Kooperkop* (Jim Copperhead) and *Brilliantin* (Diamonds). The first play centered on a mechanical figure (Kooperkop), brought in to replace human laborers. The robot unexpectedly joins the radicals and helps to vanquish their overlords.

Jim was an amalgam of Frankenstein, the medieval Yiddish legend of the Golem—a gigantic creature created by rabbis to rescue the Jews—and the screeds of Karl Marx. His story was located in a hellish America. Aronson's austere, futuristic sets evoked the overpowering atmosphere of Fritz Lang's 1927 film fantasy, *Metropolis,* with scenes of a bereaved mother losing herself in the wildness of jazz; a jobless worker starving to death; a quack; a pimp; a broker and an undertaker reaching out their hands for money. *Kooperkop* quickly attracted a cult audience of performers who jammed the theater, often crowding out the ordinary laborers it was intended to reach.

But a succès d'estime was not enough. Artef still needed that capitalistic entity called profits. *Diamonds* was intended to bring them in. The drama harked back to the grand old farces of con men who arrive in a small town, swindle the occupants, then get exposed as frauds. Here the principal charlatan was Comrade Schindel, posing as an official from Moscow in search of goods for schools and orphanages.

Actually, Schindel has come there to smuggle diamonds out of the Soviet Union. He hides the stones in *tefillin* (the leather boxes worn by Orthodox Jews at morning prayers) and accidentally loses them. Frantically, he and his assistant overpay for every pair of *tefillin* in town until they find the right ones. Then, just before the cheats can sneak away, the police collar them, leaving the thieves and townspeople sadder and wiser.

In form *Diamonds* was just another folktale, but the ending punched home a different moral: the days of the *shtetl* were over. In the new Soviet regime, provincial shenanigans were no longer to be tolerated; reeducation and comradeship would usher in a new era of progress and crime-free life.

The new production had positive reviews, but no lines appeared at the box office. Early in 1931, the *Freiheit* reported: "Because of purely technical problems the Artef management is forced, as of today, to suspend all performances for several weeks." This was fiction; the difficulty was not a lack of props, it was a dearth of popularity. No matter how good the acting or memorable the sets, ordinary Yiddish-speaking audiences wanted to be amused in these miserable times. They were made uncomfortable by harangues, political metaphors, and object lessons delivered from behind the footlights.

So they went elsewhere, to the straight plays and *shund,* the "ideological poison" of Second Avenue. There, they knew what they were getting: emotional involvement, not mass movement; entertainment, not lectures. And besides, these people had long memories. The incident of the "Zion orgy" was not something they could dismiss out of hand.

Only one thing could have reconciled traditional Jews with the non-religious communists—a common enemy. Someone, or some movement, that could threaten the very existence of their *landsmen.* In the early 1930s this seemed plausible but unlikely. The czar had been dead more than a dozen years. To be sure, there were rumors of mob violence in the East, not unlike the pogroms of the past. And everyone knew stories of anti-Semitism reasserting itself in the West. But these were minor incidents. Leon Blum, a Jew, headed the French Socialist Party. In Germany the city of Ulm had put up signs for Einstein-strasser, naming the street in honor of its most famous citizen, a Jewish physicist. True, the entire world struggled with hard times. Yet America, where one third were ill-clothed, ill-fed, ill-housed, had not dissolved into chaos. Why should the older nations? As civilizations advanced, what men, what countries would be capable of destroying European Jewry? And why on earth would they wish to do so? It would be some time before the Jews awakened to reality. The years of sleep-walking would be the most tragic in their long, winding history.

CHAPTER TWELVE

✦

THIS BASTARD IS
UNDERPLAYING
ME TO DEATH!

i

A MAJORITY of the early film producers and scenarists had grown up in Yiddish-speaking homes. Consciously or unconsciously they were familiar with the classic themes of the Yiddish Theater—the sanctity of the family, the precariousness of life, the importance of education. Louis B. Mayer, one of the founders of

MGM, was typical in this regard. He grew choleric when he saw a gangster film that violated the idea of motherhood: "Knock the mother on the jaw! Throw the little old lady down the stairs! Throw the mother's good, homemade chicken soup in the mother's face! Step on the mother! Kick her! That is art, they say. Art!" Mayer, Samuel Goldwyn, the Warner brothers, and many other foreign-born producers found their ideal in Samson Raphaelson's *The Jazz Singer*. America's first sound movie unreeled in 1927, making silent film obsolete and changing every aspect of show business.

An opening title card set the scene: "The New York Ghetto, throbbing to that rhythm of music which is older than civilization." In this roiled neighborhood a battle gets under way between Jakie Rabinowitz and his father, a fourth-generation cantor. He expects his son to carry on in the family tradition. Jakie refuses. A frightful row takes place, and the boy leaves home. Years pass, and in that time he becomes famous as Jack Robin, cabaret entertainer (Al Jolson). When Jack comes home his mother embraces him. The cantor wants no part of his celebrity son. Robin returns to show business, going from strength to strength until, on the opening night of his first Broadway show, he learns that the old man is dying. Should Jack go onstage anyway? Or should he return to his parents? Naturally, he chooses the latter course, his blackface makeup still clinging to his skin as he goes down on one knee and sings:

> *I'sa comin'*
> *Sorry I made you wait.*
> *I'sa comin'*
> *Hope and pray I'm not too late.*
> *Mammy! Mammy!*
> *I'd walk a million miles*
> *For one of your smiles*
> *My Mammy!*

Even in those palmy days, filmmakers were made uncomfortable by scenes of parent worship—unless it could be expressed in disguise. The black mask was ideal: audiences knew the singer was a Jew, played by a man who was himself the son of a cantor. But in the movie Jack Robin could also get himself up in burnt cork and pretend to be a Negro. As such he could express the raw emotion of mother love and a fear of death. (A Freudian interpretation of *The Jazz Singer* changed the letter "a" to the letter "o"—from "Mammy" to "Mommy.")

The Yiddish filmmakers were overjoyed. At last, the *mamaloshen* could be heard as well as seen. And forget about burnt cork, they told one another. Yiddish actors needed no Jolson-like masks; they would never disguise themselves as another race. The headliners had been emoting for fifty years; audiences expected to see them go over the top.

Two years into the sound era, two New York businessmen, Louis Weiss and Rubin Goldberg, founded a new company called Yiddish Talking Pictures. It might have been named Yiddish Talking Picture— they produced only one film, *Uncle Moses*. Maurice Schwartz had recently starred in his own stage adaptation of the Sholem Asch novel; naturally he was chosen to do the screenplay and take the title role. Filming took place at the East Coast version of Hollywood—a studio in Fort Lee, New Jersey, just across the Hudson from Manhattan. There were only minimal sets, big parts, sharp dialogue, and best of all, a relevance to the current climate of distress.

The main figure, played by Schwartz, is a venal and lecherous clothing manufacturer. Back in the European ghetto of Kuzmin he had been a butcher with a bloodstained apron. In America, with a combination of luck, gall, and manic energy, he has become a benevolent despot, a man who pays for his *landsmen* to come to America—and then engages them in his sweatshop for fourteen-hour days and subsistence pay.

Two of Moses' relatives provide the counterpoint to the boss's dominant personality: his father and his nephew. The old man is a kind of Shakespearean fool, speaking truth in comic asides. He sings constantly, but the cheerful *nign* (melody) carries references to his son as a modern-day pharaoh, cruelly using his Jewish prisoners. The nephew, Sam, is a totally Americanized operator, running the day-to-day operations of the factory, and dreaming of when he'll inherit his bachelor uncle's property.

Moses devotes much of his leisure time to the wooing and winning of a beautiful seventeen-year-old employee, Mascha. She is in love with Charlie, a labor organizer, but marries her aging boss in order to liberate Mama, Papa, and all her siblings from abject poverty. Mascha becomes pregnant, and Moses revels in his prospective fatherhood. Historical forces are at work, however, and they will soon overwhelm him.

On the day Moses' son is born, a strike is declared. The workers hail Charlie as the *true* Moses, the one who will lead them out of wage-slavery. To counter their moves, Sam hires hooligans to break the strike. The idea of Jews attacking other Jews is too much for Uncle Moses. He suffers a severe heart attack, ages overnight, and undergoes a moral reformation. He alters his will, leaving 25 percent of his estate to his abused employees, and agrees to divorce Mascha. The young mother will at last be liberated from her chains, free to marry her heart's desire.

In the closing scene Uncle Moses returns to the factory and speaks to the workers in the resigned, all-is-vanity tone of Ecclesiastes: "I was walking past the Great Synagogue. I walked in and heard a rabbi delivering a sermon. He was talking about 'man.' He spoke for an hour and never said what 'man' is all about. So I asked him: 'Mister, what is a man? He builds houses, factories, brings his countrymen to America, and after all, the grave awaits him. He builds, he makes a commotion, and the grave still waits.' "

In *Bridge of Light,* J. Hoberman remarks on the film's strange agnosticism. "Religion is present largely as an absence—it's striking that even after Moses renounces his worldly goods, he does not turn to God. In the harshest ending of any Yiddish film, Moses asks one of his old workers to sing the *nign* he sang for his father and the melody is drowned out by the roar of the machines."

Uncle Moses had none of the polish associated with Hollywood features. The cast was solid but plain, the montage a collection of crowd scenes, two-shots, and close-ups. And yet, in the year the film was released only one English-language talkie had the same visceral impact. It also opened in April 1932. As Maurice Schwartz spoke the words of Uncle Moses, the Yiddish Theater's first crossover star, Paul Muni, filled the screen as Tony Camonte—*Scarface.*

ii

MUNI HAD TAKEN a winding trek to the big time. At the age of twelve he entered his parents' touring Yiddish Theater company. First Salche and Nachum Weisenfreund played in Eastern Europe, then came to the United States. Their son had a certain knack in adolescence: with an adroit use of powdered chalk and charcoaled wrinkles he could impersonate codgers with sly immigrant faces and timeworn physiques. Backstage they called him Old Man Makeup. Out front, few cottoned to the fact that they were watching an adolescent.

But Nachum wanted something better than a scrambling show business life for his boy. Muni had shown some talent for the violin; what if he were to be another Misha Elman, the Jewish kid who had played himself out of a Russian *shtetl* and onto the recital stages of the world? Muni was forced to take lessons and to play his instrument two hours a day—until the moment his father unexpectedly came home to find the boy making faces in the mirror and experimenting with makeup. His violin lay under a bunch of discarded underwear.

Nachum picked up the instrument. "Why aren't you practicing?"

Muni hesitated. "I—I no longer care for the violin, Papa. I don't have time for it. I want to be an actor—I can't do both!"

Without another word, Nachum took the violin in his hands and broke it over his knee. Yiddish melodrama once again reached into real life: save for the lines they exchanged onstage, father and son did not speak to each other for the next two months. By then Nachum realized that Muni's ambition was an irresistible force. There was nothing he or anyone else could do to impede it.

Muni's work drew the attention of provincial theater managers; they won the apprentice numerous walk-ons and cameo roles as a doddering geezer. A decade later, when Muni was on his own in New York, Maurice Schwartz arranged an audition at the Hebrew Actors Union. Again the young man played an elderly figure. One committee member was less impressed than his fellows: "Let him in—he'll never put anybody out of work, except himself. And if Schwartz wants him, that's Schwartz's funeral." In a way, it was.

Muni quickly made himself at home in the city. He married young—to Boris Thomashefsky's niece Bella—and she became his most important audience. Preparing for a show at the Yiddish Art Theater, he developed an offstage routine. When Bella went shopping, he would sometimes arrange to shuffle by her on the street, a wrinkled beggar *in extremis*. If she walked on without a sign of recognition, he knew his stage persona would pass muster. Muni liked to call on his mother-in-law with much the same purpose.

Emma had been bound in a wheelchair since that horrific day Morris Finkel aimed at her lover, shot his wife by accident, and then turned the gun on himself. These days she rarely got out to the theater, but fancied that she could still spot a false beard and windowpane glasses from a hundred feet away. Not when Muni wore them. More than once she failed to spot him beneath the clothes and manner of a doddering rabbi. "Mama," he would chortle after the revelation, "I'd rather fool you than the critics."

On a summer afternoon he played a similar game at City Hall. Muni's principal biographer, Jerome Lawrence, reports that the actor went through the final naturalization ceremony as if it were a play. Bent over, apparently from years of arthritis, he spoke in "a halting and heavy *mittel Europa* accent, squinting his eyes as if he didn't quite understand each question." During the interrogation he gradually straightened up, and his accent diminished. The final answer was delivered in impeccable English. Muni smiled at the astonished judge. "Your honor, it's remarkable. Now that you've made me a citizen, I can speak perfectly!"

Praise from family and friends was ratified by professional critics. By the mid-1920s Muni had enough encomia to fill several scrapbooks. For no matter how minuscule the role, he always managed to draw the most curtain calls, the closest attention of reviewers, and the wariest regards from fellow actors. Only a few months into the first season with Muni, Maurice Schwartz came to regret the thumbs-up decision at the Hebrew Actors Union. Luther Adler put it succinctly: "Muni was too visible. He would walk onstage and Schwartz would disappear, as if you'd turned off the light on him."

Schwartz assigned minor parts to Weisenfreund—and, to his surprise, the younger man was happy to play them. Somehow, even in walk-ons, Muni would manage to use up all the oxygen on the stage. And he seemed to do it effortlessly. A fellow actor complained, "This bastard is underplaying me to death!" Schwartz thought there was a different reason for Muni's charisma: makeup. When the period piece *Hard to Be a Jew* was staged, he cast himself as Shapiro, a patriarch with a long beard and slow speech. Muni was assigned the role of the clean-shaven Russian gentile, Ivanov. In the play Ivanov attempts to pass as a Hebrew in order to understand what the Jews are going through in the czar's country. Muni was terrified. "I've never been to Russia. I'll be a terrible flop. It'll ruin the play and ruin me. I've never played a part with my bare face hanging out. My God, I'll catch cold!" During rehearsals he turned into an insomniac, endlessly complaining to Bella, "A Jew playing a Christian playing a Jew—I won't know who I am!"

On opening night he knew very well who he was; so did the audience and the journalists. Even the hard-bitten Abraham Cahan suggested that Second Avenue's "Heroic Era" had been given a premature obituary. "Muni Weisenfreund put his name in the Golden Book of the Yiddish Theater," he wrote. This Ivanov "makes him one of the most talented actors our theater has ever had." A few weeks into the run, Schwartz changed his mind and summoned Muni to his dressing room. "Weisenfreund," he stated, "you were quite right. You are far better suited to the part of old Shapiro. You can have your wish, beard and everything. And I shall play the part of the young Ivanov."

Muni stepped into the new role without complaint. Actually, he welcomed the chance to play behind heavy makeup once again. The reviewers were ecstatic about the new Shapiro and only lukewarm about the new Ivanov. Whereupon Schwartz made his most drastic anti-Muni move. He produced and directed Romain Rolland's *Wolves*, a vivid panorama of the French Revolution. The impresario cast Weisenfreund as Du Arun, an overdressed aristocratic snob. For the entire evening, the actor would not face front. His performance was to be played upstage, a symbol of decadence in retreat.

According to Lawrence, "At first Muni was appalled at the idea. How could he play a role when the audience never saw his eyes? He boiled inside, certain he was being tossed to the wolves by a jealous and vindictive actor-manager." In the brief respites between rehearsals he contemplated revenge. As he and a colleague sat on a park bench, he suddenly exclaimed: "Watch! I'll sit that way, and I'll arch my back, stiffening it when one of the scum passes in front of me." He slapped the seat of the bench. "By God, I'll do it! I'll keep my back to the audience during the whole goddamn play, and I'll take it away from Schwartz anyway."

The thievery began when the curtain rose and found Muni facing away from the seat holders, and climaxed when Schwartz, as leader of *la Révolution,* demanded Du Arun's sword, ripped the epaulets from his uniform, and ordered him to the guillotine. "Swine!" Schwartz shouted contemptuously. "You swine!" Muni's back went rigid. He quivered. His neck seemed to extend as he faced the back wall in defiance, disdaining to ask for mercy. He remained in that position as the curtain fell, and when it rose he *still* refused to face forward, bowing to the rear of the stage. It was a true *coup du théâtre,* duly noticed and lauded. Muni was not asked back for the next season. After he departed from the Yiddish Art Theater, a story went around that Schwartz had taken the part of Du Arun, playing as Weisenfreund did, with his back to the audience. He abandoned the role when the questions of a Second Avenue habitué came back to him: "Schwartz has a pimple on his face, he doesn't want us to see it?"

By this time Muni's reputation had reached Broadway, but no offers came in. To put food on the table, and his name on the marquee, he agreed to appear in a series of Yiddish-language operettas at the National Theater. Musical comedy was not his strong suit; it seemed a long, sad way down from his dramatic turns at the Yiddish Art Theater. Yet it was Sigmund Romberg's *The Student Prince* that supplied the break he needed.

In the part of an elderly and infirm waiter, Muni incorporated some Chaplinesque bits, walking gingerly across a polished floor as if he hardly dared to set foot on it, dandling a plump waitress on his lap until her weight nearly crushed him. The crowds loved his clowning; they had never seen the actor do this sort of farcical turn. At the urging of colleagues, the uptown producer Sam H. Harris decided to summon this comedian, this Weisenfreund that everyone was talking about. Perhaps he could play a part in *We Americans,* a Broadway play currently in preparation. When Muni showed up at his office, Harris felt he had made a horrible mistake. "Too young," he snapped at the playwright and the director. "Are you out of your minds? He's just a kid."

Muni had an answer. He approached Harris's desk with infirm steps and palsied hands. "Oh sir." His voice quavered. "We old bastards shouldn't let any of those young punks into the theater. What do they know—still wet in the diapers?"

Amused, the producer turned to his director. He received a two-word response: "Sign him."

He turned to the author. "You want him?"

"Very much. I think he'll be a sensation."

The next day, Muni pleaded his case with his employers at the National, and won a release from their contract. And so it was that the thirty-one-year-old followed his destiny uptown. Under the new name of Paul Muni he would establish a second reputation as an "American" stage actor, and a third as an international film star. He would never return to the old arenas. Not everyone understood or forgave, but most did. The *Forward* offered the most sympathetic rationale: "Weisenfreund is an actor, first and last. On the Yiddish stage, his scope is naturally limited. Here, if you are not a star-manager you have to limit yourself to roles offered by the director who is susceptible to whims and caprices." Nevertheless, Muni never failed to acknowledge his roots, and gallantly saluted the man who had so often tried to suppress him. "Schwartz was daring on many occasions," he insisted. "There was always something new and different, an adventure, a challenge. Most of all, he trouped; he helped promote theater. Sometimes working with him was a struggle. But he was an artist."

CHAPTER THIRTEEN

✦

A JEWISH PETER PAN

i

AT ABOUT THE SAME TIME Muni Weisenfreud was learning his craft, the daughter of a Yiddish Theater costumier was growing up in Philadelphia. Like most Jewish girls, Molly Picon deeply respected her mother, who was raising her family alone. And like most Jewish girls in the ghetto, she enjoyed the local sport: making fun of her elders. Indeed, Molly built a stand-up routine from her mother's malapropisms and gaffes.

"In Italian bakeries, there was often a priest in the store. The baker would say, 'Mama Picon, I want you to meet Father.' And Mama answered, 'Hello, Father, how is Mother?' "

At the funeral of a producer, the mourners walked solemnly past the casket and mumbled a few words of respect. "Mama was the last one." She was expected to add some folk wisdom about death. "In a voice clear as a bell, she said, 'Yes, Edelstein, there's a first time for everything.' "

Molly strung some of her best bits together, along with comic songs, and began entertaining between reels at the nickelodeons. From there she went into Yiddish vaudeville, and after the Great War took up with a touring company of actors. In the winter of 1918 she got off the train in Boston only to find the city in the throes of the influenza epidemic then sweeping the nation. Schools, stores, and theaters were shut down by the city's board of health. But one venue had escaped: a place so decayed that the inspectors hadn't bothered to look within. The seedy old Grand Opera House under the El quietly went on with its program of wrestling matches on Tuesdays, boxing on Thursdays and Fridays, and "Jewish Theater" on Saturdays. Molly wangled an interview with the manager/director/writer, an immigrant named Jacob Kalisch.

Luck was running her way; he had once seen Miss Picon perform in Philadelphia, and found her a job with the little troupe of Yiddish-speaking actors at the Opera House. It turned out to be an extraordinary group. Muni Weisenfreund was in it, along with a new comedian named Menashe Skulnik, and the Bernardis, a family of character actors. There was also a hanger-on, Sheike, a somewhat retarded mute, who served as the company gofer, forever getting food and coffee and helping with the props. Sheike fancied himself an actor, and after the final bows had been taken and the theater emptied of customers, he would look out at the unoccupied seats, go to center stage, and make the gestures of a star in mid-performance. Kalisch had once thought to take advantage of the man's love of theater. He communicated with him in deaf-and-dumb language, requesting a group of some twenty of Sheike's friends to act as supernumeraries for the opening night of a period comedy. On the appointed evening, Sheike appeared with the requisite crowd of friends. Kalisch handed out costumes, and as they put them on, gave instruction: "When the King makes his appearance, raise your hands high and shout, 'Hail to the King! Hail to the King!' Now go!" He shoved them onstage. A few moments later the King entered. The extras remained in place, silent. In the wings, Kalisch frantically flailed his arms and yelled: "Shout. Shout! 'Hail to the King! Hail to the King!' " The extras copied his gestures, but no sound issued from their mouths.

Sheike had invited every one of his mute friends.

In the midst of this chaos and improvisation, Molly thrived. She was now twenty and had reached her maximum height of four foot eleven, thus making her a natural for juvenile roles, male and female. In one production the twenty-two-year-old Muni played her father, and she had a chance to watch him as he developed a character in rehearsals. The actor, she noted, "never enjoyed his success. He was never good enough for himself, and was always digging into himself for more and more. I don't know why he couldn't get more joy out of acting." Molly, on the other hand, was quite happy with her own work, and this blithe attitude turned out to be a liability. No Yiddish Theater producer in New York made an offer because her reputation had already been established—professional showfolk considered the young woman a comedienne rather than an actress.

Molly stayed on in Boston, the one place that guaranteed steady work. Two seasons later she married Kalisch. The transplanted Romanian knew his bride had talent and energy to spare; he also knew that as long as she stayed in America she would always be considered a piece of fluff. Molly resisted change. Europe was what the American Jews had fled. Going back there would be a retreat, a surrender. When she got pregnant, her arguments took on new force. Why raise a child anywhere but here? And then she miscarried. She went into a steep melancholia. Kalisch could not stand to see her suffer. One day he put on a bright face and told her: "I'm turning the theater over to new management, and I'm taking my little star to Europe, where she will become a big star." She was too weak to argue.

Over the next two years, Molly slowly recovered. Applause helped. She played Paris, Lodz, Vienna, Bucharest, most often in *Yonkele,* a play Kalisch shaped to her tomboy talent. She took the role of a Jewish Peter Pan, with, as she put it, "a slight difference. Whereas Peter Pan doesn't want to grow up, Yonkele desperately wants to grow up and make a better world for our people." In 1923 the maturing actress ventured into the new medium of silent movies. Codirected by Sidney Goldin, an experienced filmmaker, *Ost und West* (East and West) was a comedy of colliding cultures and mistaken identities. It was accurately publicized as "The adventures of an American girl in Poland."

The girl, of course, was Molly. From her first appearance, the girl provides shock treatment for her insular, deeply religious relatives. Hoberman accurately observes that "nothing in the film is more American than its star." Molly not only conceals a dime novel in her prayer book during Yom Kippur service, she also tiptoes into the kitchen and violates the fasting day with great mouthfuls of food. Later, the girl derisively labeled "That American *Shiksa*" teaches *yeshiva* boys how to Charleston, and attends her cousin's wedding dressed as a boy—Picon's trademark shtick.

At the end of the ceremonies, Molly drags an excruciatingly shy student, Ruben (Jacob Kalisch), under the wedding canopy and pretends to marry him. But when he places a ring on her finger before two witnesses, according to Jewish law the couple is officially wed. Separation follows, when Molly returns to New York. Tradition dictates that a divorce can take place only after five years. During that time Ruben leaves the *shtetl* and fetches up at his uncle's house in Vienna. The progressive Austrian convinces his nephew to abandon the long black cloak, yarmulke, sidelocks, and beard in favor of a modern look.

Flash-forward five years. Ruben is now the celebrated author of a bestseller entitled *East and West*. At a party in his honor, Molly, playing a pretty American tourist, wanders through the crowd. She looks around, searching for a familiar face. The young lady fails to recognize the clean-shaven, impeccably tailored Ruben—to whom she is instantly attracted. She wants to keep company with the young man but cannot; mock marriage though it may be, she belongs to another. Ruben recognizes *her,* however, and the next day, disguising himself as an old-style Hasid, takes her out. In a grand finale, he peels away the disguise to reveal himself as the once bashful youth she wed in Poland. They joyously embrace. Fade to black.

Ost und West became a smash hit in the Jewish sections of Austria and Poland, outpulling Chaplin's *The Kid* in the summer of 1923. That fall the Kalisches returned to New York, full of plans for films and theater pieces. They began by renting a Second Avenue theater for one evening. It sold out in a matter of hours. The manager, curious about the lines outside the box office, asked some of the patrons why they had come. Said one, "My uncle in Warsaw wrote me when Molly Picon appeared in *Yonkele* to go and see her." Another added, "My cousin from Bucharest wrote me not to miss Molly's *Yonkele*." Others had seen or heard about *Ost und West*. The European sojourn had paid off richly. Wrote Picon, "We had a subscription audience before I even started."

Because of that auspicious beginning, the couple rented the theater and stayed on to produce their own shows. Jimmy Walker, the new mayor of New York City, attended one performance. The movie director D. W. Griffith, invariably dressed in cape and high hat, became a steady customer. After seeing one of their shows he invited himself up to the Kalisches' apartment. Griffith had in mind a film project built around Molly. "He wanted Jacob to work on the script with him because he felt Jacob had the tempo that he himself hadn't acquired. He tried to raise a million dollars, but he was on the way down—a has-been to backers—so nothing happened. We remained in the Yiddish Theater, which was then thriving."

That year she had other reasons not to appear on celluloid. In the fall of 1923 *Ost und West* opened in New York, now dubbed *Mazel Tov* and equipped with up-to-the-minute English titles. Members of the New York State Motion Picture Commission pounced on it. In their opinion it was "filled with scenes which tend to bring the religion of the Jew in ridicule and disrespect," and they singled out Molly for shimmying "in her underclothes." Kalisch agreed to excise three scenes, and offending lines like, "You know as much about the Jewish law as Moses knew about Prohibition." The uncut version unreeled in "private" screenings. Footage was added before and after, in an attempt to placate the inspectors. They showed a grandmother telling the story of Molly to a group of children, as if the impudent girl's adventures were just a fantasy told by a harmless old lady.

None of this was lost on Maurice Schwartz. If Europe could furnish Molly Picon with a new and higher stature, why couldn't he get the same results with a little side trip to the Old World? He had profoundly miscalculated the situation. By the time he and his troupe arrived, circumstances had changed. Polish, French, German, and Yiddish companies were now thriving in their own theaters. A touring American group held little interest for European audiences, and by the time Schwartz & Co. reached Vienna they were broke. A frantic wire to the Hebrew Actors Union followed. Bailed out with a long-term loan, the chastened players returned to New York.

Their impresario, however, stayed on in Austria. Remembering the publicity surrounding *Mazel Tov,* he signed for a starring role in *Yizkor* (Prayer of Remembrance), also directed by Goldin. Schwartz was an ideal choice to play the hero in this eighteenth-century tragedy: he had starred in a stage version the year before. Set in a small Ukrainian village, the film focuses on the travails of a dashing Jewish guardsman, Leybke, in service to the local Count. He has eyes only for his intended, Kreyndl, an innkeeper's daughter. But the Count's daughter has other plans. Lovestruck, she uses all her wiles to seduce Leybke.

When he proves immune to her vamping she goes into hell-hath-no-fury mode, accusing him of attempted rape—just as Potiphar's wife did when she failed to seduce Joseph in the biblical account. On the eve of his wedding, police arrest Leybke. He escapes and flees with his fiancée. In response, authorities hold the entire Jewish community hostage. Leybke surrenders, and is forced to amuse the onlookers by putting on a bearskin and dancing in it—a common amusement of anti-Semitic Poles at the time. His humiliation acts as a goad for the onlookers. Egging each other on, they bury him alive. The Countess, mortified by the cruelty she has incited, takes her own life.

Yiskor did well enough in the Jewish neighborhoods of Europe, and much was expected of it in America. A Yiddish Theater journalist gave Schwartz reason to hope when he wrote that the Jews in attendance at an advance screening "could not help but shed a tear" and that "the film is likely to make an even stronger impression on the Gentiles for, in addition to suspense and human interest, they will find the appeal of the exotic." The feature opened on the Lower East Side, with extravagant fanfare—and flopped. "Inept distribution may have been one factor," Hoberman speculates; another, perhaps more important, was the reviewers' general disdain. The man at the *Jewish Theatrical News* was the most derisive; he compared Schwartz to "a ghost playing Hamlet."

The actor had a rhinoceros hide; he staged more theater productions and made plans to appear in yet another movie. For this one he would not only star, but direct. *Di Gebrokhene Hertser* (Broken Hearts) had previously been done by a Polish organization and shown with modest results. The new one would be made in America by Jaffe Art Films, a company that existed only on the letterhead of its stationery. Real estate speculator Louis N. Jaffe was a cinema-struck producer who claimed to be in the business in order "to present the Jew . . . done in an artistic manner." Actually a commercial hit was what Jaffe and

Schwartz were after, and the bathetic *Broken Hearts* seemed the ideal vehicle for both of them.

The actor/director played Benjamin Rezanov, a radical writer forced to flee the Alexandrine pogroms. His wife, Esther, is supposed to follow him, but upon arrival in New York City, Rezanov hears that she has died in the Old Country. The Russian Revolution takes place during the requisite mourning period, during which Benjamin marries Ruth, the daughter of an impoverished rabbi. Soon after, he learns that the information about his first wife was false. She was arrested by the Cossacks but freed by the Bolsheviks, and is alive after all. Bound by his vows, Rezanov sails for Russia.

He arrives too late. Now Esther truly *is* deceased; even the great Soviet doctors could not save her from a lethal disease. Back goes Benjamin to Manhattan, hoping to make amends with the pregnant Ruth, who has been supporting herself by working in a sweatshop. She is nowhere to be seen. Shamed and alone, she has given birth far away from the city. On the eve of Yom Kippur she returns to visit her beloved parents and behold! There is Benjamin, armed with the good news: he and his now legitimate wife and baby can live happily ever after.

Schwartz didn't believe his name would be enough to attract an audience. Therefore, in addition to the regulars in his company he hired an established cinema actress to play Ruth. Lila Lee came armed with great credentials. A performer since childhood under the sobriquet Cuddles, Lee had been featured as the servant wench in Cecil B. DeMille's *Male and Female* in 1919, and starred opposite Rudolph Valentino in the bullfight melodrama *Blood and Sand* three years later. It was assumed that she would bring *shiksa* appeal to the production, thereby roping in gentiles as well as Jews. Lee did indeed earn good reviews—the *New York Times* lauded her work, as well as the film's "sincerity" and "restraint." But her affecting turn was not enough to make *Broken Hearts* a hit. The same *Times* critic thought Schwartz the director was too deliberate, too measured in his tempo. And though the *Jewish Theatrical News* had more positive things to say about the film, it found Schwartz the actor devoid of the requisite passion, "listless, a trifle stunned, a wee bit too careful. This is especially noticeable in the love scenes."

Broken Hearts lasted one week in a first-run uptown theater. Nevertheless, it paid dividends for Schwartz. Jaffe was so impressed by his own production that he took a lease on the Folks Theater on Second

Avenue and 12th Street. This, he told the Jewish community of New York, would be the permanent home of Maurice Schwartz's Yiddish Art Theater. The actors, designers, and businessmen moved in, secure for the first time in their lives. In the subsequent months they found much to praise in their boss's attitude and generosity.

The Yiddish Art Theater manager wrote that whenever Schwartz barnstormed he took costumes, electrical equipment, and various props with him. "But he never brought any back to New York. He left them with the local troupes." A designer claimed that Schwartz had "remarkable theatrical instincts." And outside the little company a similar feeling became widespread. Critic John Mason Brown thought that, by and large, American theater had become predictable and vulgar. By contrast, he wrote, the Yiddish Art Theater was "one of the few playhouses in New York that has shown a steady humility in its approach to the theater. It has been untiring and patient in its work. And it has been directed by Maurice Schwartz, one of the few really creative directors that this country knows."

In a feature piece, the *Times* asked, "Would it be perilous to declare that Schwartz has welded players, theme and scenery into monumentally impressive works?" Given this new buzz, *Theater* magazine expressed a renewed interest in the goings-on of Second Avenue, and secured an aisle seat for the Yiddish Art Theater's adaptation of Goldfaden's play *The Tenth Commandment*. The reviewer thought Schwartz "directed with great gusto" and "an intensification more common to Berlin than Broadway." There could have been no higher compliment.

ii

GROUCHO MARX never allowed Irving Berlin to forget about his past—particularly about songs that he had written in the old days, numbers like "Yiddle on Your Fiddle Play Some Ragtime" or "Sadie Salome," about a young lady who takes to the stage, to the distress of her fiancé:

Don't do that dance, I tell you Sadie
That's not a business for a lady!
Most everybody knows
That I'm your loving Mose
Oy, oy, oy, oy
Where is your clothes?

Like many another Jewish youth, the comedian had learned these
tunes by heart, as he and his brothers gathered at the parlor piano. In
the 1930s, Julius Henry Marx sang them at parties. More than once,
the embarrassed Berlin dangled a $100 bill; all Groucho had to do was
just shut up and sit down. If Marx was feeling expansive he took the
money and sang numbers by lesser composers, among them "The
Yiddisha Rag" and "Under the Matzos Tree, A Ghetto Love Song."
These never reached the Hit Parade, but remained great favorites on
the Lower East Side. There were also such self-satiric Western numbers as "Yonkle, the Cow-Boy Jew" and "I'm a Yiddish Cowboy." After
them came songs about assimilation: "It's Tough When Izzy Rosen-
stein Loves Genevieve Malone," followed by a plea to Jewish maidens,
"Marry a Yiddisher Boy."

The subject of anti-Semitism rolled around, and the songsmiths
addressed that as well, giving it an eccentric lilt, as if the whole thing
were some kind of joke. "Since Henry Ford Apologized to Me" was
first recorded by the singing team of Billy Jones and Ernest Hare, better known as the Happiness Boys. They specialized in topical composi-
tions, and this one took off from an incident in the automobile
magnate's long career of Jew-hatred.

Ford owned the *Dearborn Independent,* a Michigan-based newspaper
with small circulation but wide influence. The periodical had always
been home to journalists who were repelled by Jews. One of his
reporters, Patterson James, attended a Jewish vaudeville and quoted an
unnamed "esthetic" companion who "foamed with rage at what he
called Kike race appeals." The *Independent* serialized the bogus *Protocols of
the Elders of Zion,* using it as "proof" that an international Jewish conspiracy was out to control the world's economies.

The series came as no surprise to Ford's inner circle. The old man
had forbidden the use of brass in his factories—he called the amalgam
"a Jew metal." Confronted with his bias, Ford replied that he was "only
trying to awake the Gentile world to an understanding of what is going

on. The Jew is a mere huckster, a trader who doesn't want to produce, but to make something out of what somebody else produces." Several articles followed, accusing some Jewish businessmen of Bolshevism.

One of them decided that enough was enough and sued the industrialist for libel. Months of damning evidence followed until Ford, anxious to avoid a public relations nightmare, ordered his executives to issue an apology in his name. The satiric number followed, performed with heavy Jewish intonations by the gentile team of Jones and Hare. Their record was played to general amusement in the early 1930s:

> *I vos sad and I vos blue,*
> *But now I'm just as good as you*
> *Since Henry Ford apologized to me.*
>
> *That's vhy you threw away*
> *Your little Chevrolet*
> *And bought yourself a Ford coupé?*
>
> *I told the superintendent*
> *That the* Dearborn Independent
> *Doesn't have to hang up vhere it used to be.*
>
> *You're heppy now because he settled hop the case?*
> *Uh-huh, I'm sorry I cut off my nose to spite mine race.*
>
> *Are you glad he changed his point of view?*
> *Yes, I like even Edsel, too*
> *Since Henry Ford apologized to me.*

In the past, this kind of satiric warbling brought a nervous assurance: comedy was the best antidote to bias. Now, as a new presidential administration came in, they felt that politics was the answer. And so began the long and perhaps endless love/hate relationship between American Jewry and Franklin Delano Roosevelt.

The first years saw nothing but uncritical awe. As a group, American Jews had never been happy with the string of Republican presidents— Harding, Coolidge, Hoover—even though a small number of Jewish plutocrats appreciated their pro-business attitudes. The rank and file were under-salaried laborers who needed more in the way of fair work-

ing conditions and a decent paycheck, more in the way of social opportunities for their families. To a great many, the bosses were the enemy,
represented by the GOP. If not directly responsible for the Depression, Hoover and the other leaders of his party had proved indecisive
and callous. Now one third of a nation was ill-clothed and ill-fed and
ill-housed. Roosevelt knew it and he would do something about it. In
this effort he would be aided by brilliant Jews, among them financier
Bernard Baruch, jurist Felix Frankfurter, and Secretary of the Treasury
Henry Morgenthau. Surely FDR was a man to follow into fire, and
from 1932 on the Jewish vote went Democrat and stayed Democrat.

Those in the president's inner circle knew a different figure. Roosevelt's mother, Sara, was a lifelong anti-Semite, and raised her son to
distrust those who, in her term, were NOKD—"not our kind, darling."
Nevertheless, FDR was the very definition of a political animal, and
when he felt that Jewish intelligence was necessary for his administration's "brain trust," he put his biases aside for the good of the nation. It
was only later that his personal feelings came out, and then only in private circumstances. He was heard to say that America "is a Protestant
country, and the Catholics and the Jews are here on sufferance." And
when Adolf Hitler began to move against German Jewry he would
condemn the reichschancellor in speeches, but otherwise offered no
help. To placate the isolationists in and out of his party, he suggested
that Jewish immigrants be "resettled" in Venezuela, Ethiopia, or West
Africa. Allowing them into the United States was out of the question.

None of this news reached the average Jewish citizens. Even if it
had, they would probably have clung to their faith in the leadership of
their country. For both they and the leadership failed to understand
the nature of the new enemy. Early news reports made clear distinctions between the brutalities of the past and present. In the *New York
Evening Post,* the paper's Berlin correspondent left little to the imagination: "Not even in Czarist Russia, with its 'Pale,' have the Jews been
subject to a more violent campaign of murderous agitation. An inde-
terminate number of Jews have been killed. Hundreds of Jews have
been beaten or tortured.

"Thousands of Jews have fled.

"Thousands of Jews have been, or will be, deprived of their liveli-
hood.

"All of Germany's 600,000 Jews are in terror."

Yet at this juncture hardly anyone wanted to deal with the news from

Europe in a realistic manner. Walter Lippmann, the most respected political columnist of the time, called one of Adolf Hitler's speeches "statesmanlike." And when books were burned in a public bonfire in May 1933, he wrote that the persecution of his fellow Jews, "by satisfying the lust of the Nazis who feel they must conquer somebody," was "a kind of lightning rod which protects Europe." Decades after the fact, the executive editor of the *New York Times* acknowledged that "No article about the Jews' plight ever qualified as the *Times's* leading story of the day, or as a major event of a week or year. The ordinary reader of its pages could hardly be blamed for failing to comprehend the enormity of the Nazis' crime."

On the rare occasions when members of the Roosevelt administration criticized the racial policies of Nazi Germany, warnings came from America Firsters—among them the iconic Charles Lindbergh. The aviator was to make a public statement enumerating the troublemakers in the United States. "The three most important groups pressing the country toward war," he warned, "are the British, the Jews, and the Roosevelt administration." In his judgment the Jews were the most dangerous of the trio because of "their large ownership and influence in our motion pictures, our press, our radio and our government."

Moreover, it was not only the see-no-evil journalists and officials who turned away from the obvious. Stephen Wise, then the most prominent rabbi in America, obtained an audience with President Roosevelt. During the interview Wise declared that tourists just back from Germany "tell me that they saw the synagogues were crowded and apparently there is nothing very wrong."

Even blinder than the self-styled authorities were the entertainers, who still insisted that mockery and derision would neutralize hate, no matter how virulent, no matter how local. Picon was typical of her profession. She was fond of describing an incident in Portland, Maine. Fresh from the railroad station, she asked her cabdriver to stop at a rather grand hotel. He turned around and inquired, "Are you Jewish?" Molly chirped, "I've been Jewish for years." The chauffeur got serious: "They won't take you in there, lady. No Jews and no dogs."

She found a more tolerant place and went her own way. She was an autonomous sort, had been since childhood. When she got back to New York, Molly urged her fellow performers to ignore the insults of anti-Semites and find their own place regardless of the hotel owners and the politicians. There was plenty of room for Jews in America, she pointed out; you just had to have a thick skin and an attitude of self-reliance. Her message echoed the subtext of one of Sigmund Freud's favorite anecdotes, related in *Jokes and Their Relation to the Subconscious.*

"Itzig had been declared fit for military service in the artillery. He was clearly an intelligent lad, but intractable and without any interest in the service. One of his superior officers who was kindly disposed toward him took him to one side and said, 'Itzig, you're no use to us. I'll give you a piece of advice: buy yourself a cannon and make yourself independent.' "

The reigning paradox of the moment was that everything depended on independence. The country was trying to make its way out of the Depression. Who had time to worry about the Jews except the Jews themselves? And among the American Jews, who had time to worry about what was going on overseas? True, many an immigrant had relatives who wrote, complaining of racial laws and smashed storefronts. But these were incidents, not a trend. The tribe of Hebrews had outlasted the Egyptians, the Babylonians, the Romans. The Nazis would pass like all the other enemies, and everything would be the way it was.

CHAPTER FOURTEEN

✦

A GIANT MADE OF CLAY

i

CHILDREN OF IMMIGRANTS naturally picked up American habits and spoke the language of their host country. In the 1930s, even the most insular parents and grandparents began to employ a Yiddish peppered with Anglicized words like "allrightnik" and "subvaystop." Maurice Schwartz needed no charts to tell him that the demographics on the Lower East Side were undergoing a drastic change.

The flow of immigrants had become a trickle. Depression or no Depression, the Jews were moving out as fast as they could—uptown and to the outer boroughs. Very well, let them. From now on Schwartz would present two versions of standard Yiddish Theater works, one in the original tongue for the traditionalists, the other in English for the modernists. Up went Israel Joshua Singer's *Yoshe Kalb*. Singer's younger brother, Isaac Bashevis, once spoke of the novel's genesis:

"Father told about a rabbi's son named Moshe Haim Kaminer, who deserted his wife. When the husband, Moshe, came back years later, the people accused him of being someone else, a beggar named Yoshe Kalb who had deserted his own wife, a woman of low origin. A story which is as dramatic as this had to be told in a dramatic way."

I. J. Singer told it with all the flair at his command, resurrecting the departed world of Polish Hasidism, with its violent clashes of fervor and repressed emotion. The book created a furor when it was excerpted in the *Forward*. Schwartz, who recognized an epic when he saw it, quickly came up with a sixty-two-role adaptation. It received the kind of notices producers dream about. When the Yiddish-language rendition was done in the spring of 1933, Charlie Chaplin dropped in; so did Albert Einstein. The elegant *Arts and Decoration* magazine labeled Schwartz's direction and acting "theater at its best." Uptown producer Daniel Frohman said the play offered "a cross-section of life that no Broadway production equals in intensity and originality" and planned to bring an English-language version to Broadway.

Brooks Atkinson, emerging as the *Times*'s most discerning theater critic, filed a long rave: "If *Yoshe Kalb* looks and sounds exhilarating at the Yiddish Art Theater, it is because Jewish actors understand that sort of mystical drama and Jewish audiences are kindled by it." While the Anglo-Saxon stage was preoccupied with musicals and empty chatter, "the Yiddish stage can still tell a full story and invigorate the scenes with pictorial figures. Mr. Schwartz's theater is alive."

Producers, adaptor, and cast naturally assumed that the Frohman production would be a smash. That December, when it debuted, they were traumatized to see notices like the one in the *American*: "Down on Second Avenue this product of Mr. Schwartz's talents was hailed, hallowed and pronounced a classic. Here at the National on 41st St. it is, I fear, simply so much gefilte fish out of water."

Harsher appraisals followed. Though Israel Joshua Singer kept his opinions to himself, Isaac Bashevis Singer grumbled about the presentation. Schwartz, he said, "was by nature a kitsch director or dramamaker. He wanted everything to be like a super-colossal Hollywood production. So he made it more sensational than my brother wanted it to be." The Yiddish Theater production ran for more than three hundred performances; the Broadway one closed after four. Schwartz was not much for lost causes; he returned to the place he knew best, and that knew him best, Second Avenue.

ii

AS THE IMPRESARIO TRIED to reestablish himself in a narrower scope, a new kind of Jewish expression began to work its way from the Yiddish Theater into a wider world. Jacob Adler's daughter Stella had appeared in more than one hundred Yiddish productions, as well as several Broadway plays. Dissatisfied with the kind of acting she saw around her, she joined a new American company called the Group Theater, founded by three young idealists, Harold Clurman, Lee Strasberg, and Cheryl Crawford. Strasberg had been introduced to the world of performance when, as a child, he was taken to see David Kessler—"Clearly an actor of great temperament," he told his colleagues. Clurman recalled his first exposure to theater on the Lower East Side where his father practiced medicine. The actors "were among the best I have ever seen. Most stimulating of all were the audiences. For to the immigrants in the early years of the century, the theater was the one center of social intercourse. Here the problems of their life, past and present, could be given a voice; here they could get to know and understand one another."

Adler immediately felt at home in the Group; so did another young actor, Clifford Odets, who would eventually find his voice as a playwright. Odets's idiom contained the trenchant intonations and inversions of Yiddish: "For myself I don't feel sorry"; "If it rained pearls—who would work?"; "Strong as iron you must be"; "To your dying day you won't change."

An admiring actor said that the young man seemed to have written his scripts with a baseball bat, and he intended it as a compliment.

Waiting for Lefty, Awake and Sing!, Till the Day I Die supplied the galvanic jolt the Group Theater had been seeking, and heralded a new generation of playwrights, mostly Jewish, mostly from the left—Albert Maltz, Samuel Ornitz, and others who would be heard from in New York and later in Hollywood. These writers wanted to express themselves in English, and radical as they were, stayed clear of the Artef—they had too much individuality to be swallowed up by the communist no-headliners approach to theater.

iii

BECAUSE OF THE WRITERS' independent attitude, the struggling Artef found itself without any homegrown talent. The troupe turned to the Soviet Union for *Rekrutn* (Recruits). This play shared the title of the old Goldfaden service farce, but otherwise the two works had nothing in common. The script, adapted by a Bolshevik writer, had a serious intent interspersed with sarcastic asides and musical interludes.

The year is 1828, and the czar has decreed that the *shtetl* of Niebivala ("Anywhere" in Russian) must furnish the army with one of its sons. Aaron Klinger, the richest man in town, argues that this is a good sign—Jews are about to be recognized as citizens. He suggests the man for the role of soldier: Nachmen, a radical, troublemaking tailor, who represents the new spirit of labor agitation. The youth is the sole support of his blind mother, but this means nothing to the capitalist Klinger. Through a series of connivances and subplots, he convinces the town leaders that Nachmen must go, entices the tailor to a place where he thinks his sweetheart is waiting, and hands him over to the Cossacks. In the penultimate scene, Nachmen's mother gropes her way through the streets, crying, "Give me back my son, give me back my son!" That was the way the original play ended, but it would not do for Artef to have such a downbeat finale. An additional scene was tacked on, in which one of the betrayers, consumed with guilt, turns on the townspeople for collaborating with the rich.

Doctrinaire communists gave *Recruits* the backs of their hands; the reviewer of one publication remarked that no one would be prompted to go to the barricades after watching the production, and that revolutionary activity must be the aim of proletarian theater. To do what Artef had done, at a historical moment "seething with class conflict," was a *shanda,* a scandal. This was a time "When every ounce of energy in our cultural front ought to be devoted to the organization of the emotions of the masses in the direction of our ideology, in the direction of a Soviet America—at a time like this taking a leap of 100 years in the past, and in addition offering no more than a beautiful spectacle . . . means going in a false direction."

Outsiders disagreed. They admired the acting, the direction, the scenery, the costumes. Theater people had been fans before this, but *Recruits* attracted bigger names than ever before. One of Artef's historians marveled at the presence of a major producer and two Hollywood stars in the audience. He wondered "whether it was Sam Jaffe or Herman Shumlin or Edward G. Robinson, or all of them, or just a natural concatenation of events which brought the Artef into the high glare of fame. Because they started to pour in—the people from Broadway and the people who had hitherto thought all Yiddish theater was restricted to the carnival noise and glitter of Second Avenue."

By now the Artef had already outlasted most of its detractors. Some, of course, would never forgive the company for its opposition to Zionism, but these were in the minority, drowned out by the cheers from mainstream newspapers and magazines. A reporter from the *World-Telegram* went on about the sets and lighting; he thought they suggested "something out of Rembrandt . . . the necessity of understanding Yiddish as good as disappears while a performance of *Recruits* is under way." The *Daily Mirror* reviewer praised the company's "joyous bawdiness." After attending the Artef play, the *Daily News* critic had bad news for the Yiddish Art Theater: "I came away from the second act with a profound conviction that Maurice Schwartz had better be looking to his laurels, if he is interested in laurels."

iv

IT SO HAPPENED that Schwartz was currently indifferent to laurels. It went without saying that art was first among equals, but what was wrong with fame and money? These last had not been forthcoming after the Broadway failure of *Yoshe Kalb,* and Maurice was forced to look elsewhere for them. Hollywood had shown some interest in Shakespeare following the critical success of *The Taming of the Shrew* with Douglas Fairbanks and Mary Pickford in 1929, and *Romeo and Juliet,* starring Leslie Howard and Norma Shearer, in 1936. It was known that Warner Brothers was exploring the possibility of filming *A Midsummer Night's Dream,* directed by Max Reinhardt. Schwartz got it into his head that he would be an ideal interpreter of the Bard, revising his opinion of Shylock as an anti-Semitic caricature, and fancying himself as an attractive and plausible King Lear.

Negotiations with MGM began. While the agents and executives bickered, the actor/impresario embarked on a European tour. He left his troupe behind, and they carried on in his name with a hastily assembled theater company called the Yiddish Ensemble Art Theater. The troupe had big plans: a classic Yiddish tale had been working its way, yet again, into the public consciousness, and the members voted to bring it to the stage.

In the Middle Ages, when anti-Semitic scourges were fevered and sadistic, a legend gained wide circulation among the Jews. *The Golem,* a fantasy that took literary form in the seventeenth century, told the story of a giant made of clay and brought to life by fervent prayers and mysterious rites. These were conducted by one Rabbi Loew of Prague, who had come upon the secret of the *Shem-ha-Meforash,* the hitherto undiscovered and therefore unutterable name of God.

Loew's intimidating, nonhuman monster rose up from the ground to become a protector of defenseless Hebrews, keeping their enemies at bay by the use of force. Plots against the Jews were continually foiled by the Golem; in one of the most typical, he overhears evildoers planning to hide bottles of blood in the synagogue before Passover. They intend to plant a child's corpse in the temple, "evidence" that the Jews employ Christian blood in the baking of their matzohs. Thanks to the giant, the plotters are revealed and killed.

The Golem's power is uncontrolled and uncontrollable, however; as time goes on, he destroys as much as he protects. In the end, the Jews have to acknowledge that the creation of life is not the province of man—even a holy man. Rueful and chastened, Rabbi Loew breaks down what he had made, lest the Jews be cursed by God for trespassing into His territory.

In outline, the tale was not dissimilar to the story of Mary Shelley's *Frankenstein,* written 150 years later. The essential difference lay in the subtext. Shelley's version implied a criticism of science without conscience and experimenters without ethics. The Czech story had no such lofty aims in mind; it was simply the consoling wish-dream of a tormented people.

The Golem was to have many resurrections over the years, surfacing whenever there were pogroms or blood libels against the Jews. Leivick Halper, who later assumed the nom de plume H. Leivick, wrote the Yiddish version that seized the imagination of theater directors and filmmakers. For him the Golem had a very personal meaning. In 1895, when he was seven, he strolled to *cheder*—Hebrew school. "I passed a large market square," he remembered, "and turned off into the street on which stood the Polish church. As I passed the church entrance a tall burly Pole bounded over to me, slammed his fist across my head, tore my hat off and threw both it and me to the frosty ground. He beat me, shouting, 'Dirty Jew! When you pass our church you have to take your hat off! You dirty Jew!' I got up with difficulty, grabbed my hat from the ground, and ran off to *cheder* in tears. My heart cried out within me: Why did that big Pole beat me, a child of seven years? And why is it that when he, a gentile, passes a synagogue, no one makes him put *on* a hat?"

Leivick's experience was echoed by thousands, if not hundreds of thousands, of Jews at that period. It would have been abnormal for them not to imagine scenarios of revenge. Some twenty years later, the playwright gave form to their feelings. To the traditional materials of the Rabbi, the clay monster, and the malefactor Taddeus and the monk who serves as his henchman, he introduced his own flourishes. Jesus makes an appearance in the free-verse drama; so does Elijah.

What emerged, notes Leivick's translator, Joseph C. Landis, was "far more than a play about an incident in Jewish history. It is a play in which the Jews become symbolic of a mankind suffering innocently, suffering in spite of its innocence, suffering *because* of its innocence." *The Golem* is "not only a philosophical morality play; it is also a political parable about the relationship of ends and means in which the figure of Force, the Golem, reveals the dangers inherent in violence."

The subject was a natural for cinema, and in 1920 a grave, overacted German version appeared, with the monster galumphing through the flickering twilight. In the mid-1930s a French company offered a subtler version. But it was on the Yiddish stage that the Golem made the deepest impression. Hershel Zohn, who was in the ill-fated Broadway company of *Yoshe Kalb,* recalled the ensemble's production of *The Golem* as "a great cultural event. The German director Egon Brecher was engaged. A guest artist from Europe, Alexander Granach, was brought over to portray the unusual character of the Golem. The rehearsals, one recalls, were most exciting. So were the performances."

But only up to a point. One weekend, an hour before the Saturday matinee curtain was due to rise, the stage manager reported that Granach was not in his dressing room, nor was he at his rented apartment. No one knew where he was. Backstage hysteria, so much a part of Boris Thomashefsky's time, was assumed to be a thing of the past. Not so. Granach, it came out, had been pining for a lost love. The reason he was not in his dressing room was that he was on the Atlantic Ocean, headed back to his European amour without so much as a note to his colleagues.

An oversize actor, Avigidor Packer, took over the difficult role at the last minute and brought it off. The reviews were uniformly good—and yet not one of them discussed the very obvious parallels between the sorrows of seventeenth-century Jewry and the fate of its twentieth-century descendants. The reason had been stated three hundred years before by the French duke François de La Rochefoucauld (a real-life contemporary of the Golem): "*La soleil ni la mort ne se peuvent regarde fixement.*"—Neither the sun nor death can be looked at with a steady eye.

v

IN THE FIRST ACT of *The Golem,* the Rabbi of Prague addresses "Joseph," the bewildered creature he has just created. A tragic blood libel has circulated, along with planted "evidence" that the Jews use Christian blood to make their matzohs. The entire ghetto appears to be doomed. The Golem is ordered to "see through walls and floors and into the hearts of those that would destroy us."

Empowered by Kabalistic magic, Joseph Golem slays one of the conniving enemies with his ax. Outraged, an anti-Semitic mob marches on the neighborhood ghetto. One by one the monster cuts them down. But after his vengeful triumph, a second tragedy occurs. All the Golem knows is violence and destruction, and even his attempts at tenderness turn lethal. After the battle he finds himself alone with the Rabbi's beautiful daughter, Devorale. Aroused, confused, he burbles uncontrollably:

GOLEM: We could twine together into one
And huddle in the covering of emptiness.
And I would open my eyes and see
The wind shredding your garments into tatters,
The lightning laying bare the whiteness of your skin,
The emptiness overflowing with your warmth:
And I would bite into your limbs
And suck your white flesh into myself—

DEVORALE (*Striking his shoulder*): No—stop it—Don't speak to me this way—!

(*He attempts to embrace her. She struggles to liberate herself from his grasp, but each attempt leaves her weaker until finally she slumps in his arms, suffocated.*)

Guilty and bewildered, the Golem heads for the synagogue, ax in hand. The Jews who try to stop him are felled by his blows. Burdened with guilt, the Rabbi addresses heaven:

RABBI (*Addressing heaven*): I refused your faith and your commandment that
WE MUST WAIT AND SUFFER AND ENDURE.

(*There is but one solution open to him. With special words and movements he returns the monster to the clay from which he came. Choking, Joseph Golem whispers his last words.*)

GOLEM: Do not forsake me . . .

RABBI: Not a living soul? Perhaps.
Death and murder were his birthright.
And now they are ours.
As Abraham built an altar to offer up his son,
So we shall have to build
A thousand altars before we're done.

(*As kaddish, the prayer for the dead, is recited, an old man enters cradling the body of Devorale in his arms. He and she remain in the shadows, unseen by the others as the Rabbi shouts in anguish.*)

OLD MAN: Who will save us?

(*All slowly turn to look but before they can see the awful sight, the stage lights are extinguished. The final curtain is lowered in total darkness.*)

In the introduction to his modernized version of *The Golem*, playwright David Fishelson speaks of "the anguish that comes of fighting fire with fire." He quotes the agonized demand of the character who confronts the Rabbi: "Won't those who lift the sword fare worse? In doing so won't they lose their share of the world to come?" The Rabbi's equally distraught reply: "Whether in this world or the next: There may be no tomorrow for Jews who meekly lay their heads on the block." The drama of the Golem lasted on the boards for nearly three months. The entreaty "*Who will save us?*" was shortly to be amplified. The answer would remain eternally elusive.

CHAPTER FIFTEEN

✦

TOTAL, UNQUESTIONED
CHUTZPAH

i

JOSEPH BULOFF HAD COVERED a considerable distance since his days with Schwartz's players. He had not only acted in a troupe visiting from Vilna, he also turned his hand to directing. Artef hired him to lead its performers in a Leivick play called *Keytn* (Chains). The realistic drama charted the sorrows of political prisoners behind bars in czarist Siberia. One of them, Levinai, is an *homme engagé* who organizes a violent plan of escape. The march to the barricades is turned back by the guards. Undiscouraged, he plans a larger uprising. Dissent breaks out, and Levinai ruthlessly suppresses anyone who dares to oppose him, even betraying former comrades who waste time and energy in fruitless debates, delaying action and weakening morale. The organizer eventually gets what he wants, but the prison-wide clash amounts to mass suicide—the well-equipped czar's troops outnumber the prisoners six to one. Levinai survives and makes no excuses when the Cossacks put him in chains. Proudly he marches to his fate: death before a firing squad. He is the first martyr of the Bolshevik Revolution to come.

To the communists *Keytn* was red meat in every sense. The trouble was that Buloff believed in the primacy of the actor and the credibility of the text. That was all very well with the uptown critics who lauded the production and hailed Buloff as a "director of genius." The *Daily Worker,* the communist newspaper, disagreed. "The acting," it said, "lacks that community of playing that has always distinguished the Artef. There is too little of the ensemble, too much of the individual." In other words, the Buloff version failed to glorify the masses, and committed the sin of stating that political movements may be comprised of vastly differing personalities and temperaments.

He moved on to another company, the New York Art Troupe. Its most audacious production was an adaptation of *The Trial,* by the late and still obscure Czech writer Franz Kafka. Audiences scarcely knew what to make of the story. What kind of drama was that—a man whose crime was unspecified, yet whose guilt was a foregone conclusion? At the end of the 1936 season, the Art Troupe went out of business—just in time for Maurice Schwartz to reenter the scene, fresh from his last European tour. For the season of 1938, he produced a play about an assimilated Frenchman who turns back to his Jewish roots when the fever of anti-Semitism reaches his city. The playwright, Jacques Berson, was unavailable for interviews; evidently he had remained in France. Later it was discovered that he did not exist. Berson was one of Schwartz's many noms de plume.

The next season Schwartz ventured uptown again with a new all-Yiddish company. They played at the Venice Theater at Columbus Circle, a place where Al Jolson had capered for many years. I. J. Singer's *The Brothers Ashkenazi* was his production of choice. This panorama told the story of a patriarch and his twin sons in Lodz, Poland, scrambling for recognition and material success. The Ashkenazi family experiences the benefits, and the soul-destroying aspects, of the industrial revolution. Later its members deal with the rise of capitalism, the advent of communism, the ravages of the Great War. At no time are they untroubled, because whenever Poland is devastated by events, the Jewish community always suffers the blame.

Singer offers a despairing view of the future, as if he had some premonitory sense of the Holocaust to come. Schwartz related the tale as faithfully as he could, with more than twenty of the actors doubling and tripling in their parts. Naturally, he played one of the principal roles, prompting a story to go around: a friend of the impresario overhears someone accusing him of monopolizing all the best roles, and gets defensive. "On the contrary, Mr. Schwartz has been exceedingly generous with leading parts. Take, for example, *The Brothers Ashkenazi.* Did he play both brothers?"

In the beginning the spectacle attracted large audiences. A second wave came and applauded—and then, suddenly, attendance dwindled to half-filled houses. A postmortem showed that the patrons of Yiddish art theaters had been expecting several plays per season, not just one. They didn't mind attending *Brothers* twice; there was no way to take it all in at once. But the second time around they noticed severe flaws. Schwartz had allowed his cast to settle into the roles much too comfortably. Speeches had become flat, and movements mechanical.

In addition, as one actor put it, Schwartz had made a grave error at the outset, when he "attempted to satisfy with one and the same play people of different political philosophies." In short, there was no way he could make the communists happy merely by showing a few revolutionaries bearing red flags onstage, and no way he could stimulate tired businessmen with a melancholy pageant, no matter how loud or flagrantly illuminated.

Schwartz was never one to acknowledge a mistake; he merely gave out the word that next season there would be an entire repertory of plays—four at the bare minimum. But what plays? Maurice was of two minds about Sholem Asch: he was probably the best-known Yiddish writer, but he was also the most controversial one. Asch was known to be attracted to the utterances of Jesus, for example, though he had never converted to Christianity. As for his most talked about powerful drama, *God of Vengeance,* it had gotten a lot of people in trouble when it was staged on Broadway fifteen years before.

The drama concerned a Jewish brothel keeper in America. Yankel

Chapchovich lives upstairs over the whorehouse he operates, convinced that he can literally raise his pretty daughter Rivkele above it all, keeping her chaste and observant. Translator Joseph C. Landis observes that "Like Jay Gatsby he seems to have remained strangely uncontaminated by the evil of the world in which he moves and with which he deals." And, like Gatsby, Yankel is undone by his own illusions.

Rivkele becomes a wanton lesbian, and her father's bitter acknowledgment shocked audiences when the play was first performed on Broadway back in 1923. Addressing a prospective in-law:

> YANKEL: I have a virginal Jewish daughter. (*He goes into Rivkele's room and drags her out by the arm. She is half undressed, her hair disheveled.*) A virginal Jewish maiden will be marrying your son. She'll bear chaste Jewish children, like any other Jewish girl. Isn't that so? (*Laughs wildly*) Yes, indeed, my friend, she'll be a chaste Jewish wife. My wife will lead her to the wedding canopy . . . down to the whorehouse! Downstairs! To the house! (*He drags Rivkele to the door by her long tresses.*) Down to the house!

References to sapphism, the explicit candor of the whores' dialogue, and the unhappy ending were enough to rouse the authorities. New York City police shut down *God of Vengeance* for "immorality," and some of the actors spent a night in jail. The playwright was accused of indecency and anti-Semitism. Asch's defense was the terse self-appraisal "I am not a Jewish artist, I am a universal artist," which failed to placate his accusers. The drama never reopened. Still, that was almost a generation before, and it had been staged uptown, where the censors were tougher.

Surely it could be performed in Yiddish now, in these enlightened times. Then again, maybe not. In the end, cold feet prevailed and another Asch project was chosen. Strictly speaking, *Three Cities* was not a play at all. It was a triptych of novels centering on the Russian Jewish experience of the late nineteenth and early twentieth centuries. The three cities are Warsaw, St. Petersburg, and Moscow. Within his works Asch includes the Hasidic villages, the fatal insensitivities of the Russian upper classes, the internecine strife within the White and Red armies on the eve of the Revolution, the plain folk and aristocrats, everyone vainly attempting to keep up with events.

As Asch scholar Ben Siegel observes, "they scurry often, for fate, in the guise of the Russian Revolution, cuts across all personal goals and pleasures to render them virtually helpless by a rapid succession of blows. Inevitably, character and plot soon diminish." In short, it was just the sort of epic Schwartz loved to bring to the Yiddish stage: Cecil B. DeMille writ small. He hired a large group of actors, convinced Jacob Ben-Ami to star, and worked out a stage adaptation, battling Sholem Asch—or more accurately, Asch's wife, Matilda—at every turn.

Recollecting that time, Schwartz complained, "What trouble with Mrs. Asch! I had worked out a magnificent finish—75 people and a projection of five hundred more. What a finale!" But Mrs. Asch pointed out that the novel had no such conclusion—it ended quietly and on a small scale. Schwartz pleaded with the author, but "he said he was helpless and would not fight with his wife." On opening night the grand penultimate scene was greeted with cheers. Then came an anticlimactic coda. "The day after the opening," Schwartz bitterly recalled, "the English language press said, 'At 11:10 last night, Schwartz met his Waterloo at the Jolson Theater.' "

The later reception was even worse. The *North American Review* described Schwartz as a pseudo-artist who seemed to have "everything there is to make the usual great big Hollywood director and adaptor. He can't write, he has the taste of a haberdashery salesman, and his notion of the perfect performer is the loud speaker." All of Schwartz's productions were two-dimensional processions, and *Three Cities* was more of the same, "a lowly comic strip conception of the sufferings of the Jews in Eastern Europe. Lacking in dignity, devoid of dramatic unity, burdened with Mr. Schwartz's vulgar direction, it leaves one wondering what has happened to the Yiddish Theater of such first-rate actors as Paul Muni, the Adlers and Jacob Ben-Ami." The latter was "made by Mr. Schwartz to act the part of a lover of his fiancée's mother. In one scene he shrieks out his love and grapples with the matronly lady of his heart in the same style that the heroes of the older films used to lasso a mustang."

ii

EDGAR GEORGE ULMER, set designer for the 1920 version of *The Golem,* had come to America with big plans back in 1923. With a combination of persuasive patter and genuine, if limited, talent, he talked himself into jobs at Universal Studios in Hollywood as a production assistant and art director. In the 1920s and 1930s he worked with such future luminaries as Billy Wilder and Fred Zinnemann. In 1934 he made an outstanding horror feature, *The Black Cat,* starring Boris Karloff and Bela Lugosi, and later he directed several film noirs. On a visit to New York, Ulmer attended several Yiddish Theater productions and became aware of "a second Broadway down there." Cognizant of the large Jewish audiences in Manhattan and the outer boroughs, Ulmer guessed that there were Yiddish-speaking viewers all across America thirsting for a well-made movie. Sooner or later somebody would provide one, he reasoned; why not me, and why not now, in 1937? His choice was *Grine Felder* (Green Fields), a kind of folktale by Peretz Hirschbein.

This was an unusual choice; then again, Ulmer was an unusual man. Although the moviemaker was born a Jew, his parents had sent him to a Jesuit school in Vienna. He knew no Yiddish. He needed help in casting, in understanding the script, in communicating with the actors. To that end Ulmer hired Jacob Ben-Ami to co-direct and aid with the casting—some performers from the Yiddish Art Theater, some from Artef, and not a bona fide star among them. From the beginning the two men were uncomfortable with each other, but they agreed on one thing: *Grine Felder* was going to take the high road. "I'm not going to do what Schwartz does," declared Ulmer. "I'm not going to do the cheap things which Picon does. I'm going to have my own style and I'm going to do it like I see it—dignified, not dirty—not with beards where they look like madmen. The same decision which Sholem Asch made, which Chagall made."

Like most of Peretz Hirschbein's dramas, *Grine Felder* looked back to his childhood in rural Lithuania. The Jews of that area led the severe, fundamental lives of farmers everywhere, and the budding author couldn't get away from them fast enough. In time, though, he came to regard those simple people as the true practitioners of *mentchlekhkayt,* the abiding moral obligation to one's family and neighbors. They were the last believers in the literal message of the Torah—that in the near future, the Messiah would arrive to deliver the Jews from injustice and deprivation, as promised in the scriptures. That trust in Holy Writ gave them a purity of faith undisturbed by circumstance or self-pity.

The romantic view of rural life is a Russian credo; in the nineteenth century Tolstoy made it a cornerstone of his art. But his was a Christian interpretation, and no comparable voice existed for the Jews. All they had was Baron Maurice de Hirsch. The German philanthropist believed that peasants were not only a repository of goodness, they were a solution to the age-old Jewish Problem. He issued a series of grants "to give a portion of my companions in faith the possibility of finding a new existence, primarily as agricultural workers, and also as handicraftsmen." His warm statement was tinctured with more pragmatic considerations. "All our misfortunes come from the fact that the Jews want to climb too high," the baron confided privately. "We have too much brains. My intention is to restrain the Jews from pushing ahead. They shouldn't make such great progress. All the hatred against us stems from this."

Grine Felder crystallized those sentiments in a tender, Chekhovian manner, following a young rabbinical student, Levi Yitzchok, on a trek through the countryside. Levi encounters two semiliterate Jewish farming families—lowest on the social ladder, disdained by the townspeople who are better educated and possess more marketable skills. Both families have young daughters. Predictably, the girls compete for this most eligible bachelor. But Levi is uncomfortable with each of them. "It's not my real life here. Here I don't have any holy books. I don't have the things I need. I miss the voices of the scholars in the study house early every morning. I miss the light in the faces of the pious Jews. It's for the sake of their merits that the world exists."

Over the course of the summer, he learns that piety can be found in places other than the synagogue. In a poem H. Leivick described the Milky Way: "God's sweet scent still rides around the sun," and that was the feeling conveyed by the play. God's sweet scent can also be found below, in the country—in a heightened sense of the green crops, of the radiant illuminations on the hills, the tilled soil, the domestic animals, the steady, honorable, sunrise-to-sunset labor. Levi comes to realize that intellect alone cannot sustain him. A phrase from the Torah occurs to him: "A man without land is not a man. Heaven is the Lord's heaven and he has given the earth unto man." At the denouement the visitor speaks with Dovid-Noich, father of the barefoot farmgirl Tzineh, the most spirited of the young women.

DOVID: My father, rest in peace, was a farmer, too. Didn't know how to train the children. How could he? Barely learned to read Hebrew. He died in my house. I took him into town, and I didn't want to leave town. That must be how our Father in Heaven wanted it, that some of us live far from Jews. Just so we're buried among Jews. Can't be helped. So it goes. . . . I'd like to say: don't go away. Let things remain as they are.

LEVI: I'm not going away, Dovid-Noich. I was getting ready to tell you that maybe you should think it over.

DOVID: What is there to think over? I have nothing to think over.

LEVI: I mean whether to take me as a son-in-law. That's what I mean.

Won over by the land, smitten by Tzineh, Levi abandons his city life to marry into the farming community, setting up as a teacher. The female rival for his hand is disappointed, but all turns out well—this is, after all, a rustic romance as well as a commentary on the dignity of labor.

The play had gone over very well in the 1920s. Ten years later, as history closed in, Hirschbein's celebration of the simple life exerted a different appeal. As historian Nahma Sandrow observes, when *Grine Felder* was first presented there was no suggestion of the poverty and dislocations that occurred in the wake of World War I. The world that so enchants Dovid seemed "a faraway paradise to émigrés and even to people who stayed home. There is no anti-Semitism. The subtext is nostalgia for a lost homeland and a lost innocence." The longing was so powerful that in 1936, when Ulmer began working on the film version, the management of three Yiddish newspapers, the *Forward, Der Tag,* and the *Freiheit,* asked for an exclusive piece of the action.

Ulmer shrewdly turned them all down; he knew if one paper was allowed to back the movie, the others would have it panned upon release. He cobbled together a small bank loan, plus cash from Paul Muni and some lesser performers. Over $10,000 came in—or so the director claimed. In any case, it was enough to get the cameras rolling in the farm fields of New Jersey.

After Ben-Ami explained each scene to the cast, Ulmer took over. Recalled Helen Beverly, the ingénue of *Grine Felder,* "we were standing in a straight line in front of the little hut as actors do sometimes on the stage, facing the audience, and we were doing our parts, and Ulmer stopped us: 'No, no, no, no, no! You can't do that in front of a camera.' Then he explained the whole business of close-ups and detail shots, and how you didn't have to face the camera. You were to behave perfectly natural, and the camera would look for you to shoot you."

Herschel Bernardi, who played Tzineh's amusing thirteen-year-old brother, called the director "a school unto himself. Acting I was taught by my parents. But film making was something else entirely. Over the course of a few weeks with Ulmer I learned more than college kids do in four years." When the director wasn't moving his actors around, he was busy squeezing the budget to get the most out of every dollar. He himself took a salary of only $300, and to save money he used only one horse. The animal's front end was shown working at one place; when the scene changed to another farm, only his tail-twitching rear end was pictured.

To the surprise of some crew members, what could have been an unintentionally comic disaster turned out to be a minor classic. Though Ulmer was more at home in the film noir genre, he knew how to expand Hirschbein's script with a series of moody, evocative scenes. Manifestly, the earth, sun, and sky are intended to be members of the cast, and the phosphorescent trees and grass plains to take on a religious significance. Ulmer was no intellectual, but the Jesuits had educated him well; he was familiar with Spinoza's view of God as immanent in nature. What he showed on-screen illustrated that philosophy far more effectively than many a textbook—and, for that matter, many an ambitious and high-minded theater piece.

Beyond its obvious intent, *Grine Felder* had an unspoken purpose. In the mid-1930s the phrase "the dignity of labor" was not a bromide. It signified the epic struggle between workingmen and their bosses, between the unions and the soulless corporations. That struggle could be seen and heard all over American popular culture, much of it influenced by Jewish writers and composers.

The song "Brother, Can You Spare a Dime?," by Jay Gorney and E. Y. Harburg, had been written for a Broadway flop, *New Americana.* But two days after the show closed, Bing Crosby recorded the anthem of the workingman's predicament. Within weeks it was number one on the charts, its message strongly reminiscent of the editorials in the socialist *Forward,* its minor-key melody reminiscent of the Yiddish Theater's melancholy ballads:

> *Once I built a railroad, I made it run,*
> *Made it race against time.*
> *Once I built a railroad; now it's done.*
> *Brother, can you spare a dime?*

On Broadway, Harold Rome's score brightened the 1937 production of *Pins and Needles,* a satirical revue backed by the International Ladies Garment Workers Union. One number, "Mene, Mene, Tekel," told the story of Daniel with gospel music and Yiddish words. In another, a Jewish shop steward pled his case with a tongue-in-cheek ballad:

> *I'm on a campaign to make you mine.*
> *I'll picket you until you sign,*
> *In one big union for two*
> *No courts and injunction can make me stop*
> *Until your love is all closed-shop*
> *In one big union for two.*

Hollywood followed their lead, featuring the downtrodden as the protagonists of their new melodramas. *Dead End* pointed to slums as a breeding ground for criminals; in *My Man Godfrey,* a servant had more dignity than his snooty employers; in *Marked Woman,* a courageous hostess went up against the gangsters (read strikers vs. scabs) at the risk of her personal safety. High on the bestseller list were Ernest Hemingway's *To Have and Have Not,* whose protagonist was a maimed boat captain fighting the spoiled and murderous rich, and John Steinbeck's *In*

Dubious Battle, which concerned itinerant workers and the bosses who took advantage of their desperate situation.

Grine Felder floated on this current. The film opened at the Squire Theater in midtown Manhattan in October 1937, and immediately became a critical and popular hit. Said Ulmer, "The Jews came into the theater in the morning and wouldn't get out! We had to turn the lights on and plead with them to please leave the theater so other people could see the picture! Impossible. We had to stop the performance and empty the house with the police."

This time around the critics were led by the community. A reviewer for one Yiddish paper compared *Grine Felder* with the best movies from France, Czechoslovakia, or Hungary and said it signaled "the beginning of a new epoch in American-made Yiddish movies." Because the film had opened in a house known for its left-wing programs, the *Daily Worker* hailed *Grine Felder* as a film that "carries one back with it into the past of Russia, when Jews lived in the Pale and had to fight for knowledge, before the days of liberty and Soviets."

For left-wing Jews as for traditional ones, the past had abruptly become fashionable. Even in Berlin, where the Nazis were closing in, the Jewish Museum turned its back on current events to stage a major exhibit about the fifteenth-century Grand Rabbi of Posen. And shortly afterward, a happy Jewish song made the rounds in Germany, sung by government officials and storekeepers, just as if everything was as normal as crullers and Wiener schnitzel.

iii

THE TUNE had been written by Sholem Secunda, an experienced composer and conductor of Second Avenue musicals and operettas. He was also known as a hard-luck figure because early on in his career he had met George Gershwin at the behest of Boris Thomashefsky. The star needed a personal composer for some operettas he planned to write; Boris judged the young Gershwin "too much American and too little Jew," but thought he might work in tandem with an experienced talent like Sholem. After all, the man had already written several Yiddish Theater scores. On an upright in Thomashefsky's dressing room the older composer listened to Gershwin play a few of his own songs. Secunda shook his head; a partnership would be out of the question: "The two of us are no pair," he told his host. "We have totally different approaches to music." Gershwin went on to worldwide eminence, and whenever he ran into Secunda delighted in offering his hand and booming, "Sholem's the one I owe my present position to in the musical world. If he had agreed to become my partner, I would now be a composer in the Yiddish Theater."

Secunda was about to suffer his second hard-luck incident. By the late 1930s several of his melodies, with lyrics by the Yiddish actor/lyricist Jacob Jacobs, had become Second Avenue favorites. In the judgment of many fans, the minor-key "Bei Mir Bist Du Schoen" (To Me You Are Beautiful) was the best of them all. Eddie Cantor refused to go along. The stage, film, and radio personality listened to "Bei Mir," declared that he loved Secunda's music, but added, "I can't use it. It's too Jewish." Two black singers disagreed with his verdict. The duo billed as Johnny and George had heard the song during their tour of Catskill resorts. They learned the words phonetically, and included "Bei Mir" in their act at the Apollo Theater on 125th Street. Tin Pan Alley lyricist Sammy Cahn happened to be in the audience during their run and marked the reaction of the Harlem audience. "The theater began to undulate," he remembered. "The beat absolutely caught hold of you." Intrigued, Cahn purchased a copy of the sheet music, brought in a collaborator, Saul Chaplin, and together the two supplied the song with an English translation. Cahn then arranged for a young close-harmony trio, the Andrews Sisters, to make a recording—all without bothering to acquire the rights to Secunda's song. "Total, unquestioned chutzpah," he later confessed.

Cahn was in luck. Discouraged by Cantor's turndown, the composer and his lyricist had already peddled "Bei Mir" to their publisher for $30. The royalties now belonged to the J. and J. Kammen Music Company. Cahn and Chaplin bought the rights. Promoted by Decca Records, the song rose to the top of the charts, followed by recordings by bandleader Guy Lombardo and Benny Goodman as well as by singers as dissimilar as Nelson Eddy and Judy Garland. In a biography of her father-in-law, Victoria Secunda reports that the Andrews Sisters disk sold a quarter million records in two months—the first Yiddish song to have made the leap from Second Avenue to the Hit Parade. The rhymes resounded from radios, storefronts, and parlors:

> *Bei Mir Bist Du Schoen, please let me explain,*
> *Bei Mir Bist Du Schoen means that you're grand.*
> *Bei Mir Bist Du Schoen, again I'll explain,*
> *It means you're the fairest in the land.*
>
> *I could say "Bella, bella," even say "Vunderbar,"*
> *Each language only helps me tell you how grand you are . . .*

Business was so good at the Gaiety Music Shop on Broadway that people crowded in front of the store's clerk, gave him 50 cents, and he handed them a rolled-up copy of the sheet music to "Bei Mir," all without exchanging a word. People unfamiliar with Yiddish would ask for copies of "Buy a Beer, Mr. Shane," or "My Mere Bits of Shame." Translations came out in dozens of foreign languages, including a contraband version in Russian. In Adolf Hitler's *Deutschland* the song caught on immediately. It took some time to discover that the composer and lyricist were Jewish. After that it was banned.

Much was made about the fact that Secunda had been cheated out of a big payday. On radio he appeared with the Andrews Sisters, was interviewed about his unfortunate sale of the song for $30, and was then allowed to conduct the orchestra in a rendition of a new Secunda tune, "Dream of Me." In addition to his fee for appearing on the *Wrigley Chewing Gum Hour,* he was paid for appearing in a Wrigley ad alongside the Sisters. "How ironic," he wrote bitterly, "that I am getting a lot more money for letting myself be photographed than I am for composing the song." In public, however, he put on a face of good sportsmanship. The *New York Post* stated that the composer "isn't worried about the profits. He's a gentle musical soul, free of greed and overweening ambition. He's glad he has a steady job." The job was with Maurice Schwartz's Yiddish Art Theater, though "steady" was not quite accurate.

CHAPTER SIXTEEN

✦

A LOW DISHONEST DECADE

i

I N 1938 MAURICE SCHWARTZ received some more bad news. MGM had decided to leave Shakespeare to other studios and concentrate on less lofty scenarios. Translation: the Yiddish actor was unwelcome on the soundstages of Hollywood. Meantime, the patrons of Second Avenue seemed to be headed away from the legitimate theater and toward the movie palaces. Were large, loud celluloid images to be the way of the future? Was Schwartz, who had done so much for the Yiddish Theater, to be left onstage, gesturing to half-empty houses?

He retreated to the Café Royal, where he could ask those questions of devoted listeners and fans.

On the Lower East Side, politicians and radicals gathered at the Monopole. The main topic of discussion was the Popular Front, an attempt by communists to enlist liberals to join Russia in the fight against fascism. Aesthetes and *luftmensch,* talkers who would rather bombinate than write or paint, hung out at Goodman and Levine's. But for Yiddish showfolk, as well as those who hoped for a glimpse of their favorites, the Royal was the epicenter. In her autobiography, *Bronx Primitive,* Kate Simon remembered the day she was taken to the café as a child. The place was "dazzlingly lit, as noisy as a market and as brilliantly, gaudily colored as a Gypsy camp." She recognized several of the actresses, all of them in full stage makeup: "One famous tragedienne wore a tall, blaring-red turban; another, with heavily kohl-circled eyes, sported a yellowed ermine capelet, her hands buried in its matching Anna Karenina muff."

Agents and producers located their official headquarters in midtown, but the real negotiations took place within the walls of the Royal. "What didn't get spoken or rumored or kicked around there didn't count," said playwright Oscar Leonard, whose family had been involved in Yiddish Theater productions since the Goldfaden days. "The place was open all night and all day. It never closed. You could always find actors as you walked in, sitting to your right, posturing and gossiping. The writers were seated on your left, scribbling and gossiping. The musicians sat in the rear, humming and gossiping. In a back room pinochle was played in an atmosphere of smoke and intrigue. The place wasn't officially segregated, it's just the way things sorted themselves out."

Stars and hams alike, he remembered, would strut in wearing black capes and nodding to their *patriotn.* "One comedian, a Romanian named Aaron Lebedeff, had enormous energy and comic timing. He also had an ego you couldn't fit into the Coliseum. He loved to enter wearing a blue suit, white hat, white spats, and an unbuttoned cashmere overcoat around his shoulders. You could hear the murmurs of appreciation a block away. There were also actors who aspired to his status. They would pay the waiters to summon them to the telephone so their names would be called aloud, like celebrities in a Hollywood restaurant."

The most important of those employees was the headwaiter. Herman was bowlegged and cross-eyed and the odor of garlic wafted from him. No one seemed to mind; he functioned as a counselor to his celebrated customers. They considered his instincts well nigh infallible. When he refused to invest in a show, they knew they had better back away from it. When he agreed to come in, they were pretty sure they had a hit on their hands. According to actor Joseph Schildkraut, "Often it was with thanks only to his financial investment that a new production could reach the stage."

Schwartz had very little luck with Herman. Every time he brought up the subject of a new show, the name of Boris Thomashefsky arose. Boris was rarely in evidence these days, and Schwartz wanted to know why. The only answer he got was a sad shaking of heads, and a Yiddish saying: *A knoyl hot oykh en ek*—The biggest ball of twine unwinds. Boris had been the undisputed King of Second Avenue, America's Darling, a *mensch*. A scenery chewer, of course, an egomaniac; but the vitality of the man, the drive, the will to power! What could have happened to him?

Some had one tale, some another. Scandals, theatrical failures, women. It took a while for Schwartz to put the pieces together. Boris and Bessie had divorced after a long and difficult marriage, and in the early 1930s each had published excerpts from their autobiographies in rival newspapers. By then Boris had a storehouse of memories, but not much of a future. He had spent all he had earned over the years, the money ceded in legal settlements with his ex-wife, or frittered away, or given away by a man who was always generous to those down on their luck. He had sold the estate in the Catskills and the house in Brooklyn and moved back to a small apartment on the Lower East Side. More skilled performers had passed him by; younger audiences scarcely knew who he was.

He had tried Broadway one last time, in a play called *The Singing Rabbi*. It lasted one week. Who cares? Boris said; he had seen hard times before. He took a new wife, the young actress Rebecca Zuckerberg, and early in 1938 appeared with her at the Public Theater in a play of his own devising. An exercise in nostalgia and desperation, *Boris and Bessie* starred Boris as himself, and Rebecca as Bessie. They performed it three times a night at an open-air cabaret, interrupted from time to time by the roar of the Second Avenue elevated train.

Long ago Herman had stopped putting his money in Thomashefsky shows. Disconsolate, in precarious health, Boris cadged meals and spoke of big plans. It was said that his weight had ballooned to 230 pounds. The man was never slender, but at seventy he seemed unable to move without difficulty. This was no longer the star who attracted young females, or for that matter, old ones. Nevertheless he plotted and planned all spring and into the early summer. Then, as the hot weather became oppressive, he stopped showing up at the café. On July 9, 1939, complaining of a vague illness and pains in his chest, he took to his bed. A massive heart attack was under way. In the Thomashefskys' flat at 10 Monroe Street, Rebecca held her husband's hand as he drew his last breaths. The news spread over the Lower East Side in a matter of minutes. At the Royal they talked of nothing else.

The body was laid out on the stage of the National Theater. A line of people anxious to pay their last respects stretched from Houston to 14th streets. On July 12, a greater audience gathered outside the Gramercy Park Memorial Chapel on Second Avenue. The chapel itself could hold only six hundred. The rest of the 2,500 stood outside in silent tribute. A hush reigned—all the better to hear the services within, broadcast by a loudspeaker. The actor was lauded in eulogies by the heads of the Yiddish Theater unions; by Abraham Cahan, whose *Forward* had covered almost the entire Thomashefsky career; and by Maurice Schwartz, who saluted the Jewish colossus, the man who had founded an art form in New York with no training, no sponsor, no mentor—nothing but energy and the belief that an audience of refugees was crazy for theater. Schwartz made it clear that a man had passed on, not an idea, that the Yiddish Theater was still a vibrant, forward-looking enterprise. His listeners nodded, but given the news from Europe and the lack of new immigrants, they could no longer be sure of anything.

ii

DURING THE GREAT WAR, half a million readers bought at least one Yiddish newspaper every day. By the 1930s that number was nearly cut in half. Assimilation, compounded by a dearth of new immigrants, had done its work. Added to these factors was the financial distress caused by the Depression. Money was scarce and jobs scarcer. Even a few cents for a daily paper seemed excessive. As for the Yiddish Theater, tickets were priced beyond the means of all but the most loyal and prosperous followers. "We affirm the sad truth that the Yiddish Theater is on its last legs," one critic was to observe, "and there is little hope that it will ever get well."

Theatrical unions had been the mainstay of Yiddish performers, the guarantor of fair wages and decent working conditions. In the 1930s, as historian Nahma Sandrow observes, they served as albatrosses. One operetta producer was forced to hire "at least nine stage hands, ten musicians (a minimum even for nonmusical dramas), three dressers, ten ushers, two doormen for the ground-floor entrance and one for the balcony, two cashiers, a benefit manager, a general manager, a Yiddish publicity agent, a special policeman to keep order in the box office line (even when nobody was buying tickets), superintendents, bill posters, printers, scene painters, 10 choristers, and 16 actors."

To squeeze out profits, most producers put on a single show per season. The habit of attending half a dozen plays over six months went by the boards, and everyone was the poorer for it. The theater badly needed another rescuer. Hallie Flanagan briefly played the part. The staid forty-five-year-old professor of drama at Vassar had been recruited by her fellow Iowan, Harry Hopkins, head of the Works Progress Administration. He assigned her to the administration of something he called the Federal Theatre Project. It would use New Deal funds to stage comedies, tragedies, and musicals. Professional actors would appear in them, drawing regular salaries for their work. The Federal Theatre paid a mere $23.86 a week, compared with the standard minimum of $40. But the jobs were real, and the productions guaranteed by the full faith and power of the U.S. government.

Best of all for Second Avenue aficionados, the Yiddish Theater was included in the project. Professor Flanagan divided her new empire into large units: a) the Living Newspaper ("Something like the *March of Time* in the movies," Hopkins explained to Congress), b) experimental theater, c) Negro theater, d) popular-priced theater, with Yiddish, Spanish, and other foreign-language companies.

The Yiddish productions included versions of Sinclair Lewis's *It Can't Happen Here,* about fascism in America; *Day Is Darkness,* one of the first anti-Nazi dramas to be produced in the United States; and newer works including *The Treasure* and *The Tailor Becomes a Storekeeper* by the prominent Yiddish playwright David Pinski.

Inevitably the Federal Theatre became embroiled in controversy, accused of serving as an *agent provocateur* for criticizing Benito Mussolini of Italy and Haile Selassie of Ethiopia, and for espousing leftist causes. In the *Times,* critic Brooks Atkinson disparaged a Federal Theatre production as "Marxism à la Mother Goose." The *Washington Post* objected to some of the theater's "frilly artistic projects," and the *San Francisco Examiner* headed a story "Federal Theatre Communist Trend Must Be Eradicated." Matters came to a head when, after weeks of debate between cast and Congress, Marc Blitzstein's Brechtian satire *The Cradle Will Rock* was canceled on the eve of its debut. The composer fought back, playing his score on the rehearsal Steinway of an empty theater. The actors sang their roles from the audience, simultaneously skirting union rules and thumbing their noses at the WPA.

Flanagan kept vigorously defending her fiefdom, attempting to keep it free from the influence of parties left and right, but the public perception was of a federal program hijacked by radicals. Congress, never happy with the idea of government-funded arts programs, summoned Flanagan before the House Un-American Activities Committee. She addressed the members eloquently, invoking several classic dramatists who maintained their independence, sometimes at great danger to their lives. When the name Christopher Marlowe came up, Representative Joseph Starnes of Alabama leaned forward. "You are quoting from this Marlowe. Is he a communist?" This was met with derisive laughter. Without expression, the witness replied, "Put it in the record that he was the greatest dramatist in the period of Shakespeare." Her victory was momentary and Pyrrhic. On June 30, 1939, Congress voted 373 to 21 to eliminate the Federal Theatre. All of show business mourned, the personnel of the Yiddish Theater most of all. Overnight, their most significant and influential backer had pulled out, never to return.

iii

MAURICE SCHWARTZ would not allow such bad news to impede his projects. Like Adler and Thomashefsky, he always managed to con-

vince investors that applause and profits were waiting on the other side
of the lights. In a time of dwindling receipts, they backed his expensive
production of Sholem Asch's *Salvation,* an epic of Polish Jews during
Napoleon's invasion of Russia. Mainstream critics came downtown
because of the Schwartz name, but they were nowhere near as indul-
gent as in the past. The *Herald Tribune* reviewer, Richard Watts Jr., had a
little fun with the makeup and costumes: "Beards do have a way of
making actors look curiously alike. I think it would be of considerable
help to us outsiders if Mr. Schwartz would place numbers on his actors'
backs." Watts enjoyed Sholem Secunda's emotional score, but
described the acting as "florid" and its direction "curiously aimless and
undramatic." In the *Post,* John Mason Brown described the Asch play as
incoherent, even in the English-language synopsis. He said that he and
his fellow critics "might as well have been Martians for whom H. G.
Wells had forgotten to write explanatory captions."

Maurice shook off the bad notices. He decided to try the cinema
again, striking back at Hollywood with his own film production.
Between performances of *Salvation* he rehearsed a new movie, *Tevye der
Milkhiker* (Tevye the Dairyman), based on the long-cherished stories of
Sholem Aleichem. The central character, his life burdened with
poverty and daughters, addresses a series of monologues to a deaf
heaven. This time Schwartz vowed that there would be no corner-
cutting as in the Ulmer movie. Harry Ziskin, a wealthy restaurateur,
had agreed to back the feature with a $70,000 budget—an immense
sum for a Yiddish movie.

After three weeks of preparation, the cameras began grinding away
at a Long Island potato farm. Every day the cast did what all casts usually do between takes, exchanging theatrical gossip and worrying aloud
about the next role. But this August there was only one topic. Danzig
had been seized by Hitler, and the invasion of Poland seemed immi-
nent. In that case a war between Russia and Germany was certain,
probably within weeks. Perhaps days. On Monday, August 21, 1939,
newspapers disclosed that Germany's foreign minister, Joachim von
Ribbentrop, had flown to Moscow to arrange the details of a pact with
Nazi Germany. That agreement sent shock waves through the entire
Jewish community. Nine million European and Russian Jews were at
risk. The New York communists, who had been loudly voicing their
approval of American's freedom fighters, were suddenly exposed as
hypocrites, string-puppets moving at the whim of marionetteers in

Moscow. Not content with mere betrayal, the Communist Party issued a statement denouncing Germany's declared enemies, France and England.

The resolution, noted historian Melech Epstein in *The Jew and Communism,* ended "under the banner of Marx, Engels, Lenin and Stalin. Jefferson, Paine and Lincoln were dropped, casualties of the Stalin-Hitler pact." The reaction to all this was as dramatic as anything on the Yiddish stage. Jewish communists were greeted by jeering fellow workers with a Nazi salute and a withering "Heil Hitler!" The portmanteau word "communazis" was leveled at the Bolsheviks who were riding high only a month before. Fellow travelers and radicals fell away, repelled by the turn of events. Artef, the communist theater group with scrapbooks full of ecstatic reviews, was forcefully pushed to the margins of Yiddish Theater. Given the political mix of Artef and Yiddish Art Theater performers, the set of *Tevye* could easily have become a battleground. That the atmosphere remained calm was due to Schwartz's insistence on professionalism before politics—and to the fact that both sides suffered from a common adversary: noise. Stirrings of war were as close as Billy Mitchell Airfield, only a few miles away. Squadrons of army planes made it their headquarters, and filming had to be done between takeoffs and landings. Only tight cooperation between director, actors, and crew made *Tevye* possible.

It was never easy. The newspaper reportage from Europe grew so dismal that one member of the cast, Leon Liebgold, finally cracked. He played the suitor of one of Tevye's daughters, and demanded to be released from his contract so that he could go back to his family in Poland. Because *Tevye* was running behind schedule, Schwartz refused; the actor would not be released until his scenes were completed. At the latest, Liebgold was assured, he could go by the end of the month. Grudgingly, he returned to work—and got his life saved in the process. For on September 1, Germany finally did invade Poland, making the return impossible. Liebgold's relatives did not survive the Holocaust— had he been released from his contract and allowed to return home, he almost certainly would have perished with them.

Schwartz's version was at variance with the original Tevye stories. Aleichem gave the dairyman seven daughters; in the movie he has two, Hodl and Khave. Hodl is dealt with in a perfunctory manner: she breaks with her father and heads to Siberia, where her revolutionary lover awaits. The central conflict involves Khave, played by Schwartz's niece, Miriam Riselle. Unlike so many Jews in the rural Ukraine, Tevye does not live in a *shtetl*. All his neighbors are gentiles, most of them hard-drinking, anti-Semitic oafs. He maintains an uneasy relationship with the town priest (Jacob Adler's son Julius). In a discussion with the cleric, the conversation gets around to intermarriage. Tevye declares that he would sooner see his daughters "perish than see them betray our faith." Khave overhears this and collapses. She happens to be the lover of Fedya (Liebgold), a soft-centered Christian who reads Maxim Gorki and believes, like many progressives of the period, that by marching forward he will magically ascend to an atmosphere of peace and equality.

The two young people marry, much to the distress of Tevye and his wife, Goldie. The parents go through a mourning period, in effect sitting *shivoh* for their "dead" child. Sometime later Goldie, stricken with a fatal disease, passes away. Even then, Tevye's heart is too hard to allow the melancholy Khave back in the family circle; she can only look at the scene of bereavement through the windows of her childhood home.

Life goes on; Tevye endures penury and the pain of loss, Khave suffers through an unhappy marriage. The father and daughter stay irreconcilable—until, in the dairyman's old age, a pogrom takes place. The Ukrainian louts give Tevye twenty-four hours to pack and get out. This is the defining moment for Khave; she leaves her gentile husband because they're "worlds apart." She begs the aging Tevye to accept her back into the family. After she makes the requisite apologies and he consults Jehovah, Khave is once again his child. They go off, pulling the little wagon that holds a few precious possessions. Their direction is east, toward Palestine.

Tevye drew a mixed response. Almost every critic recognized that *Tevye* was technically superior to every other Yiddish movie. And to a man they praised Schwartz's virtuoso portrait of a faithful doubter, a loquacious monologist who could turn in a moment from misery to comedy, from hostility to fondness, from despair to dignity. But the communist *Freiheit* stated that while the central role was "played with deep understanding," the result was "not *Tevye der Milkhiker*"; it was "something else and something worse." The *Forward* called *Tevye* "One of the best Yiddish films made to date"—and then added that "merely a shadow of Sholem Aleichem has remained in Tevye's few external characteristics." Schwartz could hardly be blamed for asking a friend, "What the hell do you have to do in this profession to get some decent notices from the press? They're constantly demanding, 'Where are the new Yiddish playwrights? Where are the opportunities for actors? How can creative designers and good musicians find work?' Those questions are reserved for feature stories. For the reviews the tune is changed and dissatisfaction becomes the order of the day."

He was not alone in his unhappiness with the press. Another notable Yiddish movie was released in 1939, and it met with much the same reception. *Mirele Efros,* Jacob Gordin's Queen Lear, had once established Keni Liptzin as the greatest Yiddish diva in New York. The play had been filmed before in a popular silent version. The new movie starred a skilled if not subtle actress, Berta Gersten, in the title role. Though *Mirele Efros* turned out to be less cinematic than *Grine Felder,* it was more respectful to Gordin's play; almost all the original lines were retained. For his pains, director Josef Berne was criticized for being *too* deferential to the stage version. In faint damns, the *Daily Worker* allowed that "if you judge the film with the appropriate measure of tradition and historical perspective, you will enjoy it. But if you go to *Mirele Efros* as you go to a modern movie—this is not the right movie." There was no pleasing anybody these days.

The only other serious rivals to *Tevye* were the films of Edgar Ulmer. *Di Klyatsche* (The Old Mare) had been marketed to English-speaking audiences under the less dispiriting title *The Light Ahead.* Shot in Ulmer's favorite Eastern locale, the farmlands of New Jersey, it was an adaptation of old tales of Jewish beggars in Lithuania. The author of the original stories was a schoolteacher who used the pen name Mendele Mocher Sforim (Mendele the Bookseller). Unlike many later writers who romanticized the *shtetl,* Sholem Abramowitz saw it as a locale that robbed the Jews of their vitality and self-esteem. As the title indicates, he likened his people to a once proud, now spavined and worn-out nag. The film version retained only a few pieces of Sforim's plot, but much of his bitterness and dark comedy.

In the little town of Glubsk, Jewish tradition is fading fast. Impudent youths regularly scandalize the remaining handful of pious Hasids. "Better a Jew without a beard," jeers a youth, "than a beard without a Jew." Only two young people have retained their purity in this dishonored place, Hodel, who is blind, and Fishke, the lowly bathhouse attendant. The two are deeply in love, but so destitute that marriage is out of the question—until an epidemic sweeps through the town.

The elders have a plan: they will pay for the wedding if it takes place under a canopy in the local graveyard. The *Jewish Encyclopedia* explains that during cholera attacks, "marriages often took place within the cemetery, as that in Kovno of a lame young man to a deaf-mute or hunchback woman. At Pinsk, and in other communities, two orphans were married . . . the idea being that the cholera was thus conducted to the graves."

The two principals carried the film. Helen Beverly, the heroine of *Grine Felder,* proved once again that she could be a confident as well as attractive performer; and David Opatoshu, who at twenty-one had already been with the Artef troupe for four years, made the most of his poignant role. But what gave *The Light Ahead* its real power was the timing of the film's release—across the Atlantic were millions of Jews not unlike these half-medieval ones, unworldly, fearful, vulnerable. W. H. Auden caught the spirit of the age in his poem "September 1, 1939":

> As the clever hopes expire of a low dishonest decade:
> Waves of anger and fear
> Circulate over the bright
> And darkened lands of the earth
> Obsessing our private lives;
> The unmentionable odor of death
> Offends the September night.

That year there were no darker lands than those of Eastern Europe, all about to be overrun and corrupted by the Third Reich. Viewers recognized the film's subtext of dread—Glubsk stood for Warsaw, for Lodz, for all the threatened Jewish quarters—and perhaps for a lot more. In the *Hollywood Reporter,* one dispatch called *The Light Ahead* "the surprise sensation of the picture business." As far away as Kansas City, it noted, the local press "urged Gentiles to enjoy it with their Jewish neighbors, resulting in picture fans of all creeds and nationalities buying tickets."

Ulmer took further advantage of the times by working with the euphoniously named Moishe Oysher. Like his father and grandfather before him, Moishe had been trained as a cantor in Bessarabia. In America, the young immigrant sought to extend his résumé. He would not only chant in synagogues, he would be a leading man on Second Avenue. He persuaded Thomashefsky to hire him for small choral parts, and proved that his voice was glorious enough to play leading roles. He debuted in *Der Mazldiker Boykher* (The Lucky Boy), and pleased the downtown fans of *shund*. At the same time he kept up his religious affiliations, singing at the behest of a Brooklyn rabbi.

The double duty antagonized many in the Flatbush congregation. *Variety* reported that a "serious rumpus" occurred during Oysher's appearance, "with a lot of squawking and many cancellations from the synagogue membership, etc. plus a few open catcalls during the services." The subject of this controversy, the story went on, "is pretty well convinced that he is probably through as a cantor unless he forgets all about acting, but he likes acting. At the same time he hasn't been offered a star or featured part in any Yiddish legit troupes in New York, because managers feel that perhaps his presence in the cast may bother some prospective customers."

With the theater barred to him, Oysher turned to the cinema. He starred in *Dem Khazns Zindl* (The Cantor's Son), a kind of reverse image of Warner Brothers' breakthrough talkie, *The Jazz Singer*. In the Hollywood movie a young man leaves the synagogue to become a vaudeville star, reconciling with his family at the last moment, but never abandoning his show business career. In *Dem Khazns Zindl*, Oysher goes from a little Jewish village (constructed in the Pocono Mountains of Pennsylvania) to the streets of Manhattan. Success piles on success, with many musical solos accompanying the climb. But with all the compensations of money and celebrity, the hero finds his life empty. Not until he returns to Beltz, where his aged parents still live, does he feel at home. Looking back, he sighs, "I tried to find my real self but I couldn't." Setting down roots, the hero forsakes the Yiddish stage and takes a local, makeup-free bride, untainted by New York.

Dem Khazns Zindl made back more than double its investment, and Oysher's next film, *Der Zingendiker Shmid* (The Singing Blacksmith), augured well. Based on the David Pinski drama, *Shmid* told the story of a voluptuary who drinks too much, pursues wenches, blasphemes, but eventually gets tamed by the purity and love of a good woman. Ulmer confidently directed this feature with minimal assistance. Scouting locations in New Jersey he remembered that "my big staff consisted of two boys and four old Jews in a station wagon we had bought for $110." After driving for about thirty minutes they came across a monastery that seemed ageless, and therefore ideal for a background. "This was Friday, I was up to the main door in the building—the Jews kept sitting in the station wagon frightened."

They had reason to be discomfited. Like almost all Jews in New York, they were aware that a Michigan-based, rabble-rousing Catholic priest named Father Charles E. Coughlin was making anti-Semitic statements on his weekly radio program, and had just harangued his listeners with the question, "Must the entire world go to war for 600,000 Jews in Germany who are neither American, nor French, nor English citizens, but citizens of Germany?" In the tradition of Henry Ford, the prelate had backed up his broadcasts by running *The Protocols of the Elders of Zion* in his privately printed newspaper, *Social Justice.* But the monks, to everyone's astonishment, proved to be the very antithesis of Coughlin, accommodating and ecumenical. The abbot went so far as to encourage some of his bearded brethren to appear as extras. Even so, the locale was not without its worrisome aspects. When Ulmer and his crew returned, they were amused to find that on one side of them was a nudist camp—and distressed to discover that their other neighbor was Camp Ziegfried, summer quarters of the state's Nazi Bund. In order to keep the sets safe from vandals and anti-Semites, armed guards walked around the set from dusk to dawn.

The film's midtown New York opening was right out of *Abie's Irish Rose.* One half of the house was packed with Catholic clergy from New Jersey; the other half was composed of what the manager called "Oysher's Hebrew claque." Every scene was greeted with thunderous applause, and in the following weeks the Yiddish press threw bouquets. The English-language papers spoke of its charm, its elevated standards, and its improvement even over such well-made films as *Grine Felder.*

And with all this, Maurice Schwartz was still to have the last hurrah. *Tevye* outscored every other Yiddish film at the box office. Thus, observes film historian J. Hoberman, "Schwartz's epic may be considered the Yiddish analogue to those fondly remembered archetypes— *Stagecoach, Wuthering Heights, The Wizard of Oz, Mr. Smith Goes to Washington, Ninotchka, Gone With the Wind*—that led to the canonization of 1939 as the greatest year in Hollywood history." Appraising the products of Jewish cinema that year, no less a *goyische* paper than the *Herald Tribune* proclaimed, "One need no longer speculate about the proper place of these films in the many-corridored auditorium of the American theater. Yiddish films have arrived." Had they? And if so, was celluloid to be the next costume of the Yiddish Theater—or its shroud?

CHAPTER SEVENTEEN

✦

FORGETTING THE HUMAN DISASTER

i

As the yiddish theater struggled for survival, Zygmund Salkin thought he might have an answer—perhaps *the* answer. Late in the 1930s he steered a rickety sedan toward the Catskill Mountains. En route, he commiserated with his passenger, a fellow immigrant named Isaac Bashevis Singer. Salkin intended to be a great director; Singer aspired to be a full-time author. The careers of both men had stalled. The theater man had recruited a troupe of young actors, but could find no audience for their efforts. The writer had recently published a novel, *Satan in Goray,* but it did not sell well. He continued to publish pieces in the *Forward,* the newspaper's paychecks rarely rising above subsistence level. That summer, the idea of a working vacation exerted an irresistible pull for both men.

Half inspirational figure, half confidence man, indefatigable in his search for recognition, Salkin had wangled an invitation to bring his new-formed troupe to a bungalow colony in Woodridge, New York. Named in honor of the Hirschbein play and film, Grine Felder was peopled with artists and intellectuals, and Salkin intended to offer them his version of I. L. Peretz's *At Night in the Old Marketplace.* Following this out-of-town tryout, he planned to take the show to New York City, where, the producer boldly predicted, it would wow the critics. Cast, costumer, and set designer were in place; the one missing piece was the dramaturge. Singer agreed to fill that role.

In *A Place in the Country,* memoirist Martin Boris observes that Grine Felder "was no ordinary Catskill resort for the families of middle-class Jewish shopkeepers and businessmen who would come for a respite from Manhattan's swelter." By the time Salkin and Singer entered, the place had been in operation for several years and now boasted "the most concentrated assemblage of Yiddish elite anywhere on Earth." Located on thirty-five luxuriantly wooded acres, Grine Felder had forty little houses, three grand pianos, and a large auditorium dubbed the Amphion. Here, declared Salkin, would be the hatchery for a new kind of Yiddish-American Theater. It would change the world—and this was a world that needed changing.

Malvina Fainberg, a longtime summer resident, remembered that "there was a long waiting list, composed of only those recommended by *Grine Felders* already there. I was considered because my brother-in-law was one of the original founders. One had to be first interviewed, parents and children alike, by the membership committee. Next, we were evaluated by the cultural committee as to his or her possible contribution to the various cultural activities going on."

The majority of those Grine Felders were left-leaning Jewish thinkers and artists. Among the musicians were conductor Lazar Weiner, who directed the highly regarded Mendelssohn Symphony Orchestra, and Moishe Rudinow, chief cantor at Temple Emanu-El on Fifth Avenue, the largest synagogue in America. The literary and theatrical genres were represented by playwright David Pinski; Nahum Stutchkoff, an author and playwright whose radio series was running on the Jewish radio station WEVD; and Abraham Shiffrin, poet, short-story writer, and president of New York University's School of Journalism.

Shiffrin made detailed accounts of the resort activities. His reports tell of Yiddish productions, as well as performances in English of Robert Sherwood's *Abe Lincoln in Illinois.* In the evenings, attendees heard lectures by Pinski, concerts of Mozart, Brahms, and Yiddish folk music, and solo recitals by Jewish stars of the City Center Opera Company. There were also vigorous discussions of contemporary politics, and these were not so agreeable to the skeptical Singer. In *Lost in America,* he recalls that bungalows were named not only for Yiddish writers like Aleichem and Peretz, but also for such radicals as Rosa Luxemburg, Karl Marx, and Emma Goldman. The Grine Felders "seethed with those offering ready-made remedies for all the world's ills. Some still preached anarchism—others, socialism. Some placed all their hopes on Freud, while others hinted that Stalin was hardly as bad as the capitalist lackeys painted him."

For a few delirious weeks Salkin and his followers believed that *At Night in the Old Marketplace* was their gateway to security and celebrity. Patrons pledged generous cash contributions. That led to talk of leasing an off-Broadway theater, setting up an artistic company to rival Maurice Schwartz's, and staging dramas in English as well as Yiddish. Singer was not so sanguine. He saw that most members of the acting company were young, naive, and penniless, and suspected that the wallets of the so-called backers would turn out to be as empty as their promises. No theater could be rented without a sizable deposit. Also, the play needed professionally built scenery. Actors and actresses had to have salaries. Verbal assurances would cut no ice with managers and landlords. Although the novelist outwardly pretended that all was well, he couldn't lie to himself. In his view, Salkin "lacked the skills of a director and most of the boys and girls had little talent. Peretz's words emerged false, awkward, and often ridiculous from their mouths."

Labor Day approached. Most of the colonists, having spent two months noisily denouncing the status quo and endorsing radical politics and free love, quietly migrated back to the city with their wives. One by one the bungalows shuttered. Salkin assured everyone that although the money had not yet come in, fame was only months away. Singer knew better: "He had a briefcase full of papers and a head full of ideas and hopes, but deep inside we knew that it was all over."

Singer's melancholia covered more than the local events of that summer. Exactly one year before, a Yiddish columnist had written, "It seems that everyone is waiting to see which way the cat will jump." The world watched it jump that fall, when a young Polish Jew murdered a German diplomat in France. As the official lay dying in a Paris hospital, German propaganda minister Joseph Goebbels seized on the incident, encouraging Nazi party leaders to incite "spontaneous" anti-Semitic riots throughout Germany and Austria. The result was *Kristallnacht* (The Night of Broken Glass). Synagogues were burned to the ground and some 7,500 Jewish-owned businesses looted or destroyed. Two weeks later Jewish children were expelled from German schools.

On May 13, 1939, a cruise ship carrying more than 900 Jewish refugees left Hamburg, Germany, for foreign shores. When the boat reached Havana, it was not permitted to lower an anchor. It set sail for Miami—only to be intercepted by the coast guard and warned to keep moving. On June 6, the *St. Louis* returned to Europe. There, Great Britain agreed to take 287 of the passengers, Belgium 214, the Netherlands 181, and France 224. All but the ones who went to Britain were keenly aware of what awaited them.

Singer sensed what was coming and expressed it in his art. His retrospective novel *The Family Moskat* encapsulates the two attitudes of Poland's doomed Jewry. "The Messiah will come soon," says an optimist. No, says a realist. "Death is the Messiah. That's the real truth." As for the author's fellow Grine Felders, they knew what they wanted to know, and they were joined in their willful ignorance by much of the Lower East Side's population. Not that any of them could have done much for their anguished relatives in Europe. The U.S. State Department had no intention of intervening on the Jews' behalf—it had never been comfortable with the big waves of Hebrew immigration.

American Jewish organizations stood by, uncertain of what to do. While the death camps were being set up, while Joseph Stalin occupied himself with the annihilation of such writers as Isaac Babel for the crime of being Jewish, the majority of intellectuals and artists—including the populace of the Yiddish Theater—continued to avert their eyes from the actual, lived on illusions, and, in Singer's memorable phrase, gathered around the Old Idolatry. "The stone and clay idols had been exchanged for a Gertrude Stein, a Picasso, a Bernard Shaw, an Ezra Pound. Everybody worshiped culture and progress." Sadly, "at its best, art could be nothing more than a means of forgetting the human disaster for a while."

The communist Artef, troubled and battered since the Soviet-Nazi pact, suffered from a collective amnesia. Culture and radicalism became their gods. A story circulated in 1939, prompted by Artef's new choice of venue: multimillionaire Otto Kahn tours the Lower East Side in his limousine. He spots the sign for a dry cleaning establishment: "Operated by Isadore Kahn, nephew of Otto Kahn." Outraged, the plutocrat orders his chauffeur to put on the brakes, storms into the shop, bawls out Isadore Kahn, who is no relative at all, and threatens a lawsuit if the sign is not changed immediately. The next day he arranges to have the car pass by. The sign has been altered. It now reads "Operated by Isadore Kahn, *formerly* nephew of Otto Kahn."

The joke gained circulation because the Artef had rented the 679-seat Mercury Theater, recently occupied by a famous company headed by the enfant terrible Orson Welles. A quarrel resulted when the Artef announced their takeover. Welles won when the ads were revised to read: "The Artef *formerly* the Mercury Theater." At that location the new occupants of the 41st Street house performed nine times a week, including two weekend matinees. The company's initial offering was *Clinton Street,* the kind of inclusive panorama of urban life soon to be popularized by a number sung in the Marx Brothers film *The Big Store:* "The Cohens and the Kellys, the Campbells and Martinellis—they're all a part of my Tenement Symphony . . ."

Naturally, *Clinton Street* emphasized the Cohen part of the saga, but other ethnic groups were not neglected. The show traced the fall and rise of two disparate characters who seek to escape the slums: a young woman who marries a rich industrialist, even though she loves a poor youth her own age; and a man who becomes a criminal in thrall to crooked Tammany operatives.

The left-wing press generally gave the drama a pass. The *New Masses* found many of the scenes "so rich they achieve genuine folk quality," and the *Freiheit* found much to like in "a clash of ideas, a contrast of cultures, a mixture of languages, an amalgamation of customs and ways of living." The mainstream papers gave a harsher assessment. The *Daily News* critic wrote that "what starts out to be a tense, sympathetic cross-section of the people of this slum district, finally degenerates into a conventional Yiddish melodrama," and the *Times* labeled the characterizations "brittle" and added that "few individuals come up to the Artef mark" of the past.

In *World of Our Fathers,* Irving Howe judiciously compares shows like

Clinton Street to an Italian art form: "Hit the high C no matter what happens to the plot of the opera, do the bang-up scene where the father banishes his errant son no matter what the story of the play. What counted, as perhaps it always must in popular art, was the exuberance of the occasion, available every evening as cast and audience joined in a magical interchange of pleasure." No one took the plots of *Aïda* or the Ring Cycle seriously anymore; similarly no one could believe in narratives like the ones of *Clinton Street*. "But if one saw these plots as residues of traditional romance or grandiose reflections of a culture's view of itself, they might make sense, if not in their details then in their larger rhythms."

And that was exactly the way the Artef's audiences did see them. By the time the play closed on Christmas Eve 1939, more than forty thousand people had come to the theater, gazing, as their parents did, at highly tinted pictures of themselves and their surroundings. No doubt there was more than a touch of nostalgia in the enthusiastic reception—along with a retreat from the headlines. But Artef members had reason to believe that the unpleasantness surrounding the pact between Nazi Germany and Soviet Russia had been forgiven if not forgotten, and that a Jewish solidarity had returned. Avoiding any references to the present day, the organization next presented *Uriel Acosta,* the uncontroversial, century-old tale of a renowned Portuguese-Jewish martyr. Helen Beverly, the star of the film *Grine Felder,* headed an outstanding cast. Much was expected, particularly after a set of generous reviews, capped by the *Mirror*'s ecstatic endorsement of Beverly: "One of the most promising actresses on the New York stage today."

By now, however, art had been overtaken by events. The communists learned the hard way that they had not been forgiven after all. *Clinton Street* had made money because of a big advance sale. Most of those purchases had taken place before the Stalin-Hitler pact was signed. Now the anti-communist Jews knew better. They refused to waste any further money. It was a matter of principle.

Uriel Acosta, as Artef historian Edna Nahshon indicates, "was doomed even before it opened." Performances shrank to a weekend schedule and then ceased altogether. Members of the company dispersed. Some, like the budding director Jules Dassin, went on to Hollywood. Others, like David Opatoshu, joined the Hebrew Actors Union and looked for work. The war was soon to begin. The Artef was about to go under.

ii

DURING THE SUMMER of 1939 Germany erected financial barriers, making it impossible for its Jewish citizens to transfer their savings out of the country. Those who sought to emigrate found few places to go. The United States had set up iron quotas: no more than 3 percent of immigrants from any specific country, based on the 1920 census.

Pushed by his wife, Eleanor, and by several Jewish associates, President Roosevelt set up an international conference. It was meant to address the problem of refugees from Germany's harsh and widening persecutions. At the same time that the Grine Felders were meeting for lectures and the Artef was planning its final productions, representatives from thirty-two countries convened at the French resort of Evian on Lake Geneva. After nine days, all but one of the countries offered excuses rather than opportunities. Commenting on the Evian conference, the German government said it was "astounding" that foreign countries had dared to criticize the Reich for its treatment of Jews when only the Dominican Republic had agreed to accept additional refugees.

Two American officials responded. Immediately after the conference, Senator Robert Wagner of New York and Representative Edith Rogers of Massachusetts introduced bills ordering the admission of ten thousand refugee children to the United States. Another ten thousand, according to their plan, would be allowed to enter the following year. Reaction was immediate and impassioned. The American Friends Service Committee volunteered to coordinate private efforts on behalf of the young refugees. Within twenty-four hours of the offer, four thousand U.S. families said they would make room for a foreign child. Radio stations and newspapers were swamped with additional tenders of aid and comfort.

The isolationists and anti-Semites felt threatened. A consortium

of thirty "patriotic organizations" organized under the leadership of
Francis H. Kinnicutt. Among them were the Veterans of Foreign
Wars, the American Legion, the Society of Mayflower Descendants,
and the Daughters of the American Revolution. Speaking on behalf of
those parties, Kinnicutt denounced the Wagner-Rogers bill as "part of
a drive to go back to the condition when we were flooded with foreigners who tried to run the country on different lines from those laid
down by the old stock. Strictly speaking it is not a refugee bill at all, for
by the nature of the case most of those admitted would be of the Jewish race."

Mrs. Agnes Waters, representing a group called the Widows of
World War I Veterans, independently sent out word that the Children's Rescue Bill would serve to make the United States a "dumping
ground for the persecuted minorities of Europe. The refugees can
never become loyal Americans." Stirrings began in Washington. At a
Beltway cocktail party, the wife of the commissioner of immigration
told friends: "The trouble with the Wagner-Rogers bill is that 20,000
children would all too soon grow up into 20,000 ugly adults." America
Firsters lobbied for the status quo. Senator Robert Reynolds of North
Carolina introduced a bill to abolish *all* immigration to the United
States for a decade. Fearful of an uprising within the reactionary and
Southern wings of his own party, Roosevelt refused to renew the
debate about immigration. A letter to FDR from a New York con-
gresswoman urged him to change his mind; the president's assistant
sent it to a drawer marked "File—No Action." The Golden Door had
slammed shut.

CHAPTER EIGHTEEN

✦

ESCAPING *INTO*
OUR PROBLEMS

i

A T THE END OF 1939 Maurice Schwartz paid a high price for his exertions onstage and in the cinema. Stricken by a heart attack, he went south to recuperate. In Florida he was not pleased to read publicity about Edgar Ulmer's latest Yiddish movie, *Amerikaner Shadkhn* (American Matchmaker). The musical, written by Ulmer and his wife, Shirley, starred a rising young comedian. Notorious for hambone tactics, Leo Fuchs could occasionally astonish his fans by underplaying. This time out he proved the validity of his street reputation as "The Yiddish Fred Astaire" and kept a light touch throughout.

He played the title role of Nat Silver, a well-heeled clothier who lacks but one thing in life: a wife. Nat has already been engaged eight times, and is chronically unable to commit to any woman. He continues to evade and deflect, and yet something in him remains fascinated by the subject of marriage. So fascinated that Nat elevates his surname from Silver to Gold and chooses a new vocation, operating a "Human Relations Bureau" in the Bronx. The bureau is the headquarters of the new, self-appointed *shadkhn.*

For the older crowd of American Jewry, that Yiddish noun summoned up bitter memories and cynical jokes. Many a match had been arranged by brokers in the Old World. The raw materials of their work were usually impoverished parents of a bachelor seeking a suitable dowry, or luckless parents of an attractive young woman looking for a moneyed son-in-law. Love had nothing to do with it. Often one candidate couldn't stand the other, and the *shadkhn* had a lot of selling to do. In *The Joys of Yiddish,* Leo Rosten quotes the defining Old World anecdote:

A *shadkhn* told his prospective client of a glorious girl named Rebecca.

"Rebecca? The redhead?" asked the young man.

"The same."

"You must be crazy! She's almost blind."

"That you call a failing?" cried the *shadkhn.* "That's a blessing— because she won't see, half the time, what you're doing."

"She also stutters!"

"Lucky you," sighed the *shadkhn.* "A woman who stutters doesn't dare talk too much, so she'll let you live in peace."

"But she's deaf!"

"*I* should have such luck! To a deaf wife you can shout, you can bawl her out—"

"She's also 20 years older than I am!"

"Ah," sighed the *shadkn,* "I thought you were a man of vision. I bring you a marvel of a woman you can spend a lifetime with, and you pick on one little fault!"

In the United States, the elements of intelligence, sentiment, and sexual attraction entered into courtship. These drastically changed the rules of engagement. Even so, the matchmaker's profession endured for a surprisingly long time. While Ulmer was planning his film, *The New Yorker* profiled one Louis Rubin. As the proprietor of Rubin's Prominent Matrimonial Bureau, he claimed to have arranged some seven thousand marriages over a twenty-five-year span, and considered himself a bridge between the Old World and the New. He wore a silk yarmulke, but covered it with a wide-brimmed fedora. He sported a long black beard and black suits that suggested a rabbinical background, but peppered his palaver with slang.

"Timid clients," the magazine reported, "especially the younger ones with fussy American ideas, sulk and get stubborn when they first put themselves into Rubin's hands. They insist on working a certain amount of romance into the thing." For that, Rubin blamed "poets, songwriters and the movies. Pin him down and he'll concede a pinch of romance is OK."

Men like Rubin continued to be tolerated, if not honored, because they helped to fend off the dangerous temptation of intermarriage. The wedding of Jew and gentile had always been anathema for traditionalists. In the rapidly changing social and political environment of 1930s America they felt endangered. The *Forward*'s famous "Bintel Brief"—letters to the editor and advice from him—continued to reflect this apprehension. "We live in a small town in the country where we are the only Jewish family," says one characteristic plea. "We earn a good living here. But we have four daughters, all of them ready for marriage, and there is no one here with whom to make a match. Here it's impossible to marry off a girl, because there are no Jews, only Gentiles. Our daughters are fine girls. They are always in the store and behave decently. The question is, however, how will it end?" The *Forward*'s reply: "We can only tell them that many Jewish families that are in the same position leave the small towns for the sake of their children. Others, on the other hand, remain where they are."

In his introduction to Isaac Metzker's *Bintel Brief* collection, columnist Harry Golden is not so equivocal: "A Jew who has three or four daughters is in bad shape. In the small towns of the South the Jew has discovered a system. He sends his daughters up to Philadelphia or Boston or to Atlanta where she can meet Jewish boys." The boys are not so fortunate: they tend to stay home and enter the father's store or become professionals. A certain number will find Jewish mates; for others the worst will be unavoidable: "Some of them wind up marrying *shikses.*" The best antidote for this disastrous outcome was the *shadkn,* a man like Nat Gold.

As the last reel of Ulmer's film winds down, the matchmaker is ensnared by a trap of his own making. Having fallen for the attractive, impecunious Judith, Nat becomes leery of his own feelings. He finds an eligible man for her by offering to provide a dowry. But the jittery bridegroom backs off at the last minute. "Neurotic as Nat is," comments Hoberman, "he can only get married behind his own back." Rather than suffer the embarrassment of a canceled wedding, Nat steps to the altar. Whether the couple live happily ever after is irrelevant; what *is* important is that despite the pressures to abandon tradition, to speak English exclusively, to wed out of the faith, a modern Jewish couple in America has taken their vows under the *chuppah.*

Amerikaner Shadkhn opened at the National Theater in May. It was an indication of the times that Boris Thomashefsky's old venue had become a movie house, with occasional live acts accompanying the feature. Eight acts of Yiddish vaudeville were on the bill, including acrobats, singers, and comedians. They represented the last of a dying breed.

ii

VAUDEVILLIANS HAD BEEN the bane of the Yiddish Theater for almost forty years. Jacob Gordin had called it the worst imitation of American taste, "the tail of the theatrical business, with disgusting shows, demoralizing recitations, vulgar witticisms, emetic beer, and debauchery." The *Tageblatt* had claimed that the vaudeville houses were where "the city's most notorious women and dangerous men congregated," and in the *Forward* Abraham Cahan headed one piece

YIDDISH MUSICAL HALLS ARE A SCANDAL WITHOUT A BUT.

In his opinion, "One has to have talent to tell a good joke. But one doesn't need brains to make the audience laugh at dirty insinuations. It is the nature of indecent jokes that one laughs more about the filth than the joke. One just needs to wink and give a certain kind of smile at the same time. In all the songs that I heard in the Yiddish music halls, there was much more winking than humor, a lot more dirty smiles than sense or charm."

As is usually the case when moralists ring alarm bells, such editorials served only to give Yiddish vaudeville free publicity and increase the size of its audience. The Hebrew Actors Union soon got into the act, refusing to allow vaudevillians to audition. In response the outsiders formed their own Variety Actors Union. The old organization agreed to recognize the junior one—but only if the performers stayed in their own venues. None of them would be allowed to go "legit." That policy also worked for the best interests of the vaudeville personalities. They may have had little training in the classics, but they displayed more energy than the aging Second Avenue actors, and drew a younger crowd.

These days ebullient Aaron Lebedeff mixed the *mamaloshen* with the American idiom in numbers like "Oy, I'm Crazy for She, but She's Not Crazy for Me." Willie Howard, who specialized in character parts and eccentric songs, amused his fans by recalling the day "When Nathan Was Married to Rose of Washington Square":

> *Oy, what a head,*
> *I'm nearly dead,*
> *How I wish that I was home in my little bed.*
> *Highbrows, lowbrows,*
> *Philosophers with no brows*
> *And the elite*
> *Came because they knew the bride and groom,*
> *Others came there just to eat.*
> *A big cow*
> *From Moscow*
> *Danced a dance that was hot.*
> *They threw her a flower. The flower, though, came in a pot.*

Polacks, Slovacks, Hindus, hoodoos, Swedes and Yids were there
When Nathan was married to Rose of Washington Square.

Some of the vaudevillians performed on Broadway; others went to
the medium that had not put up barriers—the Yiddish cinema. Besides
Fuchs and Lebedeff there were Menashe Skulnik and Ludwig Satz, two
natural clowns; and the *zaftig* Jennie Goldstein, one of the highest-paid
stars in Yiddish vaudeville, a comic singer turned mock tragedienne
whose specialty was portraying the heartbroken loser in melodramatic
tableaux. The *Times* pointed to her as a performer who "counts a day
lost when in which she does not spend a little time either in the gutter
or in a psychopathic ward."

Edgar Ulmer's greatest rival in Yiddish cinema was Joseph Seiden,
who knew how to use these talents. It didn't matter that the performers
had no classical training; they could cross a soundstage without bump-
ing into the furniture, and that was all he needed. An experienced cam-
eraman who had filmed many sports events including the Jack
Dempsey–Gene Tunney fight in 1927, Seiden acquired a partner who
owned four major film palaces. They incorporated under the name
Judea Pictures, and went on to produce a slew of Yiddish two-reelers
and full-length movies with nothing but a few thousand dollars and a
line of persuasive patter. On one occasion in 1939, Seiden remembered,
"I didn't have the faintest idea for a story. And the Passover, three
weeks away—our best season. Then, that Saturday, in a bookstore on
Allen Street, I found this dog-eared little booklet." He bought the nov-
elette *Love and Passion* for 20 cents, spent the afternoon rewriting it, and
the following Monday started casting sessions. "I hang around the
beaneries on Second Avenue," he was happy to relate. "There's always
an actor who wants to get in the movies. I don't pay him nothing. Over
a cup of coffee, I give him a smile, a promise and he's willing."

Seiden was not the only hustler in the field of Yiddish talkies. Sidney
Goldin directed the riotous *Zayn Wiebs Lubovnik* (His Wife's Lover),
starring Satz. Loosely adapted from Molnár's *The Guardsman,* the sce-
nario was augmented by the melodies of Abraham Ellstein and billed
as "the first Jewish musical comedy talking picture." It was indeed
musical and comic, although a minor actress got most of the attention:
this was also the first film to have a black maid speaking fluent Yiddish.

But for sheer energy and invention, Seiden had no rivals. Because he
used combustible nitrate stock, the New York City Fire Department

would not certify him during regular business hours, lest he endanger other occupants of the building on East 38th Street. So he shot most of his movies at night or during holidays, when no one was watching. In his history of Yiddish cinema, *Visions, Images, and Dreams,* film scholar Eric A. Goldman cites Harold Seiden on his father's schedule. Joseph "would be shooting about four to eight weeks before the holidays and just get the picture finished for the opening. He used to run down to the Clinton movie theater on a Friday to collect money from them as an 'advance' against the picture to pay the crew. He worked with no money. He would make enough to start another picture. . . . It was a hand-to-mouth existence."

The summer of 1940 was a difficult one. Hitler's troops had already invaded and taken over Denmark and Norway, as well as Belgium and the Netherlands. France had fallen in June. Rumors of Jews rounded up in concentration camps had been confirmed. Mindful that *Amerikaner Shadkhn* was not thriving at the box office, perhaps because of the national malaise, Seiden sought to have it two ways.

Still a vaudevillian at heart, he produced several melodramas. *Motel der Operator* (Motel the Big Shot) told the story of a young labor leader crippled by strikebreakers, leaving his wife and baby penniless. To give the child a future, his mother gives him up for adoption to a wealthy couple and then takes her own life. In the tearjerker *Eli, Eli* (My God, My God), children mistreat their aged parents before reconciling at the last minute. *Ir Tsveyte Mama* (Her Second Mother), an adoption drama laden with coincidence, concerns a difficult child and the biological father she confronts in court (where she is the malefactor and he is the judge). These, Seiden felt, might appeal to the apprehensive Jewish filmgoer.

To cover all bases, he also produced the comedy *Der Groyser Eytse-Gever* (The Great Advice Giver). "The world sorely needs more laughter," he explained to a reporter, "and we therefore modeled this feature on the type of film produced by the Marx Bros." The film followed the farcical misadventures of a radio host, a scheming *shadkn* (as if there were any other kind), and three friends looking for love and luck. This was followed by *Der Yidisher Nign* (The Jewish Melody), in which a cantor's son journeys to Italy to further his musical education. There he meets a beautiful and mysterious girl who, in one of Seiden's typical crowd-pleasing finales, is revealed to be the illegitimate daughter of the synagogue president.

While all these films explored the Jewish experience, not one mentioned what was going on in contemporary Europe. The confrontation of Nazi butchery was left to Hollywood. Granted, there were many Jewish producers and executives in that town, but their personal concerns rarely reached the screen. Harry Cohn, the Neanderthal head of Columbia Pictures, let it be known that "in this studio, the only Jews in the movie play Indians." A glossy photograph of Benito Mussolini hung on the office wall of producer Walter Wanger, and Il Duce's son had recently studied the movie business under the tutelage of Hal Roach.

As all-out war approached, however, a number of studios were suddenly forced to confront the truth. Charlie Chaplin came up with *The Great Dictator,* playing the double role of a mustachioed Jewish barber and the megalomaniacal dictator Adenoid Hynkel, a jeering parody of Adolf Hitler. Warner Brothers' *Confessions of a Nazi Spy* was released under protest from the German consul general in Los Angeles.

Newspaper stories assiduously followed the controversy. A fellow mogul prudently advised Jack Warner that anti-fascist movies might reduce the overseas market for American movies. Snapped Warner, "The Silver Shirts and the Bundists and all the rest of these hoods are marching in Los Angeles right now. There are high school kids with swastikas on their sleeves a few crummy blocks from our studio. Is that what you want in exchange for some crummy film royalties out of Germany?" Frank Borzage's *The Mortal Storm* dealt with a professor who refuses to recognize a "superior Aryan race." As punishment for this exhibition of courage, the teacher is sent to a concentration camp. His family is divided between those who argue in favor of a Master Race, and those who despise the Nazis. Shortly after the film's release, MGM films were banned by the Third Reich.

With more at stake, the Yiddish filmmakers continued to blink in the face of *realpolitik.* During the winter of 1941 the first units of the German Afrika Korps arrived in North Africa, advancing under the direction of General Erwin Rommel. England was alone in its fight against the Nazis. After furious negotiations with Congress, President Roosevelt signed the Lend-Lease Act, allowing the besieged and exhausted Britain to receive armaments. In April the Nazis invaded Greece and Yugoslavia; both surrendered within two weeks. The Jews of these countries were rounded up and either murdered on the spot or sent to concentration camps in the East.

In Vichy France, chief of state Marshal Pétain announced the internment of "foreign Jews" and revoked the citizenship of Algerian Jews. These decrees were covered by the American press; *Time* magazine called them "so un-French, so very German in accent that the outside world found it hard to believe they came from the mouth of an old fighter for France." In New York, the liberal daily *PM* lamented that the "best policy for a Jew in Poland today is neither to be seen nor heard"—a policy that took place immediately after the Nazi racial policies herded Polish Jews into ghettos. *Beyond Belief,* Deborah Lipstadt's account of the coming Holocaust, offers evidence that "As the commencement of the mass murder of European Jews neared, the press had enough information to indicate that many of them were doomed to die of disease, starvation, exposure, torture and slave labor. But their own nagging doubts and those of their editors back home permeated the writing and publication of the news so that the American public would still have cause to disbelieve."

Not all writers or readers turned away. By the summer, a large protest rally took place in Madison Square Garden. Rabbi Stephen Wise, who had been slow to acknowledge what was happening to his co-religionists under German rule, was joined by New York State governor Herbert Lehman, New York City mayor Fiorello La Guardia, and AFL president William Green. Some twenty thousand people heard them speak about the Nazi killing fields. The *New York Times* headlined its coverage SAVE DOOMED JEWS, HUGE RALLY PLEADS.

Though that call was to go unanswered, the Jews of New York could no longer claim ignorance of world events. A feeling of dread and guilt ran through the community with palpable force. For once, Seiden's timing went awry. His feature *Mazel Tov Yidden* (Congratulations, Jews) was a collection of souvenirs posing as a new piece of entertainment. The compilation film, offering snippets of the director's previous short and full-length movies, died at the box office. The sources of financial backing were gone at the end of the year, and by then the audience had lost its taste for trivia. There would be no more Yiddish movies made in America until six million Jews had been murdered, Hitler was dead in his bunker, and the Third Reich lay in ruins.

iii

WITH THE YIDDISH THEATER treading water and the Yiddish film industry bankrupt, there remained one place where Yiddish-speaking performers could still find steady work: radio. Some independently owned stations in New York City were of meager wattage, barely able to reach a mile. But others were powerhouses. WEVD led the way. The station had been founded in 1927, its call letters chosen in honor of the Socialist party leader Eugene Victor Debs. Cahan sat on the station's board of directors; in dark times the *Forward* contributed $250,000 to fund the station's English- and foreign-language broadcasting schedule—everything from Japanese to Macedonian, with a heavy tilt toward Yiddish.

On Jewish radio, Zvi Scooler, a Yiddish Theater veteran, recited news items in rhyme. Molly Picon offered monologues, chatter, and songs. Moishe Oysher presented cantatorial recitals and scat-sang Yiddish popular melodies. Rabbi Samuel A. Rubin mediated disputes among Jews who were too poor to settle their arguments in court. The layman C. Israel Lutsky dispensed advice with such authority that many listeners thought he was a rabbi. A comedy series called *Happy Tho' Married* became a forerunner of the TV situation comedy. *The Forward Hour* was a blend of music, recitals, and dramatic radio plays.

But it was *Bei Tatemames Tish* ('Round the Family Table) that gave Yiddish actors the broadest scope. The plays were written by Grine Felder veteran Nahum Stutchkoff, a throwback to the tireless "bakers," Moishe Hurwitz and Joseph Lateiner, who had dominated the Yiddish Theater in its early days. For decades, Stutchkoff ground out as many as eight half-hour radio dramas a week. In "The Yiddish Radio Project," Henry Sapoznik's remarkable excavation and reconstruction of a bygone era, the radio writer is recalled as a man with an unruly thatch of hair, whose "clothing was covered in cigarette ash, and who would leave the house wearing unmatched shoes." To Stutchkoff the external world hardly mattered; emotion was everything. His children often saw him weeping over some dialogue he had just written. "If it doesn't make me cry," he explained, "then my audience won't cry either."

In its early melodramatic form, Yiddish Theater could have been defined as life on fire. Gradually, the dramatic writing matured and the actors' art grew subtle and naturalistic. Yiddish radio was a sudden throwback to the Goldfaden era, when emotions were expressed in primary colors and scripts were sprayed with exclamation points.

Stutchkoff's son Misha, who occasionally acted in his dramas, defined the difference between WEVD melodramas and the soap operas on the major networks. "Mainstream radio was about allowing listeners to escape *out* of their problems. On Jewish radio we would escape *into* our problems." Generational conflict was the staple of *Bei Tatemames Tish*. In a typical episode, a haughty Jewish matron guards the family's nouveau-riche status on Riverside Drive by passing for a gentile. The pretense works until the day her Orthodox father-in-law invites a few friends to drop by. One of them is a gnarled old man with beard and yarmulke, Reb Hirsch. The lady throws a fit, embarrassing her husband and son.

Out of sight, the grandfather overhears her words. He appears with his bags packed, to the dismay of his son and grandson.

GRANDFATHER: Don't get yourself all excited.... I'm from another world and this is—another world. In Brownsville I have my friends, my countrymen, my acquaintances. They know me, I know them. And here...a Jew spends a whole day in a non-Jewish neighborhood, sits the whole day on Riverside Drive, and has no one to share a single word with.

(*At the door*)

A person is not an animal. A person has a soul, too. No one in Brownsville will accuse me of bringing beggars home.

FATHER: I beg you—

GRANDSON: Don't go, *zaide,* please!

GRANDFATHER: Look at him. This is my dear grandchild. (*He hesitates*) Reb Hirsch, I suppose your wife will let me in after Passover . . .

(*Violin music up*)

ANNOUNCER: The grandfather remained at his son's for Passover. But will he stay after Passover? Only God knows.

These stories, almost all of them interior, family dramas, went on throughout the 1940s. There were no radio plays that mentioned the Holocaust; not a single playwright—or for that matter, novelist—dealt with the immense suffering overseas. In America there were little interruptions like the Madison Square Garden rally, or the occasional editorial in the *Christian Science Monitor*: JEWS HAVE NO CHANCE IN NAZIS' NEW 'ORDER.' Otherwise it was show business as usual.

iv

PESACH'KE BURSTEIN considered himself—correctly, as it turned out—more of a matinee idol than an actor in the style of Adler or Kessler. Watching him perform at a *Forward* benefit, Maurice Schwartz commented, "You're a fine actor, Burstein. You could have a position in my art theater, but no doubt you want billing; in my theater we don't list names, just 'Maurice Schwartz's Yiddish Art Theater.' " Burstein, with a lively concern for Burstein, did not hesitate. "That's too bad, Mr. Schwartz, you'll just have to do without me." A broad, infectious smile and purring voice were all he needed to build a loyal following among radio listeners in the United States. He gained more fans when he toured South America and Europe just before the war. Pesach'ke arrived back in Manhattan aboard the overcrowded Polish ship *Pilsudski,* one of the last passenger vessels to make it across the Atlantic without taking fire. (On the return trip, the boat was torpedoed and sunk.)

Although Burstein had by then built something of a name in New York, he was nowhere near as famous as another entertainer also heading for the States during the same period. The Bursteins had not yet learned to wring comedy from their sorry condition. Bob Hope, aboard the overcrowded *Queen Mary,* demonstrated the way to turn a situation into a routine, recalling his berth in a parody of "Thanks for the Memories"—while some passengers slept on the floor, he said, "I had 'Men' written on my door."

Burstein's wife and fellow actor, Lillian Lux, found a job on WEVD. A producer ripped the news off an AP ticker and made instant translations into Yiddish; she spoke them into a microphone, reading from his handwritten script before the ink was dry. Following that program, Burstein went on the air with his own show, singing popular Yiddish numbers. As soon as the last commercial went on, he joined with Lux for yet another interlude of songs and amiable gossip. On weekends, he operated a Yiddish theater in Brighton Beach, Brooklyn. The overwork took its toll; the exhausted couple began to bicker and the subject of divorce was broached.

Their marriage was rescued by a lucrative offer to appear in the Jewish enclaves of Montevideo and Buenos Aires. The Bursteins treated it as an extended second honeymoon. They sang, appeared on radio, and starred in operettas and plays—including a grim new one, *Der Vershaver Kanarik* (The Canary of Warsaw), about the Polish underground. It was one of the first Yiddish attempts to confront the situation of Europe's Jewry.

A year later the Bursteins returned to a New York they scarcely recognized. The elevated train on Second Avenue, whose periodic rumbles had been the bane of downtown restaurants and theaters, was being torn down. The sky, blocked out for all these years, could be seen from the sidewalk. It was a dark time for the city nonetheless. "The young, American-born comics and singers had been drafted into the army," Burstein observed in his autobiography. And the Yiddish Theater was scraping bottom. In order to work, he and Lillian headed for the Catskill Mountain resorts along with many other theater veterans. The experience of facing a Borscht Belt audience changed them all. Jennie Goldstein, who had made a good living out of Yiddish stage melancholia, cheered up and became a stylish comedienne. The entertainer Danny Lewis disliked show business, and encouraged his adolescent son to study law or medicine. One evening Danny and his wife had to appear at another hotel, leaving Burstein to conduct the weekly amateur night. "Let me go on," begged the youth. "My father won't know." Against his better judgment, Pesach'ke assented. As soon as the sixteen-year-old made his loose-jointed way across the stage the audience began to snicker; by the time he left they were weak with laughter. Jerry Lewis was on his way.

Molly Picon and her husband, Jacob Kalisch, could have made a small fortune in the Catskills, but they aimed higher. Kalisch convinced himself that in these strange days a Yiddish play might just make it on Broadway. No evidence to the contrary would dissuade him. Thomashefsky, Adler, Schwartz—they were all good men, but bless them, they didn't know how to do it. Kalisch had a plan. Working with Joseph Rumshinsky, he prepared a new musical, *Oy, Is Dus a Leben* (Oh, What a Life). Written in Yiddish, English, and Yinglish, a blend of both languages, it covered the story of Molly from childhood through her many shows and to her marriage, carrying her on to the present day.

They opened the show at the Jolson Theater, which was renamed the Molly Picon for the occasion. The grab bag of good-hearted vaudeville, melodrama, and operetta debuted on October 13, 1942, played to the expected loyalists, then gathered a new group of gentile fans and kept on going until the New Year. By that time the war news had improved; the Allies were making inroads in Europe. At home, though, Molly heard more than a few anti-Semitic slurs about Jewish wartime profiteers. And, she noticed, Negroes were still barred from many places where she was free to go. Visiting a friend on Central Park West, as she and Jacob entered one elevator, an authoritative voice sounded behind them: "You'll have to take the freight elevator," said the uniformed black operator. She turned around just as he shut the door on Mr. and Mrs. Paul Robeson. Picon's memoir of that occasion reads, "Racism, Jew bastard, war. When would we learn to follow the Bible and love thy neighbor?"

CHAPTER NINETEEN

✦

NO MORE RAISINS,
NO MORE ALMONDS

i

LATE IN JANUARY 1942, fifteen high-ranking officials of the Third Reich met at Wannsee, a lakeside villa near Berlin. The topic of the conference was the "Final Solution to the Jewish Question in Europe." Put less euphemistically, this meant the step-by-step elimination of all European Jews, the old, the middle-aged, the young, men, children, infants. Though the Wannsee Conference formalized the plans, killings had been under way for months. Mobile detachments had already rounded up and machine-gunned thousands of Jews in the German-occupied parts of the Soviet Union.

After the conference, the murders increased exponentially. The thousands of victims became hundreds of thousands, and then more. Rabbi Stephen Wise, who had gotten close enough to Franklin Roosevelt to address him informally, received specific information about the Final Solution. He sent a vexed but carefully worded letter to the president:

"Dear Boss,

"I do not wish to add an atom to the awful burden which you are bearing with magic, and as I believe, heaven-inspired strength at this time. But you do know that the most overwhelming disaster of Jewish history has befallen Jews in the form of the Hitler mass-massacres."

A twenty-page report followed. Prepared by Wise and his colleagues, *Blue Print for Extermination* was the most accurate nongovernmental account of the Final Solution, analyzing the deaths country by country. Roosevelt responded, promising to rescue "those who may yet be saved. The mills of the gods grind slowly, but they grind exceedingly small. We are doing everything possible to ascertain who are personally guilty."

The rabbi's group waited expectantly for specific action against the genocide. It never came. Roosevelt maintained a policy of Rescue Through Victory, rarely mentioning the catastrophe of European Jewry in his political speeches. Yet he remained a pantheon figure to most American Jews, who voted en bloc to elect him to office again and again and again. Only a handful found this dissonance impossible to accept.

Ben Hecht was one of them. The playwright and scenarist (*The Front Page, Twentieth Century*, etc.) refused to get along and go along. He decided to arouse America to the Jewish plight by staging a pageant, *We Will Never Die*, at Madison Square Garden. Seeking support, he addressed a private group of important Jewish writers and artists gathered at the town house of fellow playwright George S. Kaufman. In his memoir Hecht refers to that evening: "I said that an outcry against the massacre would have an important effect on the British. . . . If they heard that millions of Jews had been murdered, and that the Germans planned to kill the four million still breathing in Europe, and that most of these still-breathing Jews could be saved if the ports of Palestine were opened, the British, fine, decent people that they were, would certainly not continue to collaborate with the Germans on the extermination."

His appeal was met with silence—or worse. To suggest that America's ally, Great Britain, was somehow at fault was too much for the majority of his listeners. "Who is paying you to do this wretched propaganda," demanded novelist Edna Ferber, referring to the Nazi chancellor and his minister of information, "Mister Hitler? Or is it Mr. Goebbels?"

Of that group, only two volunteered their services, the writer Moss Hart and the composer Kurt Weill. Hecht had better luck with a handful of Yiddish Theater stars. Some forty thousand people attended We Will Never Die, a spectacle clearly influenced by the Second Avenue style. Before a backdrop of forty-foot-high tablets of the Ten Commandments, Hecht's words boomed out: "Almighty God, Father of the poor and weak . . . we are here to say our prayers for the two million who have been killed in Europe, because they bear the name of your first children—the Jews. . . . They shall never die though they were slaughtered with no weapon in their hand.

"Though they fill the dark land of Europe with the smoke of their massacre, they shall never die.

"For they are part of something greater, higher and stronger than the dreams of their executioners."

Stella and Luther Adler spoke out; so did Jacob Ben-Ami and Paul Muni. We Will Never Die rolled on to Hollywood, where Edward G. Robinson and John Garfield contributed their talents, and to Washington, D.C., where it was seen by the first lady, Eleanor Roosevelt, and several hundred members of Congress. Everyone who attended was moved, and there was talk of the War Department reversing the policy of Rescue Through Victory, of taking immediate action to save the victims. Somehow, feet were dragged and phone calls were not returned. A month later Kurt Weill bitterly assessed the situation. "What have we really achieved? All we have done is make a lot of Jews cry, which is not a unique accomplishment."

Amid all this fervor and pity there was one nation that claimed special credit for saving its Jews—Soviet Russia. Having turned back the Nazis at Stalingrad, the nation made a fresh appeal to the United States, asking for approval and aid. The communists' chief propagandist was Shlomo Mikhoels, actor and director of the Yiddish Theater in Moscow. Joseph Buloff remembered his fellow performer with considerable disdain. Throughout a monthlong visit to America, Mikhoels dressed as a Russian peasant, his wardrobe announcing solidarity with the proletariat. The two men hit it off at first, but things turned sour when Mikhoels announced that he was on his way to the capital for an official reception.

In his memoirs, Buloff writes, "I found myself expansively saying, 'Tomorrow you are going to Washington to represent your great country. Would it be right and proper for you to appear there in sagging pants and a torn shirt, without even a tie? I'll tell you what: I have a closet full of suits, stacks of shirts—colored and white alike—and a wide selection of ties. Come home with me, and I will outfit you from head to toe, well enough to meet even President Roosevelt himself.' "

Mikhoels exploded. "You louse, you think I don't have enough money do you? My government has provided me with enough funds. But I refuse to spend the workers' money on your bourgeois trappings. I spit on your lackey cravats and white shirts. Let the president see me as I am, a Soviet proletarian dressed like the people!" He walked away.

Buloff never expected to see him again. But two weeks after the explosion he received an invitation to the widely advertised Soviet-American Friendship rally, held in the Polo Grounds before a great crowd of fifty thousand. Mikhoels was accorded a hero's welcome. The Russian actor responded by performing a one-man sketch inspired by a Sholem Aleichem story. During the early days of railroading, a Jew and a Russian Orthodox priest find themselves trapped on an out-of-control train. The Jew has reason to be wary of his seatmate: the priest is a transparent anti-Semite. Forced to work together in this emergency, the two men stop the locomotive just in time, saving hundreds of lives. In the process, each comes to recognize the other's essential dignity and humanity.

The audiences responded with a mix of laughter and tears. Mikhoels held up his hand and smiled. "At this very moment, even as I speak to you, a Soviet Tiger-Tank is rolling across the steppes. At the controls are a Jewish soldier and a Gentile soldier—descendants perhaps of Sholem Aleichem's very same Jew and priest. But unlike those two, our soldiers know their machine. And they drive, they maneuver, they fire their weapons, they fight on and on against the brutal Nazi invaders. They are battling and winning—Jew and Gentile together—for a free Soviet, for a free world!"

He received a standing ovation. When the roar died down he continued: "The other day an American dandy of an actor came to me and said, 'Mikhoels, why are you in rags? Come, let me dress you like a fancy

American, in a white linen suit and a blue silk tie.' And I, as a proud Soviet Citizen, said, 'Never.' "

He indicated a large photomural of Stalin at the side of the stage. "I say to you, my friends, blessed be the hand that keeps us in rags, so that we may buy tanks and guns and bullets to fight for our homeland and kill the damned Fascist aggressors."

The speech was met with an ecstasy of enthusiasm—deafening shouts and cheers that went on for several minutes. Buloff awaited the final blow: Mikhoels would finger him as the bourgeois lackey who had offended the people's artist. He was spared any embarrassment when the speaker exited to thunderous applause.

If Comrade Stalin was grateful for Mikhoels's tribute, he chose an odd way to acknowledge it. Five years later, the Generalissimo saw to it that the actor-director was assassinated. The Jew had outlived his value to the Revolution.

ii

IN THE FALL, two more Yiddish Theater performers, Jacob Ben-Ami and the Hollywood character actor Sam Jaffe, appeared in *Miracle of the Warsaw Ghetto.* Presented at the New Jewish Folk Theater on 12th Street and Second Avenue, that epic commemorated the last days of twenty-four-year-old Mordecai Anielewicz and his compatriots. Armed with a total of nine rifles, fifty-nine pistols, and a few hand grenades, they had fought against overwhelming German forces bent on wiping out every Jew in the ghetto. The one-sided battle raged from April 19 to May 8. As *Miracle* pointed out, a number of European countries, armed to the teeth, had not defied the Nazis for that long a time. But here, too, the message was carried to the already convinced. For too many in New York City—and that included its Jewish population—the war news was serious enough without editorials expounded from the stage. Instead of confronting the massacre in Europe, they sought to hide from it, seeking refuge in that reliable painkiller, nostalgia.

iii

COMEDY, FANTASY, AND HISTORY thrived in the early 1940s. *Fantasia,* Walt Disney's overdecorated salute to classical music, became one of the top movies of the decade, along with the sagas of distant times and places, *Rebecca* and *How Green Was My Valley.* In the legitimate theater farce rose to the top, from the sweetly lethal maiden aunts of *Arsenic and Old Lace* to the psychics and ghosts of Noel Coward's *Blithe Spirit* to the wry view of the Yiddish Theater gone by in Hy Kraft's *Café Crown.*

Based on the operators and celebrities who once populated the Café Royal, Kraft's comedy was directed by a former actor, Elia Kazan. Its twenty-member cast featured Jay Adler, son of the famous Jacob, and two prominent Yiddish-speaking film veterans, Morris Carnovsky and Sam Jaffe. Stage directions described the Crown as "the last cultural rendezvous of the Jewish-American, the country store of New York's ghetto." His story revolved around David Cole (Carnovsky), a legendary superstar of the Yiddish Theater who has scattered wives and illegitimate children around the world. Cole nourishes the idea of starring in one last, grand role. He tries to enlist a café employee, Hymie (Jaffe), as his principal backer, warmly describing the play that will provide his comeback. Hymie is wary—he has been burned before, investing in classics that folded in a week. A relentless pitchman, Cole presses on with his synopsis. On the West Side of Manhattan a wealthy Jewish businessman gathers his three daughters and two sons-in-law around him:

COLE: Now he puts a question before his three daughters. Which of you loves her parents most?

HYMIE: This is a good question.

COLE: The oldest daughter Gertrude answers. "I love you more than words can wield the matter."

HYMIE: Sweet, very sweet. And the next one?

COLE: "I profess myself an enemy to all other joys."

HYMIE: Ah, it'll be a pleasure to hear such words in Yiddish. If a person can write like that, he's richer than J. Pierpont Morgan. *Nu,* and the third one?

COLE (*Dramatically*): She's silent.

HYMIE (*Disgustedly*): Ah, children. . . . It has good content. Also it's typical. So long it isn't highbrow you can count me in. How much will it cost?

COLE: It isn't your money, it's your understanding, your enthusiasm, your judgment.

HYMIE: With me, if I put money in something, I'm enthusiastic already, so long as it isn't Shakespeare. For him money I haven't got, and *my* enthusiasm *he* doesn't need.

COLE: Did Shakespeare ever write such a play?

HYMIE: But he wrote *Othello,* no? So it cost me four thousand two hundred twenty-one dollars. And *Richard One–Two–Three,* cost me twenty-five hundred dollars apiece.

After being courted, flattered, and reassured, Hymie learns that Cole's "new" drama is in fact a rewrite of *King Lear.* Memories flood back.

HYMIE: How could you do this to me, Mr. Cole? You tell me a story and suddenly it's Shakespeare!

COLE: Hymie, don't be hasty. Did Shakespeare ever write a play with an apartment on Riverside Drive?

Café Crown turned out to be the surprise hit of the 1942 season, launching the directorial career of Kazan and informing a new generation of playgoers who had never strolled on Second Avenue. From the machinations at the Cort Theater, and from the attendant publicity, they learned that there really *had* been a flourishing and vital enterprise in downtown New York, and that the Yiddish Theater still had a pulse, thanks in large part to Maurice Schwartz's still vigorous, still ambitious Yiddish Art Theater.

All during the war, the last remaining actor/impresario had remained hard at work. His artistic temperament had not mellowed over the years. Two people who giggled during a dramatic moment were lectured from the stage. Breaking out of his part as a false Messiah, Schwartz boomed, "Get the hell out of my theater! Go watch *shund* someplace else!" He ordered a stagehand to lower the curtain, after which he gave a short lecture on the importance of treating the theater as a temple.

When the couple left he ordered the curtain to rise, and went back into his role as if nothing untoward had occurred. Moments like this convinced Schwartz that people only needed a little moral instruction to make the Yiddish Theater vibrant again. He saw no reason why there would not be a Second Avenue renaissance once the Allies declared victory.

Maurice took a brief time out in Hollywood, where in 1943 he played a minor role in a major film. *Mission to Moscow* starred Walter Huston and the great character actors Oskar Homolka and Vladimir Sokoloff, but even this trio could not keep it from becoming one of the most embarrassing features ever turned out by a large studio. Produced at the behest of the U.S. government, *Mission* told the story of Joseph Davies, ambassador to Russia from 1936 to 1938. Stalin was portrayed as a warm and benevolent leader, the Soviet invasion of Finland was seen as "self-defense," and the notorious show trials were made out to be nothing more than a fair-minded conviction of "traitors." Schwartz made a convincing Soviet doctor in the few minutes he was on-screen. He took the money and ran back to New York.

The following year he resurrected his adaptation of I. J. Singer's novel *The Family Carnovsky*. The critics were kind, the attendance sparse. For the first time, the eternal optimist began to despair not only for his projects but for his community. He had the literary properties, actors, sets, venue. But where was the audience? Tyranny was destroying the Jews of Europe. In the benign United States, assimilation continued its own erosions.

iv

IN THE WINTER of 1944 Red Army soldiers discovered the abandoned Majdanek extermination camp near Lublin, Poland. The worst tales of German atrocities, long thought to be as exaggerated as they had been during World War I, were confirmed. The wire services ran pictures of a warehouse bursting with 800,000 pairs of shoes that had once belonged to Nazi victims. A *New York Times* correspondent contributed to the general information when he entered the site of the Natzweiler concentration camp and reported that Zyklon B gas had been used to kill prisoners. Other killing places were liberated, among them Chelmno, Auschwitz-Birkenau, and Treblinka.

"We are constantly finding German camps in which they have placed political prisoners where unspeakable conditions exist," said General Dwight D. Eisenhower, leader of the European Theater of Operations. "From my own personal observation, I can state unequivocally that all written statements up to now do not paint the full horrors."

In the spring of 1945, CBS reporter Edward R. Murrow reported from Buchenwald: "They showed me the children, hundreds of them. Some were only six years old. One rolled up his sleeves, showed me his number. It was tattooed on his arm. B-6030, it was. The others showed me their numbers. They will carry them till they die. An elderly man standing beside me said: 'The children—enemies of the state!'

"The manner of death seemed unimportant. Murder had been done. God alone knows how many men and boys have died there during the last 12 years. Thursday, I was told that there were more than 200,000 in the camp. There had been as many as 600,000. Where are they now?

"I pray you to believe what I have said about Buchenwald. I reported what I saw and heard, but only part of it. For most of it, I have no words.

"If I have offended you by this rather mild account of Buchenwald, I'm not in the least sorry."

The twentieth century's ultimate barbarism is common knowledge today. It was deeply traumatic then, as the irrefutable evidence piled up: the testimonies of witnesses and victims; the photographs of bodies stacked like cordwood; corpses bulldozed into mass graves; ovens in which people were sometimes burned alive; the rooms full of gold rings, false teeth, and hair taken from the prisoners before they were murdered in gas chambers; skin turned into lamp shades; soap made from human corpses—it came in a rush, and the horror was too much to comprehend. It took the cessation of hostilities, an unconditional surrender, and the trials of war criminals at Nuremberg before the public could take in the lineaments of the Holocaust. Then it reacted with powerful revulsion. Echoes of the Third Reich still could be found in Poland, where in the summer of 1946 a pogrom took place in Kielce. Some one hundred Jews were attacked and forty-nine murdered as the mob shouted slogans of rage and hatred. Save for this incident, however, anti-Semitism became quite literally unspeakable in most of the civilized world.

In the course of examining prison records, researchers came upon yet another sad irony. The name of Abraham Goldfaden, father of the Yiddish Theater, had been kept alive in the camps. The melody of his first popular song, "Raisins and Almonds," was sung as it had been in the nurseries of New York. But the lyrics had been altered. In *Ghetto Tango*, an album of wartime Yiddish Theater produced in 2000, Adrienne Cooper and Zalmen Mlotek supply the concentration camp version:

> *Nit keyn rozhinkes*
> *Un nit keyn mandlen*
> *Der tate iz nit geforn handlen*
> *Lylinke mayn zun*
> *Er hot farlozt undz un avek*
> *Vu di velt hot nor an ek.*
> *Lyulinke mayn zun*

> No more raisins
> No more almonds
> No more daddy going off to work

He's left us here and gone off far
Where the world is no more
Than another dark star
Lyulinke, my child

S'shrayen soves, s'voyen velf
Got derbarem zikh un helf
Lyulinke mayn zun.
Ergetz shteyt er un er vakht,
Mandlen, rozhinkes a sakh.
Lyulinke mayn zun.

Owls screech, wolves howl
Oh, God, comfort us, help!
I am sure your daddy's near
Waiting for me and you
Out there, somewhere.
His hands filled
With raisins and almonds,
Lyulinke, my son.

CHAPTER TWENTY

✦

YOU ARE NOT IN A LIBRARY

i

PRESIDENT ROOSEVELT'S DEATH in April 1945 called forth a great mourning from every Jewish enclave. This, despite what had been learned about the administration's refusal to permit the bombing of railroad tracks leading to Auschwitz-Birkenau, a policy that might have saved hundreds of thousands. Only after the unconditional surrender of the Germans, followed by photographs and personal accounts by Holocaust survivors, did the administration of Harry Truman agree to overhaul its immigration policies. Jewish survivors were allowed to enter the United States, most of them shattered by their experiences and bewildered by the strange, loud, unregulated world of New York City.

Inspired by this remnant of a once vital culture, the tireless Ben Hecht argued for a Jewish state in his historic show *A Flag Is Born.* Staged at the Alvin Theater on 52nd Street, it starred Paul Muni as a weary veteran of the camps, and a rising young actor, Marlon Brando, as a young Zionist. Stella Adler's favorite student, Marlon had fallen completely under her spell. Wherever she went, onstage or off, he followed, socially, aesthetically, politically. In the melodrama, the young survivor thinks of suicide after his experience in the killing fields. Soldiers come from the Middle East, offering him a home in Palestine. As he leaves the charnel house of Europe for his new country, he speaks out to the audience, indicting his co-religionists:

"Where were you Jews when the killing was going on? When the six million were burned and buried alive in lime, where were you? Where was your voice crying out against the slaughter? We didn't hear any voice. There was no voice. You Jews of America! You Jews of England! Where was your cry of rage? Nowhere! Because you were ashamed to cry as Jews! A curse on your silence."

Brando was to recall that his accusatory tone "sent chills through the audience." At several performances "Jewish girls got out of their seats and screamed and cried from the aisles in sadness, and at one, when I asked, 'Where were you when six million Jews were being burned to death in the ovens of Auschwitz?' a woman was so overcome with anger and guilt that she rose and shouted back at me, 'Where were *you?*' "

At the time, the actor went on, "there was a great deal of soul-searching within the Jewish community over whether they had done enough to stop the slaughter of their people—some argued that they should have applied pressure on President Roosevelt, for example—so the speech touched a sensitive nerve." So sensitive that contributions poured in. Before *A Flag Is Born* finished its tour of Detroit, Philadelphia, Baltimore, Boston, and Chicago, a million dollars had come in. A large portion of that money was used to buy the *Abril,* a four-hundred-ton yacht. Renamed the *Ben Hecht,* it was used to ferry six hundred Holocaust survivors to Palestine. The British government was administrating the area, and strict immigration policies were in effect. But when the ship docked, London sent instructions that the British officials were to back off rather than create an international incident. It was the start of 10 Downing Street's new Middle East foreign policy, and the first giant step in the creation of Israel.

ii

POSTWAR, the Eastern European survivors who made their way to New York City constituted a stream, not a wave. But they were enough to provide the Yiddish Theater with a new audience. A handful of veteran showfolk gratefully returned to their typewriters and pianos. Sholem Secunda composed music for *Hard to Be Honest,* a celebration of the Jewish spirit starring the aging soubrette Henrietta Jacobson and a fresh comedian, Fyvush Finkel. The *New York Post* critic derived some mild amusement from the clowns, but he was impressed by the melodies. "Mr. Secunda's synagogue background colors his popular songs as definitely as Sir Arthur Sullivan's choir boy training makes itself felt in the Gilbert and Sullivan operas."

The warm reception did not go unnoticed by Maurice Schwartz. For the first time in more than a decade the town had an influx of Yiddish speakers. They could very easily become the new audience so necessary for the Yiddish Art Theater to survive. He gambled with his remaining funds and in the season of 1945–46 presented *Three Gifts,* an adaptation of an I. L. Peretz story that took on a new significance in the wake of the Holocaust.

A poor man dies and arrives at the celestial court. Since his good deeds do not outweigh his bad ones he is barred from entry. An archangel takes pity on him: times are harsh even in heaven; some of the lesser angels can be bribed. If he can find three rare and beautiful gifts for the seraphs, he can get in.

Sent back to earth he sees a crime being committed—bandits are holding up an old Jewish businessman. They want him to hand over his greatest treasure. The robbery victim silently prays: "The Lord giveth, the Lord taketh away, blessed be the name of the Lord! You're not born with it, and you can't take it with you." The thieves continue to plunder his satchels until they come upon a small bag. He tries to shout "Don't touch that!" but when he opens his mouth he is slain. The robbers rip open the sack, expecting to find jewels and gold. Instead they find dirt—"Just a little soil. From the earth of Palestine, for his grave."

The petitioner to heaven offers this as his first gift to the angels.

The second gift is a pin. He has removed it from the body of a beautiful Jewish girl who was murdered for walking past a church on Sunday. She used the pin to keep her ripped dress from revealing her battered body, even as she was dying.

The third gift is a yarmulke, taken from the corpse of an old Jew forced to walk a gauntlet for crimes that no one can recall. During the beating his skullcap came off. Rather than go on without it, he walks back through the gauntlet of anti-Semites and is killed by them.

In the world's eyes, these presents are worth no more than a few pennies. And yet they prove valuable enough to allow a poor man to enter heaven—evidence of the power of faith over death. The rich man's bag of soil is a pledge to the Jewish people who have maintained a presence in the Holy Land since the days of Moses. The woman's modesty demonstrates that she remains human in the presence of monsters. As for the old man, his devotion to Jehovah outweighed all other considerations including pain and annihilation.

The relevance of *Three Gifts* needed no program notes. If some of the performances were overwrought, this was considered more than appropriate. In the *Times,* Brooks Atkinson complimented the production. In his view the "Yiddish Art Theater has always been one of the most interesting stage organizations in this city. It always produces plays in good taste. The style of acting is warm and excitable."

Schwartz went on to stage and star in *Song of the Dnieper,* a look back at a Russian *shtetl,* and in 1947 startled everyone by taking the part of Shylock. He had sworn never to play that Shakespearean role, and in a sense he kept his vow. This Shylock was the Bardic character, but he did not speak Shakespeare's lines. He came from an obscure Hebrew novel written decades ago, *Shylock, ha'yehudi mi'venetsia* (Shylock, the Jew of Venice).

In program notes Maurice sought to defend Shylock, and by extension all who shared his faith. "There is no case in history indicating that a Jew ever sought a pound of flesh as security for a loan," instructed Schwartz. Such an obscenity was unthinkable "due to the laws laid down by the Jewish religion. . . . Jews must salt the meat of fowl and cattle not only to make it kosher but in order that not even a drop of blood should remain in the meat. Since Shylock is a very religious man, it is impossible that he could have exacted such terms in his contract with Antonio."

Critics downtown and uptown wanted to believe those words. Even before *Shylock and His Daughter* opened, a conservative Yiddish paper, the *Morgen Zhurnal,* observed that Shakespeare's usurer was "a historical lie, a falsehood that has cost Jews very dearly." It had to be "once and for all erased." In the *New York Post,* Richard Watts added, "It would most assuredly be both arrogant and untrue to suggest that this new Yiddish drama sets out to put Shakespeare in his place. It is merely an effort to view the same story and the same set of characters from the standpoint of modern historical knowledge and to right an unintentional wrong."

Two guards set the tone in the opening minutes:

GRATIANO: Here's another Jewish devil come to Venice. Must have escaped the Inquisition. If I were the Pope, I'd burn them all in a single day—*basta*!

SALANIO: Why do you hate the Jews so?

GRATIANO: Because they are Jews.

SALANIO: Why, then, do you accept their bribes?

GRATIANO: Because my miserable wages won't buy me enough rope to hang myself.

Within the hostile environment of Venice, the widower Shylock has raised his only living child, Jessica. Now that she's come of age he has chosen a husband for her: Samuel Morro, son of a friend killed during the Inquisition.

But Jessica has been secretly keeping company with Lorenzo, the gentile manager of Shylock's bank. Gratiano and Salanio are in on the romance, and demand 3,000 ducats to keep their mouths shut. Lorenzo is not a wealthy man, and he asks his friend Antonio for a loan to silence the blackmailers.

Antonio also detests Shylock. But his money is on the ocean, heavily invested in merchant ships. And so he must go to the Jew for cash. Without knowing what the money is for, Shylock agrees to the loan. But not without answering Antonio's anti-Semitism with a paraphrase of Shakespeare's "Do we not bleed" speech:

> S H Y L O C K : You who cage us within ghettos, you who cast us alive into flames, only because we are Jews. Are not Jews and Christians alike fashioned in the image of God? Have we not the right to the breath of life as you do? Who has driven us to earn our embittered bread by usury? You.

To underline his sentiments, Shylock loftily refuses to charge interest for the loan.

> A N T O N I O : I do not want any kindness from Jews, and certainly not from you. I insist on your usual conditions—ten percent for the loan, and a bond with my seal.

> S H Y L O C K : Signor Lorenzo, please tell Signor Antonio how many worthless bonds, sealed by noblemen, lie in our safe.

> A N T O N I O : Why, then, don't you demand the same security that a merchant of Genoa, years ago, demanded of a borrower, to wit, that if the loan is not paid back on such and such a day, the debtor forfeits to the nearest creditor a pound of flesh from his breast, cut nearest his heart.

> S H Y L O C K (*Smiling*): A pound of human flesh is surely not worth as much as a pound of mutton or beef.

That smile makes the difference. Shylock is not a man seeking revenge; he is instead a master of irony, at once proud and dismissive. To no avail. Shylock learns all too soon that he will lose Jessica—not to a malady, the way his other children were lost, but to something he dreads even more: conversion to Christianity.

The moneylender is beside himself. His daughter must now be treated as dead. Embittered to the point of madness, he decides to go after the pound of flesh after all, setting himself against the church with Antonio as its emblem. An overheated trial occurs, ending with the Jew awarded his right to that pound. It is, in effect, a death sentence. The community of Jewish elders turns away in revulsion. The high churchmen plead their case, but Shylock is stone-hearted. For all those martyrs who died in the Inquisition flames, for all who were forced to convert to Christianity on pain of death, he raises his hand in vengeance.

Yet for all his passionate avowals, Shylock hesitates. Illuminated by the morning sun, he lifts the weighing scales above his head—and stops. The conclusion is abrupt and catastrophic.

SHYLOCK (*Speaking in measureless pain*): I cannot shed blood. I am a Jew!

(*The Cardinal and Bishops bend under those words. A ray of light plays about Shylock as he moves offstage. Suddenly, the voice of Morro, Jessica's intended, resounds*)

MORRO: Father! Rejoice! Our Jessica has returned to us! Forbidden to come back to her people, she drowned herself by the ghetto shore.

In its melodramatic flow, its sudden surprises, and big expostulatory speeches, *Shylock and His Daughter* was a throwback to the days of Adler, Kessler, and Thomashefsky. The extravagant emotional style can be gauged from Brooks Atkinson's comment in the *Times*: "If the acting in Second Avenue is not precisely in the grand manner, it has animation and latitude, with wide gestures and excitement; and you always know that you are not in a library.

"Without being flamboyant, Mr. Schwartz acts with boldness, using his hands continuously, waggling an eloquent forefinger and raising shaggy eyebrows to project astonishment."

But grandiloquence was not the main reason for the play's success (it ran for most of the 1947–48 season). As Joel Berkowitz details in *Shakespeare on the American Yiddish Stage,* this production "clearly struck a chord with an audience that had just lived through Hitler's attempt to find a Final Solution to the Jewish Problem." The chord was amplified in a printed introduction to the play. In a reference to the mid-sixteenth-century pope, it pointed out that "Paul IV's period was a small-scale precursor of Hitler's time, and the Nuremberg racial laws were practically a copy of Paul's Roman edicts against the Jews. A description of the time is almost a replica of the anti-Jewish practices in our own days."

There were other reasons for the play's visceral force. Jews were front and center as they had never been before. Postwar Hollywood hammered away at the notion that anti-Semitism was a poison that had destroyed the Axis, and that would threaten the United States if it were allowed to resurface. At the same time that *Shylock and His Daughter* was drawing crowds, 20th Century Fox produced *Gentleman's Agreement*. Based on Laura Z. Hobson's postwar novel, the movie starred Gregory Peck as a journalist who poses as a Jew, uncovering country-club prejudice in suburban America. Directed by Kazan, the self-congratulatory feature won Academy Awards for Best Picture and Best Director. (A stagehand wryly praised scenarist Moss Hart for the picture's "wonderful moral." Asked what that moral was, the man replied, "I'll never be rude to a Jew again because he might turn out to be a Gentile.")

A better, underpraised feature on the same subject opened that season. Directed by Edward Dmytryk, *Crossfire* concerned the killing of a civilian Jew by a sociopathic soldier. Robert Ryan played the villain, Robert Young the investigating officer, and Robert Mitchum a noncom who finally ferrets out the truth. The tough, unrelenting picture received no awards, but proved to be an immensely popular film noir.

The social conscience of the motion picture business would not be on exhibit for much longer. Shortly after those films were released, the House Un-American Activities Committee busied itself by investigating Hollywood. The congressmen went on a search for scenarists, directors, and actors who might have inserted communist propaganda in their films. Anyone who had been active in the politics of the left was suspect, some simply for being "prematurely anti-fascist" in the 1930s, others for being members of the party and lying about it. HUAC made little distinction between the two. An atmosphere of hysteria enveloped Hollywood and New York, and a blacklist was instituted by the studios and networks, barring actors and directors with "subversive" backgrounds.

Representative John Rankin of Mississippi took advantage of the situation to remind his fellow Americans of certain ethnicities. "I want to read you some of the names," he intoned in 1948. "One of the names is June Havoc. We found out from the motion picture almanac that her real name is June Hovick. Another one was Danny Kaye, and we found out that his real name was David Daniel Kaminsky. Another one is Eddie Cantor, whose real name is Edward Iskowitz. There is one who calls himself Edward G. Robinson. His real name is Emanuel Goldenberg. There is another one here who calls himself Melvyn Douglas, whose real name is Melvyn Hesselberg."

That year, the European intelligentsia buzzed about *The Plague,* a metaphorical account of France under German occupation. Novelist/philosopher Albert Camus made no attempt to explicate his work, but insiders knew it was a metaphorical account of France under German occupation. The protagonist, Dr. Rieux, represented humanity's decent impulses; the germs of disease stood for the evil buried in the life of an old, decaying culture. The last paragraph was Topic A at the Deux Magots café as well as other existentialist hangouts: "The plague bacillus never dies or disappears for good; it lies dormant for years and years in furniture and linen-chests; and perhaps the day would come when it would rouse up its rats again." For any sensitive reader in America, his point needed no underlining. Anti-Semitism, thought to be slain on VE Day, had merely been on holiday.

Zionism exacerbated the situation. The notion of a Jewish state had drawn the world's attention, accompanied by fresh controversy. The debate was not limited to Congress and the State Department. On Second Avenue itself, battle lines were drawn. Examining the audience reaction to *Shylock and His Daughter,* for example, the *Morgen Zhurnal* critic divided ticket-holders into two groups. One was linked to the Jewish vigilantes in Palestine, the other to the regular army. "Those who support the Irgun have almost the whole drama to themselves. Shylock can almost be considered one of their own: vengeance is the key to his deeds! And those who support the Haganah or who are in general soft Jews who are against bloodshed, can consider Shylock among their ranks at the end: Jewish ethics have triumphed."

Thus Schwartz had it both ways. He could reinterpret Shylock in a modern view—and yet be the classic Venetian. He could play the rancorous avenger—and yet be the righteous figure who could not take a life. Armed with this two-edged triumph he went on to produce a series of revivals, and bolstered his ego by pursuing some strange fantasies.

One of them, and perhaps the most peculiar, concerned *Death of a Salesman.* Arthur Miller audaciously placed an ordinary man—a com-

moner rather than a king—at the epicenter of tragedy. In its first production the text was abetted by Lee J. Cobb's towering performance
and Elia Kazan's inventive staging. It took some time for reviewers to
realize that despite *Salesman*'s fresh approach, it was *au fond* a classic family drama. The Broadway themes of mothers vs. daughters, husbands
vs. wives, and in this case, father vs. sons, as critic Robert Brustein put
it, "all engaged in epic battles that invariably ended in tearful reconcil-
iations, were ultimately derived from Second Avenue."

No doubt that was why Schwartz told an interviewer, "The part of
Willy Loman was written for me. The role needs close understanding,
not creating it through externals. Miller had me in mind when he
wrote *Death of a Salesman*."

The playwright was considerate enough not to deny or reinforce
that assertion. But he did not award the rights to present a Yiddish
Salesman to Schwartz. Instead they went to Joseph Buloff, who opened
his version in Buenos Aires. The city's large Jewish population made it
a smash. A year later Miller allowed Buloff to take the Yiddish rendition to Brooklyn. At the Parkway Theater, the adaptor/actor/director
played opposite his wife, Luba Kadison, cast as the long-suffering
Linda Loman. That occasion caused the playwright an unaccustomed
twinge or two. In *Commentary*, critic George Ross concluded that
despite the Irish-sounding monicker, Willy Loman's tone and style was
clearly Jewish: "The effect is remarkable. Buloff has caught Miller, as it
were, in the act of changing his name."

Brustein concurred: "What one feels most strikingly is that the Yiddish play really is the original, and that the Broadway production was
merely Arthur Miller's translation into English." Privately, the playwright objected to these reductive critiques, but said nothing. "Why
was this so?" asked a veteran of many Lower East Side productions.
"Well, the proverb puts it this way: *Az tsvey zogn shicker, zol der driter geyn
shlofen.* If two say drunk, the third should go to sleep. Which he did."

iii

THE COMPOSER OF "Bei Mir Bist Du Schoen" had always preferred Second Avenue to Broadway or Hollywood. "It's my duty to stay here," he would explain. "I owe it to the Yiddish Theater. It gave me my start." Besides, "In its heyday, the Yiddish Theater paid me $250 and my contract guaranteed me a six-week vacation. That's when Broadway paid a conductor $100 a week." Only now, in 1948, at the age of fifty-seven, did Sholem Secunda feel ready for the big time.

His debut was called *Bagels and Yox,* an American-Yiddish musical presented at the Holiday Theater on Broadway and 47th Street. The show delivered what the title promised, cheap and frequent gags, recited by a cast of Borscht Belt comedians and song belters. One number rocked the theater, when the audience joined in on a chorus of nonsense syllables set to jaunty, mock-Romanian music in a minor key:

> *I heard cousin Maxi do it.*
> *Drivers in the taxis do it.*
> *They would rather sing the song than eat*
> *In the street the shoppers do it*
> *Even traffic coppers do it*
> *While directing traffic on the beat.*
> *Chiri bim, chiri bom, chiri chiri bim bam bom.*

The *Times* considered *Bagels and Yox* "noisy mediocrity" but made a point of commending the "ancient" melodies: "Someone could make a memorable musical show out of these songs by taking them seriously and not throwing them away in a tasteless revue desperately coagulated around a microphone." In Victoria Secunda's biography of her father-in-law, she recalls that Sholem was flattered by the praise but sent a letter of complaint to the paper. The songs were not traditional, he informed the reviewer; they were composed by the undersigned.

Brooks Atkinson wrote back, "You fooled me. I thought that music was right out of the synagogues. I salute you for having given me such an exalted impression."

Secunda returned to the Yiddish Theater in 1949. The book and lyrics for *Uncle Sam in Israel* were written in three languages—Yiddish, English, and a smattering of Hebrew. Chaim Ehrenreich, theater critic of the *Forward,* took exception to the polyglot style of these revues and went so far as to confront a producer backstage. "I pulled him by the lapels into the alley outside," said Julius Adler. "Why do you knock me for making a living? If you want pure Yiddish Theater, why don't you invest your *own* money in it?" The *Forward* editors knew damn well from the size of dwindling readership, he went on, that "young members of benefit organizations are threatening to take their benefits to English theater because they don't understand Yiddish. If I don't use some English, there will *be* no Yiddish Theater!"

The attitudes of those two, the traditionalist and the realist, could be seen in the last two Yiddish movies ever to premiere on Broadway. The first was a retro work directed by Joseph Seiden. After having made films for the army for the last four years, he returned to his first love with *Got, Mentsh, un Tavyl* (God, Man and Devil), Jacob Gordin's fifty-year-old drama. Modernizing Job, folding in a touch of Faust and a sprinkling of socialism, Gordin created the moral fable of Hershele Dubrovner. The virtuous weaver buys a winning lottery ticket from the devil, disguised as a peddler. With his newfound wealth, Hershele acquires a factory that produces prayer shawls. So far, so pious.

But as he gets used to a finer life, the young man becomes more of a capitalist and less of a Talmudist. His humble origins forgotten, Hershele runs a hectic sweatshop, oppressing his employees at every turn. "They let us earn just enough so we don't croak from hunger," complains one of the abused.

After years of suffering, another confronts his tormentor: "You robbed us all, you made us unhappy, corrupted us. Reb Hershele Dubrovner, you play-acted a comedy with God." That speech prompts the boss's long dormant feelings of guilt. They proceed to destroy him. He recovers his conscience, acknowledges his sins, opens a safe, and peers in. "Look at that. A strongbox full of money, yet it will not pay the smallest debt which one man can owe another. Oh, powerful rich man, how fearfully poor you are." In a final, fitful burst of energy Hershele wraps one of the prayer shawls around his neck and hangs himself.

The film opened with the appropriate fanfare on January 21, 1950, but its theme of working-class resentment was totally out of step with the upbeat tempo of the new decade. The reviews were tepid and the public apathetic. On the same day, *Catskill Honeymoon,* a musical comedy directed by Josef Berne, made its Manhattan debut. The plot, such as it was, focused on a couple celebrating their fiftieth wedding anniversary at a mountain resort, entertained by feverish tummlers, singers, dancers, and impressionists.

The *Herald Tribune* was not impressed with this "undistinguished collection of borscht circuit performers." But Jewish viewers were not impressed with the *Tribune*'s critique. The movie, made on location at Young's Gap Hotel in Parksville, New York, ran for months and returned an immense profit. Seiden saw which way the wind was blowing and several months later released his own *Borscht Belt Follies,* a hastily assembled compilation movie also filled with tummlers, singers, dancers, and impressionists.

The jargon of the entertainment business was rapidly descending from spoken Yiddish to body Yiddish. Seiden saw it in the querulous, insistent comedy of Sid Caesar, Jerry Lewis, and Buddy Hackett, the bemused look of Ed Wynn and Menashe Skulnik, the quiet, almost scholarly style of ex-schoolteacher Sam Levenson and dialectician Myron Cohen. These men were Jewish in manner and substance; nevertheless, they did their routines in English. A story told by Cohen mordantly summed up the spirit of the age and the reason for the Yiddish Theater's troubled prospects.

Mrs. Moscowitz tells her Orthodox rabbi, "My grandchildren are driving me crazy. They want to have a Christmas tree. Could you maybe make some dispensation, a *broche* [Hebrew benediction] over such a tree?"

"Impossible," says the rabbi. "But tell me, what exactly is Christmas?"

She consults a more lenient rabbi, a Conservative.

"No," he says. "I'm sorry. But tell me, what exactly is a Christmas tree?"

She turns to the young new Reform rabbi.

"I'll be glad to," he assures her. "Only tell me: what exactly is a *broche*?"

CHAPTER TWENTY-ONE

✦

THE DEFENDING ANGEL

i

THE CAFÉ ROYAL, that was the canary in the mineshaft," lamented Seymour Rexite, president of the Hebrew Actors Union. A smile crossed his lean, intelligent face, but beneath the laugh lines was a sense of profound melancholy. The restaurant had just closed for lack of customers. In its place was a dry cleaning establishment.

It was the fall of 1953 and, truth be told, there had been precious little oxygen in the mineshaft for the last several years. The once robust Yiddish periodicals were dying, one by one. Only a couple of thousand readers took the *Freiheit*. The *Morning Journal and Day*, now merged, limped from week to week. As before, the *Forward* employed far and away the best workforce—Isaac Bashevis Singer was a staff reporter. Yet no one rejoiced at the office; the average age of the newspaper's readership was estimated to be sixty. Still the *Forward* went on publishing, just as Schwartz's Yiddish Art Theater offered regular performances despite an aging clientele and straitened budgets.

The finish of the Royal provoked comment far beyond Second Avenue and 12th Street. Harrison Salisbury, the *Times* editor who usually addressed political matters, offered a deadpan valedictory to the grapevine of the Yiddish Theater: "No more did rising young doctors and professional men make known their names and budding talent by the innocent device of being paged.

"And long since had vanished the youthful artist rebels, the brilliant socialists, the eccentrics and anarchists who poured their talents so lavishly into Great Causes like the Russian Revolution."

Actors were wont to stop by and ask Mrs. Sorokin, the S of K&S Cleaners, about the previous occupant. "The Café isn't all gone," she would inform them. "See the mirror there? That's your mirror from the café. You can still look in and see yourself—just like the old days."

Salisbury peered in the looking glass as ordered. "The mirror from the café," he remarked, "is almost the only memento of the great days along Second Avenue. You will look in vain for a restaurant that serves tea in a glass."

The survivors ignored the evidence. They had fewer places to congregate outside, but in their homes the tea glass remained half full. A committee of actors decided to celebrate the history of their art with a gala, commemorating the Diamond Jubilee of the Yiddish Theater. Whether that theater was exactly seventy-five years old or not didn't seem important. The point was to salute the glorious past, to boost the sagging morale of the neighborhood, and let the world hear the heartbeat of downtown's glorious invalid.

The fete took place at the National, where Boris Thomashefsky had once strutted to the awe of ghettoites and the mixed pleasure and exasperation of journalists. Master of ceremonies for the gala was Jacob Kalisch. He hit all the high points in his narrative—among them the fact that unlike the Greeks or the English, the Yiddish Theater had a legitimate parent. So Abraham Goldfaden hadn't reached the high moral plane of Jacob Gordin. So he hadn't created a universal folk style, in the manner of Sholem Aleichem. But he *had* invented an immortal character, Shmendrik, whose name had become a synonym for an all-thumbs loser, and he *had* written lullabies that remained in the repertoire of Jewish mothers from New York to Jerusalem.

It was to be expected that Mrs. Kalisch, Molly Picon, would come onstage to wild ovations, and that Jacob and Sara Adler's daughter Celia would put in an appearance. The surprise was eighty-year-old Aaron Lebedeff, long a star in Yiddish vaudeville and author of the song "Romania, Romania." He performed it as he always did, loudly and with great panache. Punctuating his song with the sound of corks popping, the octogenarian rejoiced in the memory of beautiful women, good comrades, and the other necessities of life, *mamaligele, pastramele, karnatzele, a glezele wayn* (a little taste of corn grits, pastrami, sausage, and a glass of wine).

Looking back at that evening, *Commentary* magazine went into defensive mode. "Seventy-five years may seem like nothing for one of the oldest peoples in the world, but the Irish had no theater before 1899, and there was no significant Russian theater before the Moscow Art opened in 1897. Our own American stage had no identity of its own before 1900." If the Yiddish Theater had produced no Synge or O'Casey, no Chekhov or Gorki, "at its best it had stood high indeed." Ansky's *Dybbuk*, the publication reminded its readers, had become "an international classic. Asch's *God of Vengeance*, a play of original power, had played all over Europe. Pinski's *The Treasure* brought him the enthusiastic interest of the general audience in Max Reinhardt's *Deutsches Theater* and in the Theater Guild in New York."

The hour was late, but the obituary a bit premature. As in Bucharest and Warsaw, the Yiddish Theater had made its way out of the ghetto. Currently it was thriving in the uptown precincts denied to Thomashefsky and Schwartz. At the Barbizon-Plaza Theater, *The World of Sholem Aleichem* played to standees. The sketches were rendered in English but the style was very much in tune with the old Second Avenue fare, putting heavy emphasis on the vigor, pathos, and anxiety of the *shtetl*.

The show starred Morris Carnovsky and his wife, Phoebe Brand. The Carnovsky name had become a familiar one at the House Un-American Activities Committee's Hollywood investigation several years before. Subpoenaed to appear before the committee, actor Larry Parks, star of *The Jolson Story*, admitted that he had been a communist in the past. That confession did not satisfy the congressmen. "I ask you again, counsel, to reconsider forcing me to name names," he pleaded. "I don't think this is fair play. These are not people who are a danger to this country."

The counsel insisted: "If you will just answer the question please. Who were the members of the communist party cell to which you belonged?"

Parks hesitated, and then broke. "Well, Morris Carnovsky, Joe [J. Edward] Bromberg, Sam Rossen, Anne Revere, Lee Cobb, Gale Sondergaard . . ."

Committee chairman John S. Wood of Georgia turned conciliatory. "You could get some comfort," he told Parks, "out of the fact that the people whose names have been mentioned have been subpoenaed, so that if they ever do appear here it won't be as a result of anything you have testified to." True enough; Carnovsky's name, for example, had already been mentioned by his onetime comrade, director Elia Kazan, in a private session with the congressmen.

Up to that point Morris had been considered one of Hollywood's prime character actors, with screen credits that ranged from the role of Anatole France in *The Life of Emile Zola* to George Gershwin's father in *Rhapsody in Blue*. After the hearings, he and his wife were barred from film work. They came to New York in search of employment, and found roles in *The World of Sholem Aleichem*. Adapted by Arnold Perl and directed by Howard Da Silva, *World* featured Jack Gilford, Will Lee, and Sarah Cunningham. That quintet had also been blacklisted for past political activities.

When no theater managers were willing to house the show, the group secured a room with a stage in the Barbizon-Plaza Hotel and opened on May Day to virtual silence. "The press," recalled publicist Merle Debusky, "were scared to death of it. Even those who wanted to do something were afraid. But the people of the left, the progressives, were willing to support it. That's where some of the money came from. And also from the people who knew and loved Sholem Aleichem. They were the audience."

Oddly enough, the *Daily News,* then a conservative tabloid, mentioned the show favorably, if briefly; so did the choleric, Hearst-owned *Journal-American.* But it was the *Times* that made the modest little show into an off-Broadway hit when, in a Sunday piece, Brooks Atkinson said *The World of Sholem Aleichem* gave the city "a time for rejoicing." He added that "a lot of skill in theater and native understanding has transmuted simple things into humor, pathos, wisdom and beauty . . . something wholly delightful."

World consisted of three one-acters: "A Tale of Chelm," "Bontche Schweig" (Bontche the Silent), and "The High School." The title was something of a misnomer; "Bontche" was actually the work of I. L. Peretz, and the disparate playlets were tied together by a narrator, Mendele the Bookseller. This was the nom de plume of the nineteenth-century novelist Sholem Yankev Abramovitch. Both men were familiar to Aleichem, however; with a little stretching, they could be considered parts of his literary cosmos.

As Da Silva played Mendele, he was a disarming font of Yiddish aphorisms: "While wisdom is no substitute for a piece of herring—a house with only fish is not a home." Shuffling along, the town elder introduced the characters of Chelm, a legendary village of comic fools.

RIFKELE: Why does the hair on a man's head turn gray before his beard?

RABBI: What would you expect? The hair on the head is 20 years older than the beard.

RIFKELE: Why is the ocean so salty?

RABBI: Don't you know that? Naturally, because of the thousands of herrings who live there.

MELAMED: Rifkele, I have been thinking. If I were the Czar, I would be richer than the Czar.

RIFKELE: How, my fine Melamed?

MELAMED: I would do a little teaching on the side.

The plot of "Chelm" involved a billy goat who was sold as a nanny goat, and the rabbi who convinced the village that a sex change was all the rage for ruminants. The curtain raiser was deliberately trivial. Act two was anything but. "Bontche Schweig" had begun life as a Yiddish moral fable. Much anthologized, it had found readers in nearly every part of the world.

The scene is the gate of heaven. A great noise has sounded, indicating that something special is about to occur—perhaps Judgment Day. But it's Judgment Day only for Bontsche, in life a poor man who had never received a single break. As God and a group of angels stand by, he faces a seraph who will defend him, and a Prosecuting Angel who will question his credentials for entry into paradise.

> DEFENDING ANGEL: Job was unlucky, but this one was even less fortunate. When he was a week old he was circumcised—and the Mohel who did the job, didn't know his business. He lived like a grain of sand, along with millions like him, and when the wind lifted him and blew him upside down, no one noticed it.

The hapless figure scratches his head and wonders who they could possibly be talking about. The Defending Angel catalogs Bontche's misfortunes. His mother died when he was thirteen. His father was an alcoholic, his stepmother a termagant who tyrannized the boy, made him chop wood barefoot in the winter, and finally rejected him. Whichever way the wind blew the young man followed. For his menial work he was underpaid and shortchanged. Fortune smiled only once, when he stopped two runaway horses. The driver died in the accident, but Bontche saved the life of the passenger and he was hired in the coachman's place. Unfortunately, he had to support the coachman's widow and child.

> DEFENDING ANGEL: When his new "wife" ran away and left him with the newborn baby, he was silent; and fifteen years later when the boy grew up and threw him out of the house—even then—silent.

> BONTCHE (*Catching on*): Do—they—mean . . . ? (*Points to himself*)

> DEFENDING ANGEL: And later when this same benefactor ran him down in the street and the carriage wheels rolled over him, he didn't even report to the police who had done it. And in the hospital, his back broken—nothing.

The man's last moments were in keeping with all that went before. He refused to enter a complaint against man or God in the hospital, where patients are permitted such things. Bontche was buried in a pauper's grave with a little branch to mark it. The wind blew the stick over the next day, and the gravedigger's wife used it to stir a pot of potatoes.

The Prosecuting Angel admits defeat. He can find no way to keep this poor Jew from his heavenly reward. The other angels surround Bontche and dress him in a celestial robe. The Presiding Angel speaks to the man who suffered and kept quiet all his life.

> PRESIDING ANGEL: You never understood that you could have cried out and your voice would have shaken the walls of Jericho, the very walls of Heaven would have fallen before your cry. You never knew your power—the strength of someone who never felt a moment's hate in his life.

He offers Bontche whatever his heart desires. Anything, everything in heaven is his for the asking. For everything within it is a reflection of his decency and forbearance. Bontche looks around, unbelieving.

> BONTCHE (*Smiling for the first time*): Well, in that case—if it's true—could I perhaps have, every day, please—a hot roll with fresh butter?

> (*A sneer appears on the face of the Prosecuting Angel. Muted laughter begins in the background. A buttered roll—is this all the man can ask after a litany of suffering and humiliation? But Bontche's abiding humility changes them all. The lights fade out, leaving only Bontche illuminated. The angels turn away, ashamed. God Himself is ashamed. Bontche smiles. Then the light on him goes out.*)

In the post-Holocaust world of the New York theater, this modest drama had enormous resonance. It was as if the story of Bontche had somehow foretold the most recent tragedy of humble, unarmed Jews going to their deaths in a silence more profound than screams. Irving Howe pointed out that in "Bontche the Silent" the archetypal *kleyne mentshele* (little man) evokes from the prosecutor "a bitter laugh, as if shamed before the paltriness of most human desire." The writer, who "does seem a little like Kafka—touches in this story on one of the major themes of modern literature, the radical, hopeless incommensurability between morality and existence, the sense of a deep injustice at the heart of the universe which even the heavens cannot remedy."

Thus far *The World of Sholem Aleichem* had represented the *shtetl* as comic turf and heartbreak house. But there was a third strand still to be examined: the Jewish insistence on social equality. "The High School," the third one-acter, was Sholem Aleichem's alone.

The place is Russia, the central characters young student Moishe Katz and his parents, Hannah and Aaron. The father is a careworn businessman, the mother a striver who wants her son to enter a secular, government high school—"*Their* high school," in Aaron's aggrieved view.

A quota permits only a fraction of Jewish candidates to enter an academy, and Moishe studies hard to outscore the gentile candidates. To ensure his son's success, Aaron bribes the local principal. Having taken the payoff under the table, the principal then decrees that he already has enough Jews. There is no redress. The only institution willing to accept a Hebrew is many miles from home. His blood up, Aaron relocates at great personal cost, selling the business at a loss—only to learn that Moishe and his gentile classmate Kholyava are truants. But the boy offers an explanation. When he arrived at school he saw scores of his fellow students on strike, carrying a sign as they marched: NO MORE QUOTAS. And their leader was a Christian. Overjoyed, Hannah embraces Moishe. Aaron refuses to share in the family's sudden enthusiasm. He knows very well what the gentile boy said—a bunch of dangerous slogans—The world is altering. A new day dawns before us. No more ghettos. No quotas. No pogroms. Education will be free in this brave new world. There will be no underdogs, no undercats, no rich, no poor, only equals.

AARON (*Derisively turning away*): So what are we waiting for? Open up the chicken coops, let out the chickens. They should be free also. And the shop: I'll open up early in the morning, and put a big sign in the window: Help yourself, it's free.

Hannah turns on him. Did he like the quotas? Did he enjoy pulling up roots, wandering the country until they found a school? Was it a pleasure, begging, *schmeering* the principal? Deep down doesn't he believe that school should be for all people, regardless of their circumstances and beliefs? The boys are at least trying to find an answer.

What is the answer that Aaron can give his son? More futile shouts and empty gestures?

AARON: I know, you don't have to tell me. Strike! Of course, strike! You don't have enough to eat, strike! The draft is taking your sons, strike! You don't like the ghetto, strike! They make a decree you can't own a certain business, strike!

(*He pauses and reflects. The others look on in silence and gratitude: Aaron, despite the bluster, is changing before their eyes. The curtain is slowly lowered.*)

To do a complete turnaround without benefit of words seemed impossible at first—the performer was being asked to show in face and posture what the playwright had failed to put into words. But Carnovsky proved to be more than equal to the task, not least because the message was one of social agitation. He and the other blacklistees had identified with Aaron from the first rehearsal. To them, the Yiddish Theater had come full circle, from the early days of tentative pushing against the oppressions of the Romanovs, to the full-throated chorus of Clifford Odets's first play, *Waiting for Lefty*—"Put fruit trees where our ashes are! Strike! Strike! Strike!"—to this earnest and desperate revival of classic tales spoken in English but *felt* in Yiddish.

ii

SPEAKING ABOUT HER FATHER in the 1940s, Svetlana Stalin remembered that "He never liked Jews, though he wasn't yet as blatant about expressing his hatred for them as he was after the war." What was once an aversion became a paranoia and loathing. In the immediate postwar period Stalin professed support for a Jewish state because he believed it would rid Russia of its Hebrews, and because it would reduce British influence in the Middle East. At the same time, he directed the secret police to begin an undeclared campaign against the

Jews. It was to culminate in the execution of thirteen Yiddish writers, each shot in the head on the night of August 12, 1952.

They had been arrested for spying for the United States, an absurd charge, but one that went unchallenged by such pro-Soviet Americans as Paul Robeson and Howard Fast. It is doubtful that any protest could have forestalled the fate of the victims, but the silence of the American left bolstered Stalin's confidence. The second prong of his pogrom occurred the next year when a "Doctors' Plot"—purported to be a ring of physicians bent on killing the Russian leader—was uncovered.

The extension of Hitler's genocide had begun on a January night in 1948. Only three months before, Shlomo Mikhoels had proclaimed, "Jews feel more physically secure in the Soviet Union than in any other country in the world." He had been an avid fund-raiser and the recipient of many medals and awards, including the coveted Order of Lenin. All this made the Yiddish actor/director too famous to criticize for "cosmopolitanism"—Stalin's code word for any specifically Jewish activity. So Mikhoels could not be dealt with in the usual manner.

He was invited to Minsk, ostensibly to meet some important theater people. Upon arrival thugs set upon him. The beating, as Stalin had ordered, was fatal. Mikhoels's body was then run over by a truck and left in a side street, to make his death appear to be an automobile accident. The physiologist who had embalmed Lenin was promptly dispatched to the scene of the crime. He removed all evidence of the brutality. A state funeral followed.

The truth did not emerge until well after Stalin's death in 1953. It was then that Joseph Buloff, who had been put down by Mikhoels on the stage of the Polo Grounds, enjoyed his moment of schadenfreude. The great Yiddish personality "was taken from his hotel, beaten to death and left in the snow," wrote the actor in his memoirs.

"Thus perished Mikhoels, slain by the hand he had blessed."

Thus also perished the Russian Yiddish Theater. Now only America played host to Jewish acting companies, and even without interference from Moscow, every one of them was in trouble.

CHAPTER TWENTY-TWO

✦

NOW HE'S EXORCISING
DYBBUKS

i

WE HAVE BEEN IN SACKCLOTH for too long, Maurice Schwartz told his colleagues. He was going to produce *The Shepherd King*, an epic with huge scenes and long speeches in the old Second Avenue style. What's more, he intended to go Broadway one better, turning the play into a musical. Who better for that than Sholem Secunda? The composer was invited to Schwartz's 8th Street apartment, along with Herman Yablokoff, who had produced a profitable "Yinglish" pageant, *Uncle Sam in Israel.* In the impresario's opinion, this was a triumvirate that couldn't lose.

He read them the play. "After Schwartz finished," Yablokoff was to remember, "we didn't have the heart to tell him what we really thought. Instead, we told him, 'Well, it's only a first draft, you'll work on it.' " Those were, and remain, some of the most lethal words in show business. The two men left 8th Street and drove uptown in silence. The composer and the producer went ahead with *The Shepherd King* anyway.

Euphoric and dreamy, Schwartz courted the press. "This is our renaissance," he told a reporter. "For this I gave thirty-one years of life, thirty-one years of talent. This is our most important attempt." His rich bass hesitated for dramatic effect. "Maybe our last attempt. If this does not work then we know where we stand." He brightened. "But I know we are on the way back to those wonderful days."

He spoke about plans to have an extended season, bolstered by a long list of patrons, including 25,000 Yiddish-speaking union members and their families. Thousands would subscribe to the Yiddish Art Theater at fees ranging from $5 to $25 a year. Finances would no longer be a concern. Art would be the only subject on the agenda. There were some fifty classic plays in the repertory just waiting to be revived. Schwartz was not worried that they would be presented in Yiddish. "After all," he reminded his listener, "the Jewish people have somehow managed to keep alive their good literature and their culture. And for those who don't speak Jewish, I don't believe language is a barrier to real art."

To back up this declaration, Yablokoff placed an article in the Yiddish papers, praising Schwartz for his new community theater. "Now, with the opening of *The Shepherd King,*" he affirmed, "the curtain rises again on the first chapter of the resurrected Yiddish Art Theater in America. The second chapter must be written by the Jewish community itself with its financial support of this cultural institution. Who is the Jewish community? You are!"

On opening night Yablokoff found himself maligned before the curtain had risen on act one. A generation later, he bitterly recalled the grumbles: "Why is so-and-so and his missus seated up front, while I and my wife are stuck in the back? Does he rate more prestige than I, in my community-run theater?" After the first act, he knew the worst. "Several dramatists eyed me with scorn, gloating as they milled in the lobby. I read in their sarcastic glances, 'Our dear Mr. Schwartz didn't want to produce my play? Fine! Now you're stuck with a turkey!' "

The Shepherd King was worse than they wished. The *Times* critic singled out one mise-en-scène for special condemnation, writing that it "wallowed in dialogue that was somewhere between Italian and soap opera." Sholem Secunda was let off the hook; he had "shaped an intelligent, sympathetic score." And the grudging conclusion noted that "a number of actors did the best they could." But their best was insufficient. Schwartz shut down the production and immediately mounted a new one, as if to erase a bad memory. His revival of *The Brothers Ashkenazi* received glowing reviews. They were too late. Burdened with debt, surrounded by indifference or outright hostility, the theater closed "for repairs." It would not reopen.

"Like the rest of us theater bugs," Yablokoff concluded afterward, "Schwartz suffered failure in the past, but, as sole boss of his theater, he carried on for years striking success again and again. The audience was willing to forgive and forget. But this was different. The enterprise was run by the people, and the blame for hammering the last nail into the coffin fell on the heads of the community."

As Schwartz's projects sank, *The World of Sholem Aleichem* took on a life of its own. One touring company starred Molly Picon and her husband, Jacob Kalisch. In 1957 they did a two-week stint in Atlantic City, with Kalisch as Mendele the Bookseller. Picon threw in a couple of songs that were not in the New York production, and the Kalisches played to standees for the entire fortnight.

Perl, having proved that Sholem Aleichem was still a bankable author, came up with a new project, *Tevye and His Daughters*. Would Jacob be interested in playing the lead role? And what about Molly? Would she like to take a part? The actors could hardly wait to read the script. When they did, however, their hearts sank. "We disliked every page," wrote Picon. "I didn't like the script or the part, and neither did Jacob. The role was too long, unfunny, and the entire play seemed labored."

Unlike Secunda and Yablokoff, the Kalisches did not suffer in silence. Jacob turned down the role, Perl fumed, and a relationship died. The show opened in September 1957, at the little Carnegie Hall Playhouse. For Molly and Jacob, any lingering doubts about their decision evaporated when they attended a performance. Mike Kellin, who later went on to a distinguished career in stage and film, played Tevye. He looked tired, and his lines seemed prosaic and lifeless—the opposite of Aleichem's appealing milkman. The Kalisches walked out at the first act intermission. Serious Yiddish Theater limped on, ill-clothed, ill-fed, ill-housed. Revues, musicals, wink-and-nudge comedies had taken over. Jacob did small parts on network television dramas, customarily playing an old Jewish merchant with a marked accent—a role for which he needed no training. When he was not rehearsing he and Molly retreated to their Catskill country house, Chez Shmendrik, where they worked on his new operetta. Kalisch did the book for *The Kosher Widow*; Molly wrote the lyrics to Sholem Secunda's melodies. A typical quatrain:

> *Toyznt vaber hot gehat*
> *Shloyme hameylekh de kliger.*
> *Fargest nisht az tsa yedn vayb*
> *Hot ir okyh gekrign a shviger!*

> A thousand wives had Solomon
> But the harem had a flaw,
> For with each lovely spouse
> Came another mother-in-law!

The show was built around her comedic abilities; for the first time she played two roles, an older wife and a young sweetheart, and this feat made her an epic box office draw. Every night, 1,500 people came to the Phyllis Anderson Theater to see Molly, even though at sixty-two she was long past her vocal prime. Looking back, she conceded that Secunda "had a little trouble writing for me, because by the time I worked with him, I had very little voice left." But time had not eroded a phenomenal stage presence and a fifty-year ability to connect with an audience. Secunda's son Gene was in attendance when Picon was in mid-song. "Suddenly there was this unbelievable crash outside the theater. Somebody had smashed a car into a store window or something, and there was this tremendous commotion and sound of things breaking.

"Molly turned to the audience and said, 'Ah, der kinder [children].' It broke up the house."

Despite its large cast, *The Kosher Widow* was really a one-woman show, and that woman had other commitments. The musical closed in January 1960, because Picon had been cast in the London production of *A Majority of One*. The banal romance, about a Japanese businessman and an aging Jewish woman, was as big a hit on the West End as it had been on Broadway.

Picon never returned to the Yiddish Theater. Even if she had wanted to, there were fewer and fewer venues to receive her. In the fall of 1958, the wrecking ball banged in the sides of the Second Avenue Theater, and bulldozers began to clear away the debris, making way for a parking lot. Nearby, the National was marked as the next theater to go; the City Council had determined that it was in the way of a new Christie Street subway spur connecting the IND and BMT lines. A last-minute reprieve allowed one more Yiddish production to take place before the wreckers moved in.

Nice People was a simple play of reminiscence, nowhere near as powerful as the memories exchanged by the actors in rehearsal. They spoke of the forty-six-year-old theater that would house them all for the last time, and of the stars who had played here—Adler, Kessler, Kalisch, and especially Thomashefsky, as flamboyant offstage as on. One of the older performers talked about Boris's many pairs of cloth shoes, each covered with material to match a particular suit. Another remembered that the superstar had the first chauffeur-driven limousine, and the first Japanese valet on Second Avenue. None of the actors mentioned a smaller auditorium in the same building.

The Rooftop Theater was currently showing *Ulysses in Nighttown,* an adaptation of the James Joyce novel. It starred Zero Mostel, another Yiddish-speaking fugitive from the blacklist. In 1958 the Rooftop meant no more to these troupers than it did to Yiddish Theater performers a generation before. In those days, the theater was known as the Minsky, featuring coarse chorines and pig-bladder comedians—strictly *traife* (non-kosher) to the crowds who had come to the National for art and uplift.

The veterans could only point to two positive signs these days, and one was ambiguous. *The Tenth Man,* Paddy Chayefsky's restatement of Ansky's *The Dybbuk,* was the hit of the Broadway season. Led by the Yiddish Theater luminary Jacob Ben-Ami, it was to be the longest running of Chayefsky's Broadway efforts, and the only one with an indisputably Jewish heart.

In it, a group of worshippers gather at a run-down Long Island temple. Beset by illness and age, they complain about their ungrateful families ("May my daughter-in-law live to be a hundred and twenty, and may she have to live all her years in *her* daughter-in-law's house") and visit their own cemetery plots. One of their number has a beautiful but schizophrenic granddaughter, and the men believe that she is possessed by an evil spirit. A Kabalist is engaged to remove it. During the rite a strange thing happens. A neurotic young lawyer, dragged in to form a *minyan*, suddenly falls to the floor, screaming. He turns out to be the possessed one, not she. After much disturbance, the pair go out into the world together, purged of their mental ailments. Two old men, Shlissel and Alper, wonder at what has just occurred. Echoes of Second Avenue fill the air.

SHLISSEL (*Sitting, with a deep sigh*): Well, what is one to say? An hour ago, he didn't believe in God; now he's exorcising dybbuks.

ALPER (*Pulling up a chair*): He still doesn't believe in God. He simply wants to love. (*They are joined by a third congregation member*) And when you stop to think about it, is there any difference? Let us make a supposition . . .

(*As the curtain falls, life as it was slowly returns to the synagogue. The three old men engage in disputation, the cabalist returns to his isolated studies, the rabbi moves off into his office, the sexton finds a chore for himself, and the policeman begins to button his coat.*)

Was the Yiddish Theater to survive only in translation and adaptation? Maurice Schwartz said no. The aging but indefatigable impresario had just taken over the Phyllis Anderson Theater to present four plays. Art was not exactly his first priority. The opener was *Loch in Kop*, the Yiddish version of *A Hole in the Head*. Arnold Schulman's Broadway comedy had been written about a Jewish widower, his son, and their Miami Beach hotel. The film adaptation starred Frank Sinatra and used Italian names, although it never bothered to change the locutions. Schwartz's production went back to the original conception. The accomplished vaudevillian Pesach'ke Burstein took the lead. *Loch in Kop* was followed by H. Leivick's *Shmattes* (Rags). Much was made of these works in advance publicity. Then they opened. The audience disliked them almost as much as the critics.

Not to worry, Schwartz assured friends. The Yiddish Theater was still very much alive. He would tour Israel, the Wandering Jew personified, looking for a home for his productions, confident that the young country would accommodate him. And when he got things going again, he would come back and make a triumphant American tour. Burstein, who had played in the Jewish state many times, begged his seventy-year-old friend not to go: "I told him how difficult it would be for him to travel daily from town to town in the hot season." Schwartz could not be dissuaded. Once in Israel he began a grand tour, finishing up each appearance by socializing with potential investors, returning to his hotel at 3:00 A.M., rising early to begin rehearsals for the next stop on the excursion.

He wrote ecstatic letters home. Despite the government's hostility to the Yiddish language (Hebrew and even English were preferred in schools and in the theater) his tour had proved "extraordinarily successful. Here indeed is where the Yiddish Art Theater can have its home." With an eye to the box office, he added that the locale had to be in Tel Aviv, home to so many Yiddish-speaking émigrés. "It is big business and better than anywhere else in the world. . . . We must have a permanent theater here and not scrounge as we do for rehearsal space."

That theater never materialized. In May 1960, Burstein learned why. "We were broken-hearted," his memoir records, "when we received the news that Schwartz had died of a heart attack. He had kept his heart ailment a secret from the world. Having known him intimately, I can honestly say that his death was also the result of a broken heart."

The tragedy had not quite played out. Sholem Secunda happened to be visiting Israel at the time of Schwartz's death, and he was asked to give the eulogy. Immediately afterward the composer wrote to his sons, "The press here resents very keenly that Schwartz's body will be flown to the U.S. for burial. They argue that real Jews leave wills stating that they be buried in Israel, and here is a Jewish artist who wishes to have his returned to be buried among *goyim,* even though he was privileged to die in Israel. Oh well."

ii

THE FOLKSBIENE, an impoverished, frail Yiddish theater company in constant danger of annihilation, had outlasted all the giants. The year of Schwartz's death the little troupe moved into the *Forward* build-ing, guaranteeing it a permanent home with four walls and a roof, plus heat in the winter, fans in the summer, and best of all, continuing sub-sidies from the newspaper and the Workmen's Circle. Sporadically, other Yiddish productions would take place in New York, but they were one-shots, musicals, and charity fund-raisers. Ensconced in their new place, Folksbiene managers claimed that theirs was the oldest con-tinuously operating Yiddish theater in the world. As proof, all past productions were listed year by year, ranging all the way back to 1915. It was an impressive roster.

Among the authors included were Sholem Aleichem, Leon Kobrin, and both Singer brothers, Israel Joshua and Isaac Bashevis; also the Russians Alexander Pushkin and Maxim Gorki; and such American authors as Theodore Dreiser, Eugene O'Neill, Sherwood Anderson, and Clifford Odets. It didn't matter how well attended those shows were, or how well acted, or the duration of their runs. The point was that the Folksbiene had survived, just as the Jewish people had sur-vived. Together, they were the keepers of the flame. It was a very small candle in a very big city.

Another occurrence in that year gave the Yiddish-speaking public an additional reason for hope. The name Isaac Bashevis Singer had entered New York's literary world, emerging from the *Forward,* where "Gimpel the Fool" first appeared. That short story had attracted the attention of Irving Howe, who encouraged Saul Bellow to translate it from Yiddish to English for the *Partisan Review.*

"This was not a big magazine," Singer was to write later, "but it appeared that everyone of significance read that issue." With the clar-ity of a folktale, "Gimpel" recounted the misadventures of a Jewish simpleton who is mocked by the crowd, cuckolded by his wife, tempted to vengeance by the devil—yet who manages through a hard and painful life to remain a purer soul than those with better minds and fatter purses. The resemblance to Bontche did not go unnoticed.

Singer was asked to contribute to *Commentary,* where his novel *The Magician of Lublin* appeared, chapter by chapter, in English translation. The protagonist is a Jewish Don Juan, working his magic in fin de siè-cle Poland by juggling not only the objects in his stage act, but the many women in his private life. Singer's prose was erotic and vigorous, his characters incandescent. *Magician* was acclaimed in newspapers and intellectual quarterlies, causing its writer to make the journey from obscurity to recognition in a matter of months.

The language in which he wrote was as defunct as Latin—or so it seemed. And then unexpectedly Yiddish came to life. *Mademoiselle* astonished its readers by publishing a translated Singer story. *Harper's* wanted in on this literary phenomenon; so did *The Saturday Evening Post, Playboy,* and the *Reporter.* At the same time, says the author's biographer, Paul Kresh, "the *Herald Tribune* and the *New York Times, Midstream, American Judaism,* and other journals were publishing Isaac's essays while articles about him were beginning to appear almost as frequently as articles *by* him." Whenever he could, Singer championed Yiddish. He made a point of reminding the public that Hebrew had been five thousand years out of date until the state of Israel resuscitated it. Why couldn't this be true of a more recent Jewish tongue?

In fact, for all his noble defense of Yiddish, Singer had benefited mightily from translations. Without them he would have remained a cult figure known only to the diminishing readership of the *Forward.* With them he had become renowned throughout the English-speaking world. That truth was taken to heart by publishers and by theater people, who sensed that the tempo and attitudes of Yiddish might still be commercially viable, *if* it could be made accessible to an American audience. Several years before, Arnold Perl had found a way with *The World of Sholem Aleichem.* Where was it written that another translator couldn't give Aleichem a fresh interpretation, this time on Broadway?

Composer Jerry Bock and lyricist Sheldon Harnick had won Pulitzer Prizes for the score to *Fiorello!,* a 1959 Broadway musical about the bygone New York City mayor Fiorello La Guardia and his war with Tammany Hall. Since that time they had written several other shows with varying degrees of success. In 1963 they began writing songs for a new project, with a book by Joseph Stein. The trio's first thought was to adapt Aleichem's Yiddish Theater novel *Blondzhedeh Stern* (Wandering Star), about a Jewish troupe during the Goldfaden era. A surfeit of subplots slowed them down, and they turned to their second choice: the Tevye stories.

The finished result, soon to be known as *Fiddler on the Roof,* attracted the attention of director/choreographer Jerome Robbins, and stage designer Boris Aronson, who knew more about the Yiddish Theater than the rest of the team combined. Borrowing heavily from the floating images of Marc Chagall, Aronson gave the show a highly tinted, romantic background. And Robbins, perching the title character on the slanted top of a *shtetl* dwelling, emphasized the precarious quality of Jewish life under the czar. Bock's melodies echoed the minor-key airs of Yiddish songs, and both Harnick and Stein caught the ironic attitudes of the language.

The out-of-town tryout in Detroit began poorly; the local reviewers found little to like, and the man from *Variety* wrote the worst critique of all: "None of the songs is memorable." After a considerable reworking, *Fiddler* opened in New York in the autumn of 1964. *Herald Tribune* critic Walter Kerr found the show inconsequential and crass: "It might be an altogether charming musical, if only the people of Anatevka did not pause every now and then to give their regards to Broadway with remembrances to Herald Square." Howard Taubman disagreed. His "money" review in the *Times* also found fault with a show that sometimes made "a gesture that is Broadway rather than the world of Sholem Aleichem." But he entered this objection "because *Fiddler on the Roof* is so fine that it deserves counsels toward perfection." Otherwise, things were "marvelously right," "faithful to its origins," "filled with laughter and tenderness," and brimming with "uncommon quality." As for Zero Mostel in the part of Tevye, his was "one of the most glowing creations in the history of the theater."

The musical took off after that. Before the year was out, no Jewish wedding was complete without a recital of the Bock and Harnick number "Sunrise, Sunset" with its sweet, derivative melody and insistent Hallmark card lyrics:

> *When did he grow to be so tall?*
> *Wasn't it yesterday when they were small?*

And Mostel's rendition of "If I Were a Rich Man" was cited by reviewers as a classic summing up of Aleichem's attitudes about money and wisdom:

> *. . . it won't make one bit of difference if I answer right or wrong.*
> *When you're rich they think you really know.*

Mostel, a larger-than-life character who reminded the *New York Times* caricaturist Al Hirschfeld of "an exploded ventricle," soon added new lore to the Broadway book of legends. For one thing, when he sang on the original cast recording, he did "If I Were a Rich Man" in only one take—an astonishing achievement for such a complicated number. But according to *Playbill* archivist Louis Botto, the "temperamental and eccentric" Zero had another distinction: he almost kept the show from its destiny. "On the opening night they had a terrible time with him because he sat on the curb in front of the Imperial and wouldn't go into the theater. Jerome Robbins had to practically drag him in." Moreover, "after the show had been running for a while, he had been ad-libbing like crazy, which drove the authors up the wall." Especially when he improvised in Yiddish, at once delighting and mystifying the onlookers—after all, the show was supposed to *be* in Yiddish, magically translated for American audiences.

Nevertheless, thanks to Zero and Co. *Fiddler* won nine Tony Awards including Best Costumes (Patricia Zipprodt), Best Producer (Hal Prince), Best Director and Choreographer (Jerome Robbins), Best Musical, Best Composer and Lyricist, Best Leading Actor, and Best Featured Actress (Maria Karnilova, as Tevye's wife Golde). The show was eventually presented throughout Europe, South America, and Asia in more than twenty languages and was a hit in every one of them. The musical went on to inspire a parody in *Mad* magazine. Entitled "Antenna on the Roof," it pictured the lives of Tevye's descendants, living in suburban America.

It took Irving Howe to cool the atmosphere surrounding this mega-hit. On the subject of Jewish history and tradition, the public intellectual had better credentials than either Bock, Harnick, Stein, Robbins, or Aronson. While others grew weak from laughter as they watched Mostel/Tevye plead with the Almighty and negotiate with his five daughters, and while record stores could barely keep up with demand for the original cast LP, Howe cast a cold eye upon *Fiddler*. Sholem Aleichem, he declared, "is deprived of his voice, his pace, his humane cleverness and boxed into the formula of a post-*Oklahoma!* musical: the gags, the folksy bounce, the archness, the 'dream sequences,' the fiercely athletic dances." No doubt the lead actor was "a genius," but an inspired performer was not enough to save this travesty of Jewish tradition. "Too many matchmakers have crossed up the union between Sholem Aleichem and Mostel: hack lyricists and composers, a choreographer whose work has become so slick as finally to be sterile."

To Howe the accolades were worse than the material. American

Jews had lost touch with their past, and the guilt was compounded by indulging themselves in an unearned nostalgia. The more they had departed from their Eastern European roots, or even from the Lower East Side experience, the more they lauded it, pathetically grateful for any scraps of ethnicity. "A politician drops a Yiddish phrase, and they roar with delight. A TV comic slips in a Yiddish vulgarism, and they regard this as a communal triumph. . . . A play like *Fiddler on the Roof* exhibits the materials of Jewish family life, and the audience goes wild."

Howe saw no way out of the paradox caused by assimilation. Jews had first been accepted and finally rewarded in America, but a price tag was attached. In a nation where, as Henry Ford had notoriously asserted, history is bunk, they had to relinquish the past and replace memories with yearnings. Howe concluded his thesis with a glum prophecy: "If a future historian of the Yiddish epoch of American Jewish life will want to know how it came to an end, we can now tell him. Yiddish culture did not decline from neglect, nor from hostility, nor from ignorance. If it should die, it will have been from love—from love and tampering."

CHAPTER TWENTY-THREE

✦

A SIGH INTO AN OPERA

i

IN 1986, riffling through a book of photographs in Van Nuys, California, Teddy Thomashefsky remembered a place three thousand miles and eighty years distant, when his father considered himself America's Darling. Along with high art and some of the most vigorous performances in New York, the backdrop of the Yiddish Theater, said Boris's oldest son, "made the Left Bank of Paris look like a convent. There was every form of degeneration you can imagine: murder, suicide, drugs, sex deviations of all kinds. These were the emergent

Jews, after years of living a Torah-cloistered existence, suddenly free—and drunk with it."

The intoxication had lasted for more than a hundred years. But by the 1980s, the Yiddish Rialto had become Hangover Square. A *Times* reporter stopped by the Hebrew Actors Union to check out the morale of the few survivors of Second Avenue's apogee. He ran into a hostile response. A veteran actress complained about the depressing stories in the newspapers. "Why do they bemoan us?" demanded Miriam Kressyn. "Why do they say we are dead?" A colleague chimed in: "If I'm buried I don't feel it." Ben Bonus cited a list of positive items, showing that their profession was alive and well. All right, not well. But at least kicking.

Union bylaws specified that every off-Broadway musical had to employ a minimum of six musicians. Not so the people of the Yiddish Theater. By special arrangement, they could make do with one pianist. Actors were permitted to do the work of stagehands, and they could also design their own illumination and sound. Moreover, the New York State Council for the Arts had just promised the Folksbiene troupe a yearly grant of $10,000.

Bonus held up a clipping. The *Times* itself had just commended their new production: "The surprise is the general youth of the cast, as a result of which romantic leads are of appropriately youthful demeanor." This is "no mean achievement in a theater where until recently, aging audiences commonly saw aging performers still playing the ardent lovers they had personified four decades ago."

But truth to tell, that cast was not so springy. One of the stars, Zypora Spaisman, had been with the company twenty-eight years. When she was not onstage the elderly diva served as a Folksbiene executive. In her downtime she liked to regale the younger players (quite a few of them middle-aged) with stories of the old days. Zipora's favorite concerned her debut in *The Lonesome Ship,* a drama about the doomed voyage of the *St. Louis.* "The director cast me as a German with a Jewish husband. In the play I was on the ship with the old people. They were crying and asking for help, and I was a spy, giving signals to help the German submarines find the Jewish ship.

"The play was so realistic that I had to leave the theater disguised; the audience outside wanted to kill me for being a spy. 'What the hell is she doing in the Folksbiene?' they asked. Here I was the victim of a concentration camp myself.

"And I want to tell you, at the time we didn't have a theater, we played in the Y on Stanton Street. Downstairs, they're playing Ping-Pong. Upstairs they're playing handball. And every time they bounced the balls, it made the 'ship' rock. It was so realistic. People wanted to know how we did it! They thought it was part of the set."

Eyes rolled; she had related these stories many, many times. But the listeners responded out of more than mere politeness. This was a woman who had seen what they could only imagine: the last great moments of an art form expiring before her eyes.

ii

THE JEWISH REPERTORY THEATER came full circle in the 1980s. In the past, writers and musicians had forced songs into the unlikeliest dramas, among them *King Lear* and Tolstoy's *Redemption.* Now Jacob Gordin's earthy drama *Mirele Efros* was renamed *Pearls,* and supplied with arias and choreography.

Hirschbein's *Green Fields* was revived at the Young Men's Hebrew Association on 92nd Street. The Congress for Jewish Culture invented and presented "Goldy" awards, silver statuettes named for Abraham Goldfaden. These productions and prizes were given with great fervor and hope. None had any staying power.

Abe Lebewohl, owner of the Second Avenue Deli, tried to put a funny face on the situation in the mid-1980s. On the sidewalk outside his restaurant, thirty Stars of David were outlined in the cement, Hollywood-style, glorifying the names of Adler, Thomashefsky, Schwartz, Picon, and other top personalities of the Yiddish Theater.

By the time 1988 rolled around, Joseph Papp, impresario of the Public Theater and a Yiddish Theater enthusiast, wanted to have a final word. He mounted a revival of *Café Crown,* Hy Kraft's 1942 comedy about the Café Royal and its denizens. Frank Rich, the *Times* drama critic, cannily appraised the production as a "sentimental journey back through time, into the warm glow of two nearly extinct forms of theatrical endeavor." The two forms were a) a twenty-person "straight" play, once a Broadway staple and now too prohibitive for uptown. And b) the Yiddish Theater itself. This version of *Café Crown* proved "an occasion not just for laughter but for paying a grand, departed theatrical universe affectionate final respects."

In 1992, playwright Herb Gardner also looked back with affection in his Broadway play *Conversations with My Father.* The protagonist, Charlie, is dissatisfied with what he hears in everyday life.

> CHARLIE: English don't do the job. Sure, you can say "Rise and shine!" But is that as good as *Slof gicher, me darf der kishen,* which means "Sleep faster, we need your pillow"? Does "You can't take it with you" serve the moment better than *Tachrich macht me on keshenes,* which means "They don't put pockets in shrouds"? Can there be a greater scoundrel than a *paskudnyak,* a more screwed-up life than one that is *ongepatshker*? Why go into battle with a punch, a jab, a sock, and a swing when you could be armed with a *klop,* a *frosk,* a *zetz,* and a *chamalia*? Can poor undernourished English turn an answer into a question, a proposition into a conclusion, a sigh into an opera?

That year also saw the irrepressible Fyvush Finkel starring in a one-man off-Broadway show, *Finkel's Follies.* The septuagenarian spoke of his debut at the age of nine. It took another thirty-four years for him to make his first appearance on the American stage. By then he could tell old jokes that Jews knew and the *goyim* hadn't heard yet: " 'Doctor, doctor,' *kvetches* the woman. 'My arm hurts in two places. What should I do?' Doctor: 'Don't go to those places.' "

Finkel was one of the few crossover actors who had leapt from Second Avenue to Broadway and then to television, and he had no regrets. Looking back only made him bitter. Gazing at the Hebrew Actors Union building one afternoon, he shook his head. "That was a barbaric place," Finkel said. "They could literally make you or break you."

The barbaric place no longer threatened; it had fallen on very hard rocks. Inside, Seymour Rexite, president of the union, sat among old photos of headliners and famous visitors: Albert Einstein, Charlie Chaplin, Mayor La Guardia, Frank Sinatra. "There isn't much for me to do anymore," the old man confessed. "All the great stars, it seems, have passed on." Paul Muni, long gone; Joseph Buloff, Luther Adler,

Herschel Bernardi, Molly Picon, Ida Kaminska—yes, and Miriam Kressyn and Ben Bonus, too. The sons of Boris Thomashefsky, Harry and Teddy—father of the conductor Michael Tilson-Thomas—gone as well. And as if there were not enough sad news, in early 1996 Abe Lebewohl, restaurateur and worshipper of Yiddish performers, had been murdered while bringing the day's receipts to the bank. "The deli is still in operation," Rexite observed. "It isn't the same, of course. But then, down here what is?"

iii

AS THE 1990S came to a close the Folksbiene edged toward bankruptcy. Most of the board of directors were in their seventies and eighties, stubbornly clinging to the notion that the old repertoire would keep their organization afloat. Two younger members, composer Zalmen Mlotek and director Eleanor Reissa, disagreed. They believed that new plays, new styles, new approaches were the key to survival.

A power struggle took place. In the end, youth prevailed. The board elevated Mlotek and Reissa to the position of co–artistic directors and eliminated Zypora Spaisman's title of executive producer. The injured party resigned. Historian Nahma Sandrow called it a "multi-generational drama" not unlike the ones that used to be put on the Second Avenue stage. She listened to both sides of the story. "We wanted the Yiddish Theater to have a future, not to take it away from her," Mlotek insisted. "We wanted to honor her work, her stubbornness that had kept it alive." Reissa explained that having two Folksbiene artistic directors was difficult enough. "Three isn't possible. We wanted to have her on the board and as a consultant. Performing, if there was a part. We tried to give her honor. She's a formidable presence, she devoted her life to this, but it was just time for the theater to move on."

Spaisman was having none of it. "They wanted to give me a nice party, to get money in my name and give it to the Folksbiene. And I should step down. My heart was bleeding. They say I retired. I never retired."

The severance was too deep to mend. The Folksbiene began the 2000–2001 season with *An Amerikaner Mishpokhe* (An American Family), an adaptation of a Broadway show with musical interludes and bright English-language supertitles above the curtain. Spaisman's splinter group, the Yiddish Public Theater, presented the honored chestnut *Grine Felder*. More plays were scheduled by the latter organization. Plans were scuttled when on May 18, 2002, Zypora Spaisman suddenly died. Obituaries quoted the Polish refugee: "My whole life has been about preserving the Yiddish language. Hitler didn't kill it. Neither did Stalin."

Five months later Rexite passed away at the age of ninety-one. Sharp-minded to the end, he had stopped performing after the death of his wife. Although his voice remained in shape, he couldn't bring himself to go onstage anymore. Appraising the situation of his life and art, he said sadly, "I have nothing to sing about."

Neither did Caraid O'Brien. An Irish Catholic immigrant, the actress had fallen in love with Yiddish drama as an undergraduate at Boston University. The unlikely student learned the language well enough to render a couple of Sholem Asch works into English, and lecture knowledgeably about the history of the Yiddish Theater. "I have a long, long list of plays I'd like to translate," she told a reporter in 2004. "It's hellish work. It makes me want to tear my hair out. My advisers are dying."

iv

ALMOST EVERY MONTH the papers ran an obituary for a bygone celebrity of the Yiddish Theater. Ultimately there came a valedictory for the institution itself. In an article for the English-language *Forward*, Robert Brustein paid homage to the vanished performers and to the dramas in which they starred. But he refused to mourn what had been.

In "American Theater's Debt to Yiddish Stage" the Yale professor pointed out that "in the theater, the Jewish theater particularly, everything comes round, and everyone and everything is an influence."

His point was inarguable. In the theater, as with history itself, nothing entirely dies. It is subsumed by the next culture, the next movement. Through the centuries Latin refracts into English, Italian, French. The Grecian idea of democracy does not perish with Ancient Greece. It is taken up and revised by the Romans, and when their empire falls, finds expression in the Magna Carta in England, the Declaration of the Rights of Man in France, the Constitution of the United States.

In America, Yiddish is spoken fluently by only a few thousand. But hundreds of words, along with the attitude embedded in their syllables—*mavin, shlepper, chutzpah, shtick,* etc.—have entered and altered the American vocabulary. The language has an academic existence as well. Harvard, Columbia, and Ohio State offer full-fledged programs in Yiddish. According to the Modern Language Association, enrollments in these courses are almost twice the rate of growth of other foreign-language studies.

Even postmodernism has found a place among doctoral candidates: "I'm currently writing a chapter on the cross-dressing work of Molly Picon for my dissertation," reads one Web item. At a Yale University conference on Sholem Asch, a paper is concerned with "The Brothel As Symbolic Space in Yiddish Drama"; another is titled "The Ambiguous Muse: Lesbianism and Torah in *God of Vengeance.*"

For generations, as we have seen, the shadow of the Yiddish Theater fell across the stages of Broadway and the soundstages of Hollywood. Its lineaments appear in the family plays of Clifford Odets and Arthur Miller and Neil Simon. Its resonances can be heard in the tunes written by two men whose fathers were cantors in Yiddish-speaking homes. Harold Arlen fused the Jewish lament with the sounds of the blues in a manner so unprecedented that George Gershwin called him "the most original of all of us." Irving Berlin, of course, was the preeminent tunesmith of the Lower East Side. Although he married a Roman Catholic, he remained militantly proud of his ancestry. When Irving's prospective father-in-law rejected him for his undistinguished background, the composer replied that he could trace his family back to Exodus. ("Here's another exodus for you," grumbled Clarence Mackay. "Get out!" But Ellin Mackay became Ellin Berlin anyway.) And there was always a subversive Second Avenue element in Berlin's deceptively simple lyrics. In *Operation Shylock,* Philip Roth mordantly observes, "God gave Moses the Ten Commandments and He gave to Irving Berlin 'Easter Parade' and 'White Christmas.' The two holidays that celebrate the divinity of Christ—the divinity that's the very heart of the Jewish rejection of Christianity—and what does Irving Berlin do? Easter he turns into a fashion show and Christmas into a holiday about snow."

Today, the Yiddish Theater's tone and style can be discerned in the works of the Pulitzer Prize–winning playwrights Donald Margulies (*Dinner with Friends*), who recently translated Sholem Asch's *God of Vengeance,* and Tony Kushner (*Angels in America*), who did his own version of *The Dybbuk.* "Our generation is forging new versions of Judaism," Kushner believes. "The assimilationist experiment has run its course."

The Yiddish Theater remains present in the performances of Al Pacino, whose attention was caught by Paul Muni in a revival of the 1932 film *Scarface.* "The film just stopped me in my tracks," he remembered. "All I wanted to do was imitate the central character. The acting went beyond the boundaries of naturalism into another kind of expression. It was almost abstract what he did. It was almost uplifting." Several years later, Pacino assumed the title role in Brian De Palma's remake. Thirty years later his acting still bears traces of Muni's stark performance.

Marlon Brando's words retain their power: "If there wasn't the Yiddish Theater, there wouldn't have been Stella Adler. And if there hadn't been Stella, there wouldn't have been all those actors who studied with her and changed the face of theater—and not only acting, but directing and writing."

Among the Adlerians were John Garfield, Lee J. Cobb, Clifford Odets, Sanford Meisner, who was to become another influential acting teacher, as well as the Greek immigrant's son Elia Kazan (an honorary Jew to the Yiddish Theater people), who would forsake acting in favor of directing.

The Yiddish Theater style found its way into the work of Harold Clurman, a devotee of Lower East Side productions. Stella's feisty ex-husband directed more than forty Broadway and off-Broadway plays, including Odets's *Awake and Sing!,* Maxwell Anderson's *Truckline Café* (Brando's breakthrough role), William Inge's *Bus Stop,* Eugene O'Neill's *A Touch of the Poet,* and Arthur Miller's *Incident at Vichy.*

The Yiddish Theater could also be felt in the work of Sidney Lumet, whose father, Baruch, was an actor in Second Avenue productions. The boy planned to follow Lumet Sr. onstage but changed his mind as an adolescent. Like Kazan, Sidney moved from acting to directing, working on Broadway and Hollywood with Henry Fonda, Katharine Hepburn, and Paul Newman.

The Yiddish Theater contained the manic clowning of Sigmund Mogulesko and Aaron Lebedeff, and the styles of those men were reborn in the comic art of Mel Brooks and Robert Klein and Woody Allen and Mike Nichols and Elaine May—whose father had directed Yiddish plays in Philadelphia.

The Yiddish Theater had its effect on the Broadway star Mandy Patinkin (*Evita, Sunday in the Park with George*). Untutored in the language, he learned Yiddish for *Mamaloshen*, a bestselling album of songs by Secunda, Rumshinsky, et al.—along with a Yiddish version of "God Bless America."

The Yiddish Theater showed itself in the efforts of Lee Strasberg, the legendary director of the Actors Studio. His students included Anne Bancroft, Maureen Stapleton, Sidney Poitier, and Dustin Hoffman. Strasberg's famous "Method" (of using personal memories to intensify a performance) had two bases. One was the discoveries of Konstantin Stanislavsky, the other, the naturalistic acting of David Kessler.

Brando cordially detested Strasberg; he claimed that the Method man stole credit away from Stella and "constantly told the world he was the mentor, the teacher, the worshipped philosopher and the possessor of the Holy Grail" of acting. Unfair, perhaps, but what would the Yiddish Theater be without an internecine quarrel?

Yet the Yiddish Theater had an additional, and perhaps more significant, role in America. It was one that had nothing to do with showfolk. The plays and musicals of that art form held a mirror up to the immigrants, helped them define who they were and what they might become in their adopted country. The options offered by the New World were not always attractive. *God of Vengeance* related a story of sexual temptation in the wide-open Promised City. *God, Man and Devil* and *Uncle Moses* addressed the corrosive nature of money in America, the sin of avarice that turned Jew against Jew. But along with these melodramas came other tales—uplifting stories of newcomers who triumphed over destitution and despair. In the end, those stories were the audience favorites, the ones that spurred them on.

Morris Raphael Cohen, who was to become a prominent professor of philosophy at City College in New York, was uncertain of his birth date. As the boat from Eastern Europe passed the Statue of Liberty on July 25, he impulsively chose that day, because, he wrote, "my mother, my sister and I reached the harbor of New York and a new chapter of my life began." Many another immigrant regarded the Lower East Side as a kind of Holy Land, reached after much painful wandering, a land that would allow them to be born-again Jews.

In "Ballad of the Children of the Czar," poet Delmore Schwartz portrayed these Jewish immigrants as American royalty:

> *O Nicholas! Alas! Alas!*
> *My grandfather coughed in your army*
> *Hid in a wine-stinking barrel*
> *For three days in Bucharest,*
> *Then left for America*
> *To become a king himself.*

The Yiddish press did much to promote the regal notions of opportunity and status, of social and legal justice, of business and professional careers. But it was the Yiddish Theater that gave those ideas three dimensions and a human voice. It's all very well to recall the long list of performers and writers, designers and directors shaped by the ambitious immigrants—men and women who invented themselves and their art while the world watched.

But the Lower East Side housed more than entertainers. It contained a nation within a nation, a people who were transformed by America, and who then fanned out across the country to work their own changes wherever they settled down. Those alterations and modifications continue today, in politics, society, and the arts.

And so, although six generations have passed since Abraham Goldfaden's self-described "hodge-podge" astonished onlookers at the Green Tree in Jassy, Romania, the curtain has still to be lowered. The lights have not gone out. The stardust is not lost. Scattered to the winds, perhaps—but lost? Never.

BIBLIOGRAPHY

YIDDISH THEATER HISTORIES AND MEMOIRS

Adler, Jacob. *A Life on the Stage: A Memoir.* Applause, 2001.

Aleichem, Sholem. *The Jackpot: A Folk-Play in Four Acts,* trans. Kofi Weitzner and Barnett Zumoff. Workmen's Circle Education, 1989.

Beck, Evelyn Torton. *Kafka and the Yiddish Theater: Its Impact on His Work.* University of Wisconsin Press, 1971.

Berkowitz, Joel. *Shakespeare on the American Yiddish Stage.* University of Iowa Press, 2002.

Bernardi, Jack. *My Father, the Actor.* W. W. Norton, 1971.

Brown, Phil, ed. *In the Catskills: A Century of Jewish Experience in "The Mountains."* Columbia University Press, 2002.

Burstein, Pesach'ke, and Lillian Lux. *What a Life!: The Autobiography of Pesach'ke Burstein, Yiddish Matinee Idol.* Syracuse University Press, 2003.

Kadison, Luba, and Joseph Buloff with Irving Genn. *Onstage, Offstage: Memories of a Lifetime in the Yiddish Theatre.* Harvard University Press, 1992.

Kaminska, Ida. *Ida Kaminska: My Life, My Theater,* ed. and trans. Kurt Leviant. Macmillan, 1973.

Kobrin, Leon. *Recollections of a Yiddish Dramatist: A Quarter Century of Yiddish Theater in America* (in Yiddish). Committee for Kobrin's Writings, 1925.

Lawrence, Jerome. *Actor: The Life and Times of Paul Muni.* Samuel French, 1974.

Lifson, David S. *The Yiddish Theatre in America.* Thomas Yoseloff, 1965.

Lipsky, Lewis. *Tales of the Yiddish Rialto: Reminiscences of Playwrights and Players in New York's Jewish Theater in the Early 1900s.* Thomas Yoseloff, 1962.

Miller, James Albert. *The Detroit Yiddish Theater, 1920–1937.* Wayne State University Press, 1967.

Nahshon, Edna. *Yiddish Proletarian Theater: The Art and Politics of the Artef, 1925–1940.* Greenwood, 1998.

Picon, Molly, with Jean Grillo. *Molly! An Autobiography.* Simon & Schuster, 1980.

Pinski, David. *The Yiddish Drama* (in Yiddish). New York, 1901.

Rosenfeld, Lulla. *Bright Star of Exile: Jacob Adler and the Yiddish Theatre.* Thomas Y. Crowell, 1977.

Rumshinsky, Joseph. *Notes from My Life* (in Yiddish). Society fun Yidishe Kompositorn, 1944.

Sandrow, Nahma. *Vagabond Stars: A World History of Yiddish Theater.* Syracuse University Press, 1996.

Schildkraut, Joseph, as told to Leo Lania. *My Father and I.* Viking, 1950.

Secunda, Victoria. *Bei Mir Bist Du Schön: The Life of Sholom Secunda.* Magic Circle Press, 1982.

Siegel, Ben. *The Controversial Sholem Asch: An Introduction to His Fiction.* Bowling Green University Popular Press, 1976.

Singer, Isaac B. *Lost in America.* Doubleday, 1981.

Thomashefsky, Bessie. *My Life Story* (in Yiddish). Varhahayt Publishing, 1916.

Thomashefsky, Boris. *My Life Story* (in Yiddish). Trio Press, 1937.

Waife-Goldberg, Marie. *My Father, Sholem Aleichem.* Simon & Schuster, 1968.

Warembud, Norman H., ed. *The Great Songs of the Yiddish Theater.* Quadrangle/New York Times, 1975.

Warnke, Nina. "Immigrant Culture as Contested Sphere: The Yiddish Music Halls, the Yiddish Press, and the Process of Americanization, 1900–1910." *Theatre Journal,* vol. 48, issue 3, 1996.

Yablokoff, Herman. *Der Piatz: Around the World with Yiddish Theater.* Bartleby, 1995.

Young, Boaz. *My Life in the Theater* (in Yiddish). YKUF, 1950.

Zeitlin, Steve, ed. *Because God Loves Stories: An Anthology of Jewish Storytelling.* Simon & Schuster, 1997.

Zohn, Herschel. *All the World's a Stage.* Yucca Free Press, 1992.

———. *The Story of the Yiddish Theatre.* Privately published, 1995.

Zukofsky, Louis. *Autobiography.* Grossman, 1970.

Zylberzweig, Zalmen. *Album of the Yiddish Theater.* Privately published, 1937.

Zylberzweig, Zalmen, ed. *Lexicon of the Yiddish Theater* (in Yiddish). Vols. 1–5. Hebrew Actors Union, 1931–1967.

TEXTS OF PLAYS FROM OR ABOUT THE YIDDISH MILIEU

Ansky, S. *The Dybbuk and Other Writings,* edited and with an introduction by David G. Roskies, with translations by Golda Werman. Yale University Press, 2002.

Chayefsky, Paddy. *The Tenth Man.* Samuel French, 1988.

Gardner, Herb. *Conversations with My Father.* Doubleday, 1986

Goldberg, Isaac, ed. and trans. *Six Plays of the Yiddish Theater.* John W. Luce, 1916.

Kraft, Hy. *Café Crown: A Comedy in Three Acts.* Dramatists Play Service, 1952.

Kushner, Tony. *A Dybbuk and Other Tales of the Supernatural,* translated from S. Ansky by Joachim Neugroschel. Theater Communications Group, 1998.

Landis, Joseph C., ed. and trans. *The Great Jewish Plays.* Horizon Press, 1972.

Lessing, Gotthold. *Two Jewish Plays by Gotthold Lessing,* trans. Noel Clark. Oberon, 2002.

Levick, H. *The Golem,* adapted by David Fishelson from a translation by Joseph C. Landis. Dramatists Play Service, 2001.

Lifson, David S. *Sholem Aleichem's Wandering Star and Other Plays of Jewish Life.* Cornwall, 1988.

Margulies, Donald. *God of Vengeance,* adapted from the play by Sholem Asch, basic translation by Joachim Neugroschel. Dramatists Play Service, 2000.

Odets, Clifford. *Six Plays.* Random House, 1939.

Perl, Arnold. *Tevye and His Daughters, Based on the Tevye Stories of Sholem Aleichem.* Dramatists Play Service, 1986.

Pinski, David. *Three Plays,* trans. Isaac Goldberg. B. W. Huebsch, 1918.

———. *The Treasure, A Drama in Four Acts,* trans. Ludwig Lewishohn. B. W. Huebsch, 1915.

Sandrow, Nahma, trans. *God, Man and Devil: Yiddish Plays.* Syracuse University Press, 1999.

Schiff, Ellen, ed. *Awake and Singing: Six Great American Jewish Plays.* Applause, 2004.

Schwartz, Maurice. *Shylock and His Daughter: A Play Based on a Hebrew Novel by Ari Ibn Zahav*, trans. Abraham Riegelson. Yiddish Art Theater, 1947.

Stein, Joseph. *Fiddler on the Roof.* Pocket, 1972.

———. *Rags, A New Musical.* Unpublished manuscript, 1983.

YIDDISH CINEMA

Cohen, Sarah Blacher, ed. *From Hester Street to Hollywood: The Jewish-American Screen.* Indiana University Press, 1983.

Friedman, Lester D., ed. *Unspeakable Images: Ethnicity and the American Cinema.* University of Illinois Press, 1991.

Goldberg, Judith N. *Laughter Through Tears: The Yiddish Cinema.* Fairleigh Dickinson University Press, 1983.

Goldman, Eric A. *Visions, Images, and Dreams: Yiddish Film Past and Present.* Ergo Media, 1988.

Hoberman, J. *Bridge of Light: Yiddish Film Between Two Worlds.* Museum of Modern Art/Schocken, 1991.

Stern, Bill. *You Don't Have to Be Jewish: Commentaries on a Selection of Jewish Content Movies.* Lugos, 2002.

CROSS-CURRENTS OF THE YIDDISH THEATER IN AMERICAN SHOW BUSINESS

Adler, Stella. *Stella Adler on Ibsen, Strindberg and Chekhov.* Vintage, 2000.

Charyn, Jerome. *Gangsters and Gold Diggers: Old New York, the Jazz Age, and the Birth of Broadway.* Four Walls Eight Windows, 2003.

Clurman, Harold. *The Fervent Years: The Group Theater and the Thirties.* Da Capo, 1983.

Cole, Toby, and Helen Krich Chinoy, eds. *Actors on Acting: The Theories, Techniques and Practices of the World's Greatest Actors, Told in Their Own Words.* Three Rivers, 1970.

Epstein, Helen. *Joe Papp: An American Life.* Da Capo, 1996.

Epstein, Lawrence J. *The Haunted Smile: The Story of Jewish Comedians in America.* Public Affairs, 2001.

Erdman, Harley. *Staging of the Jew: The Performance of an American Ethnicity, 1860–1920.* Rutgers University Press, 1997.

Frommer, Myrna Katz, and Harvey Frommer. *It Happened on Broadway: An Original History of the Great White Way.* University of Wisconsin Press, 2004.

Gottlieb, Jack. *Funny, It Doesn't Sound Jewish: How Yiddish Songs and Synagogue Melodies Influenced Tin Pan Alley, Broadway, and Hollywood.* State University of New York Press, 2004.

Herr, Christopher J. *Clifford Odets and American Political Theatre.* Praeger, 2003.

Kaktov, Norman. *The Fabulous Fanny: The Story of Fanny Brice.* Alfred A. Knopf, 1953.

Lyman, Darryl. *Great Jews on Stage and Screen.* Jonathan David, 1987.

Mast, Gerald. *The Comic Mind: Comedy and the Movies.* University of Chicago Press, 1979.

Most, Andrea. *Making Americans: Jews and the Broadway Musical.* Harvard University Press, 2004.

Samuels, Charles, and Louise Samuels. *Once Upon a Stage: The Merry World of Vaudeville.* Dodd, Mead, 1974.

Sapoznik, Henry. *Klezmer!: Jewish Music from Old World to Our World.* Schirmer, 1999.

Snyder, Robert W. *The Voice of the City: Vaudeville and Popular Culture in New York.* Oxford University Press, 1989.

Stein, Charles W. *American Vaudeville, as Seen by Its Contemporaries.* Alfred A. Knopf, 1984.

Strasberg, Lee. *A Dream of Passion: The Development of the Method.* Penguin, 1987.

Toll, Robert C. *The Entertainment Machine: American Show Business in the Twentieth Century.* Oxford University Press, 1982.

Tucker, Sophie. *Some of These Days.* Doubleday, 1946.

Winokur, Mark. *American Laughter: Immigrants, Ethnicity and 1930s Hollywood Film Comedy.* St. Martin's, 1996.

THE LOWER EAST SIDE AND ENVIRONS

Bettmann, Otto L. *The Good Old Days—They Were Terrible!* Random House, 1974.

Birmingham, Stephen. *"Our Crowd": The Great Jewish Families of New York.* Harper & Row, 1967.

———. *"The Rest of Us": The Rise of America's Eastern European Jews.* Little, Brown, 1984.

Burroughs, Edwin G., and Mike Wallace. *Gotham: A History of New York City to 1898.* Oxford University Press, 1999.

Cahan, Abraham. *The Education of Abraham Cahan,* trans. Abraham Conan, Lynn Davison, and Leo Stein. Jewish Publication Society, 1969.

———. *The Rise of David Levinsky.* Harper & Bros., 1916.

Diner, Hasia R. *Lower East Side Memories: A Jewish Place in America.* Princeton University Press, 2000.

Douglas, Ann. *Terrible Honesty: Mongrel Manhattan in the 1920s.* Farrar, Straus & Giroux, 1995.

Epstein, Melech. *The Jew and Communism.* Trade Union Sponsoring Committee, 1959.

Hapgood, Hutchins. *The Spirit of the Ghetto: Studies of the Jewish Quarter in New York.* Funk & Wagnalls, 1965.

Henderson, Mary C. *The City and the Theatre: The History of New York Playhouses, a 250-Year Journey from Bowling Green to Times Square.* Backstage Books, 2004.

Howe, Irving. *The World of Our Fathers: The Journey of the East European Jews to America and the Life They Found and Made.* Phoenix, 1976.

Kanfer, Stefan. *A Summer World: The Attempt to Build a Jewish Eden in the Catskills, from the Days of the Ghetto to the Rise and Decline of the Borscht Belt.* Farrar, Straus & Giroux, 1989.

Kazin, Alfred. *Starting Out in the Thirties.* Little, Brown, 1965.

———. *A Walker in the City.* Harcourt, Brace, 1951.

Libo, Kenneth, and Irving Howe. *How We Lived: A Documentary History of Immigrant Jews in America, 1880–1930.* Richard Marek, 1979.

———. *We Lived There Too: In Their Own Words and Pictures—Pioneer Jews and the Westward Movement of America, 1630–1930.* St. Martin's/Marek, 1984.

Manners, Ande. *Poor Cousins.* Coward, McCann & Geoghegan, 1972.

Marqusee, Mike, and Bill Harris, eds. *New York: An Anthology.* Little, Brown, 1985.

Mendelsohn, Joyce. *The Lower East Side, Remembered and Revisited.* Lower East Side Press, 2001.

Metzker, Isaac, ed. *A Bintel Brief: Sixty Years of Letters from the Lower East Side to the Jewish Daily Forward.* Vols. 1 and 2. Doubleday, 1971, 1981.

Morris, Lloyd. *Incredible New York: High Life and Low Life of the Last Hundred Years.* Random House, 1951.

Riis, Jacob A. *How the Other Half Lives: Studies Among the Tenements of New York.* Penguin, 1997.

Rischin, Moses. *The Promised City: New York's Jews, 1870–1914.* Harper & Row, 1970.

Roskolenko, Harry. *The Time That Was Then: The Lower East Side—an Intimate Chronicle.* Dial, 1971.

Sanders, Ronald. *The Downtown Jews: Portrait of an Immigrant Generation.* Harper & Row, 1969.

———. *Shores of Refuge: 100 Years of Jewish Immigration.* Henry Holt, 1988.

Schoener, Allan, ed. *Portal to America: The Lower East Side, 1870–1925.* Holt, Rinehart & Winston, 1967.

Simon, Kate. *Bronx Primitive.* Viking, 1982.

Simon, Robert A. *Bronx Ballad.* Simon & Schuster, 1927.

Spewack, Bella. *Streets: A Memoir of the Lower East Side.* Feminist Press, 1995.

THE YIDDISH LANGUAGE

Ayalti, Hanan J., ed. *Yiddish Proverbs,* translated from the Yiddish by Isidore Goldstick. Schocken, 1949.

Blesch, Rabbi Benjamin. *The Complete Idiot's Guide to Learning Yiddish.* Alpha Books, 2000.

Burgin, Richard. *Conversations with Isaac Bashevis Singer.* Doubleday, 1985.

Kogos, Fred. *The Dictionary of Popular Yiddish Words, Phrases and Proverbs.* Citadel, 1995.

Kresh, Paul. *Isaac Bashevis Singer: The Magician of West 86th Street.* Dial, 1979.

Kumov, Shirley, ed. *Words Like Arrows: A Treasury of Yiddish Folk Sayings.* Warner, 1984.

Lansky, Aaron. *Outwitting History: The Amazing Adventures of a Man Who Rescued a Million Yiddish Books.* Algonquin, 2004.

Neugroschel, Joachim, ed. and trans. *No Star Too Beautiful: An Anthology of Yiddish Stories from 1382 to the Present.* W. W. Norton, 2002.

Rosten, Leo. *The New Joys of Yiddish.* Three Rivers, 2001.

Samuel, Maurice. *In Praise of Yiddish.* Cowles, 1971.

Shepard, Richard F., and Vicki Gold Levi. *Live and Be Well: A Celebration of Yiddish Culture in America.* Rutgers University Press, 1982.

Sinclair, Clive. *The Brothers Singer.* Allison & Busby, 1983.

Stevens, Payson R. *Mishuggenary: Celebrating the World of Yiddish.* Simon & Schuster, 2002.

Swarner, Kristina. *Yiddish Wisdom.* Chronicle, 1996.

Weinstein, Miriam. *Yiddish, a Nation of Words.* Ballantine, 2001.

Wex, Michael. *Born to Kvetch: Yiddish Language and Culture in All of Its Moods.* St. Martin's, 2005.

JEWISH HISTORY

Allen, Frederick Lewis. *Since Yesterday: The Nineteen-Thirties in America.* Bantam, 1965.

Antin, Mary. *The Promised Land.* Random House, 2001.

Ausubel, Nathan. *Pictorial History of the Jewish People, from Bible Times to Our Own Day Throughout the World.* Crown, 1953.

Bloomfield, Sara J. *The Art and Politics of Arthur Szyk,* curated by Steven Luckert. United States Holocaust Museum, 2002.

Davidowicz, Lucy. *On Equal Terms: Jews in America, 1881–1981.* Holt, Rinehart & Winston, 1982.

Dimont, Max I. *The Indestructible Jews: An Action-Packed Journey Through 4,000 Years of History.* New American Library, 1971.

———. *The Jews in America: The Roots, History, and Destiny of American Jews.* Simon & Schuster, 1980.

Dinnerstein, Leonard. *Anti-Semitism in America.* Oxford University Press, 1994.

Eban, Abba. *My People: A History of the Jews,* adapted by David Bamberger. Behrman House, 1978.

Eliach, Yaffa. *There Once Was a World: A Nine Hundred Year Chronicle of the Shtetl of Eishyshok.* Little, Brown, 1998.

Elon, Amos. *The Pity of It All: A History of Jews in Germany, 1743–1933.* Henry Holt, 2002.

Feldstein, Stanley. *The Land That I Show You: Three Centuries of Jewish Life in America.* Anchor/Doubleday, 1978.

Fried, Albert. *The Rise and Fall of the Jewish Gangster in America.* Columbia University Press, 1993.

Gantz, David. *Jews in America: A Cartoon History.* Jewish Publication Society, 2001.

Glenn, Susan A. *Daughters of the Shtetl.* Cornell University Press, 1990.

Goldberg, M. Hirsch. *The Jewish Connection.* Bantam, 1976.

Graetz, Heinrich. *History of the Jews.* Resource Publications, 2002.

Greenbaum, Masha. *The Jews of Lithuania: A History of a Remarkable Community, 1316–1945.* Gefen, 1995.

Johnson, Paul. *A History of the Jews.* HarperCollins, 1987.

Karp, Abraham J., ed. *Haven and Home: A History of the Jews in America.* Schocken, 1985.

———. *The Jewish Experience in America.* American Jewish Historical Society, 1969.

Leff, Laurel. *Buried by the Times: The Holocaust and America's Most Important Newspaper.* Cambridge University Press, 2005.

Lipstadt, Deborah E. *Beyond Belief: The American Press and the Coming of the Holocaust, 1933–1945.* Free Press, 1986.

Mendes-Flohr, Paul R., and Jehuda Reinharz, eds. *The Jew in the Modern World: A Documentary History.* Oxford University Press, 1980.

Oring, Elliott. *The Jokes of Sigmund Freud: A Story in Humor and Jewish Identity.* University of Pennsylvania Press, 1984.

Plesur, Milton. *Jewish Life in Twentieth-Century America: Challenge and Accommodation.* Nelson-Hall, 1982.

Poliakov, Leon. *The History of Anti-Semitism, Volume 1: From the Time of Christ to the Court Jews.* University of Pennsylvania Press, 1975.

Potok, Chaim. *Wandering: Chaim Potok's History of the Jews.* Ballantine, 1983.

Reik, Theodor. *Jewish Wit.* Gamut, 1962.

Rosten, Leo. *Treasury of Jewish Quotations.* McGraw-Hill, 1972.

Rubenstein, Joshua, and Vladimir P. Naumov, eds., trans. Laura Esther Wolfson. *Stalin's Secret Pogrom: The Postwar Inquisition of the Jewish Anti-Fascist Committee.* Yale University Press, 2001.

Schoener, Alon. *The American Jewish Album, 1654 to the Present.* Rizzoli, 1983.

Schwartz, Leo W., ed. *The Menorah Treasury: Harvest of Half a Century.* Jewish Publication Society, 1964.

Sklare, Marshall. *Observing America's Jews.* Brandeis University Press, 1993.

Spalding, Henry D., ed. *Encyclopedia of Jewish Humor from Biblical Times to the Modern Age.* Jonathan David, 1969.

Spiro, Ken. *World Perfect: The Jewish Impact on Civilization.* Simcha, 2002.

Stahl, Sidney. *The World of Our Mothers.* Schocken, 1990.

Vital, David. *A People Apart: A Political History of the Jews in Europe, 1789–1939.* Oxford University Press, 1999.

VIDEOTAPES AND DVDS OF RELATED INTEREST

Actor: The Story of Paul Muni, 1978.

Almonds and Raisins: A History of the Yiddish Cinema, 1983.

American Matchmaker (Amerikaner Shadkhn), 1940.

The Cantor's Son (*Dem Khazns Zindl*), 1937.

The Comedian (*Der Komediant*), 2000.

The Dybbuk, 1937.

The Forward: From Immigrants to Americans, 1989.

God, Man and Devil (*Got, Mentsh, un Tavyl*), 1950.

The Golden Age of Second Avenue, 1968.

The Golem, 1920.

Green Fields (*Grine Felder*), 1937.

His Wife's Lover (*Zayn Vaybs Lubovnik*), 1931.

The Jester (*Purimshpieler*), 1937.

Kol Nidre, 1939.

A Letter to Mother (*A Brivele der Mamen*), 1938.

Little Mother (*Mamele*), 1938.

Mirele Efros (the Jewish Queen Lear), 1939.

Mothers of Today (*Hayntike Mames*), 1937.

Tevye, 1939.

Uncle Moses, 1932.

The World of Sholem Aleichem, 1978.

The Yiddish Cinema, 1991.

A Young Jew with a Fiddle (*Yidl Mitn Fidl*), 1932.

CDS

The Best of Yiddish Vaudeville, 2000.

Bonsche the Silent, 2000.

Ghetto Tango: Wartime Yiddish Theater, 2002.

Great Songs of the Yiddish Stage, 2000.

Joseph Buloff: On Stage, 1985.

The Yiddish Radio Project, 1999.

WEB SITES

www.Folksbiene.org

www.Jewishvirtuallibrary.org

www.brown.edu/Facilities/University_Library/exhibits/yiddish/links.html
(Yiddish Theater song sheets)

www.laits.utexas.edu/gottesman/theatreindex.html
(University of Texas Yiddish Theater background)

www.nypl.org/research/chss/jws/yiddishintro.html
(Dorot Yiddish Division of the New York Public Library)

INDEX

INSERT PHOTOS

Jacob Adler as Shylock: Marianne Barcellona/Time & Life Pictures/
Getty Images

Boris Thomashefsky portrait: from the Archives of the YIVO Institute for Jewish
Research

Boris Thomashefsky as Hamlet placard: The Dorot Jewish Division, The New York
Public Library, Astor, Lenox and Tilden Foundations

David Kessler: Museum of the City of New York, The Theatre Collection

Abraham Goldfaden: The Granger Collection, New York

Maurice Schwartz with Charlie Chaplin: from the Archives of the YIVO Institute
for Jewish Research

Maurice Schwartz filming *Tevye der Milkhiker*: Museum of the Moving
Image/Lawrence Williams Collection

Bertha Kalisch: Museum of the City of New York, The Theatre Collection

Jacob Ben-Ami in *Idle Inn*, the Jewish Art Theater: Museum of the City of New York,
The Theatre Collection

Molly Picon, Second Avenue Theater: Museum of the City of New York, The
Theatre Collection

Celia Adler, Paul Muni, Marlon Brando: Eileen Darby/Time & Life Pictures/Getty
Images

Automatic Vaudeville: Museum of the City of New York, The Byron Collection

Grand Theater, New York City: The Granger Collection, New York

Irving Place Theater: Museum of the City of New York, Federal Art Project,
"Changing New York" (#306)

Jewish Audience cartoon of both a Yiddish Theater presentation and an American
play: The Dorot Jewish Division, The New York Public Library, Astor, Lenox and
Tilden Foundations

A NOTE ON THE TYPE

The text of this book was set in Requiem, created in the 1990s by the Hoefler Type Foundry. It was derived from a set of inscriptional capitals appearing in Ludovico Vicentino degli Arrighi's 1523 writing manual, *Il Modo de Temperare le Penne.* A master scribe, Arrighi is remembered as an exemplar of the chancery italic, a style revived in Requiem Italic.

COMPOSED BY
North Market Street Graphics, Lancaster, Pennsylvania

PRINTED AND BOUND BY
Berryville Graphics, Berryville, Virginia

DESIGNED BY
Iris Weinstein